WOODEN LEG

A Warrior Who Fought Custer

Interpreted by

THOMAS B. MARQUIS

UNIVERSITY OF NEBRASKA PRESS
LINCOLN AND LONDON

"I OFTEN THINK THAT IF I WERE AN INDIAN I WOULD GREATLY PREFER TO CAST MY LOT AMONG THOSE OF MY PEOPLE WHO ADHERED TO THE FREE OPEN PLAINS RATHER THAN SUBMIT TO THE CONFINED LIMITS OF A RESERVATION, THERE TO BE THE RECIPIENT OF THE BLESSED BENEFITS OF CIVILIZATION, WITH ITS VICES THROWN IN WITHOUT STINT OR MEASURE."

—*From page 18 of General Custer's book,* MY LIFE ON THE PLAINS, *published 1876, a few months before his death.*

The Author's Statement.

The Indian story of Custer's last battle has never been told, except in a few fragmentary interviews that have been distorted into extravagant fiction. There were no white men survivors of that most thrilling of American frontier tragedies, so the veteran hostile red warriors have exclusive possession of the key to the mystery as to how it happened.

The present author, sixty-one years old and a resident of Montana throughout the past forty-one years, decided in 1922 to apply himself at probing into this matter. He served a few months as agency physician for the Northern Cheyennes, a tribe allied with the Sioux in the annihilation of Custer. Since then, the investigator has been in close association with these Indians. He has learned the old-time plains Indian sign-talk to a degree enabling him to dispense with interpreters, except in rare instances. He has held out continual invitation for Custer-battle veteran warriors to visit his home, partake of his food and smoke his tobacco. After a long siege, they began to come. Later, they began to talk, but only a little. Still later, after they had found out that this ingratiating white man was not scheming to entrap them into fatal admissions, they told the whole story. Not only did they answer all questions, but they added spontaneous information concerning every detail of the battle and of the entire hostile Indian movements during that eventful summer of 1876.

Sixteen hundred of these Montana Cheyennes were with the Sioux horde in the battle camps beside the Little Bighorn river. All of the Sioux were settled soon afterward in the Dakotas, and they stayed there. The Cheyennes were located on a reservation in the heart of the region where had been the conflicts. During the subsequent more than fifty years they have viewed over and over the central historic spots. Thus they have kept their memories fresh or have kept each other prompted into true recollections. This advantageous condition has rendered them the best of first-hand authorities. Up to late 1930, seventeen Cheyennes who were adult warriors at Custer battle were yet alive.

Wooden Leg became the author's favorite narrator. It seemed that his lifetime biography should surround his special battle story, so that readers might learn what kind of people were the hostile Indians of that day. Hour after hour, on scores of different occasions in recent years, the elderly white man doctor has sat enthralled by the well-connected and vivid sign-talk recountings of this companion so congenial. Wooden Leg's gestures often were supplemented by his dainty pencil drawings and by his sketched maps—papers now treasured as precious documents. A few stray English words from his extremely scant vocabulary of them were besprinkled through the efforts at full expression.

The principal story-teller's statements of essential facts have been amalgamated with those of his fellow tribesmen who fought as companions with him. Groups of them, with him as the leader, took the author many times into assemblage. Thus all points of importance have been checked and corroborated or corrected. The helpers have been Limpy, Pine, Bobtail Horse, Sun Bear, Black Horse, Two Feathers, Wolf Chief, Little Sun, Blackbird, Big Beaver, White Moon, White Wolf, Big Crow, Medicine Bull, the younger Little Wolf and other old men, as well as some old women and a few Sioux, all of whom were with the hostile Indians when Custer came.

THOMAS B. MARQUIS, M.D.

CONTENTS

I	Boyhood Wild Days	1
II	Roamers in the Game Lands	20
III	Cheyenne Ways of Life	56
IV	Worshiping the Great Medicine	123
V	Off the Reservation	155
VI	Swarming of Angered Indians	177
VII	Soldiers from the Southward	193
VIII	On the Little Bighorn	208
IX	The Coming of Custer	217
X	The Spoils of Battle	258
XI	Roving after the Victory	272
XII	Surrender of the Cheyennes	295
XIII	Taken to the South	310
XIV	Home Again on Tongue River	325
XV	A Tamed Old Man	348
XVI	Clearing the Docket	375

Boyhood Wild Days.

Seventy-three years ago (1858) I was born when my people were camped by the waters of the Cheyenne river, in the Black Hills. Both of my parents were of the Northern Cheyenne tribe of Indians. My father had two names, as often is the case among us. He sometimes was called Many Bullet Wounds, because of such marks of warfare on his body. But his preferred name was White Buffalo Shaking Off the Dust. My mother's name was Eagle Feather on the Forehead. Marriage during the old Indian days did not change any woman's name, so all through her lifetime this same term was used for her.

My father's father went to Washington, as a delegate from our tribe, before I was born. He was known as No Braids. The differing words to indicate my grandfather, my father, my mother, and myself show our old way of keeping individuality, regardless of parentage or marriage. My brothers and sisters each had a name different from mine and from our father and mother.

I was known, during my boyhood, as Eats From the Hand. But this baby name was set aside during my youth. The change came about in this manner:

On a certain occasion, many years before my birth, the Cheyennes were camped on the western side of the middle part of Powder river. At this same time the Crows were assembled on a branch of what now is known as the Mizpah river, which flows into the lower part of the Powder river. They were only two or three days of travel from our camp. The Cheyennes organized a war party and went to fight the Crows. As a result of the battle the Cheyennes captured five Crow women and one boy about ten years old. The women were made wives for their captors. The boy was adopted as a son of one of them. All of these captives stayed permanently thereafter with our people.

The Crow boy liked Eagle Feather on the Forehead, who then was only a little older than he. He said, "This girl is my sister." She accepted him as a brother. In later years the girl was married to White Buffalo Shakes Off the Dust, and these became my parents. The Crow boy came to manhood and married a Cheyenne girl. Myself and my brothers and sisters were taught to look upon him as our uncle,

2

since he had been an adopted brother of my mother. He was an admirable man, brave and capable. All of the Cheyennes had a high regard for him. He knew he was born a Crow, but he never showed any desire to leave us for returning to them. He went, though, to the Southern Cheyennes, following the great warrior Roman Nose. He died there, in Oklahoma, a very old man.

This Crow-Cheyenne Indian man was a wonderful traveler on foot. Even as a boy he could outwalk and wear down most of the young men who journeyed with him. His capabilities in this regard were so noticeable that people said: "His legs must be made of wood, since he never becomes tired." Then they fixed upon him a name, Kum-mok-quiv-vi-ok-ta— Wooden Leg.

I also was a youthful wonder in the matter of walking. By the time I was fifteen years old I could go all day following in the footsteps of my uncle Wooden Leg. I was tall and gaunt, and I grew yet taller in young manhood. Friends began jokingly to apply to me the name of this enduring uncle, who then had become a middle-aged or elderly man. I liked the name, I liked the man who bore it, and I liked the honor of comparison with him. I told my father I wished to be known as Wooden Leg. It was a common custom to pass down names to junior relatives. My father told me that when the right time came he would confer upon me the new name. The time came when I was about seventeen years old.

The Cheyennes then were camped far up the Tongue river, on a small creek branch at its western side. It was in winter, there was deep snow and the weather was cold. One morning we discovered that twenty of our horses were missing. A blizzard was whirling, so we could only get glimpses of the trail of the thieves. We supposed them to be Crow Indians, of course. Thirteen Cheyennes, including myself, mounted ponies and set off in pursuit. We struggled all day through the blinding snowstorm. We got the general direction of the trail, so we kept on going during all of the succeeding night. None of us slept. The following morning was clear, but a cold north breeze was sifting the snow along as if it were sand. We then were far up the valley of the Little Bighorn river.

We saw two Indians driving a band of horses out of the valley and upon the benches to the westward. It was evident they were Crows urging our lost animals toward their camp west of the Bighorn. We approached them as rapidly as possible while concealing our presence. When we arrived on the benchland we found the two men had stopped in a sheltered gulch, had dismounted and were preparing to light

4

their pipe for a smoke. We charged upon them. One of them got to his horse and dashed away, but Black Eagle's rifle brought him down dead. The other one was surrounded and cut to death with knives and hatchets. We got back all of our horses and their two horses in addition.

My companions informed my father that I had shown great bravery in rushing upon and helping to dispatch our Crow enemy. My father gave a feast to honor me, and at this feast he proclaimed: "Henceforth the name of this son of mine is Wooden Leg."

As a little boy I used to ride in a travois basket when the tribe moved camp. Two long lodgepoles were crossed over the shoulders or tied to the sides of a horse. Thus they were dragged over the country. Buffalo skins were used to stretch across between the widely gaping poles behind the horse. Upon or into these bagging skins were placed all of the family property, in rawhide satchels or as separate loose articles. The smaller children also rode there. I have fond recollections of this kind of traveling. Many an hour I have slept in that kind of gentle bed. Roads were not needed for this kind of vehicle. A travois can be taken anywhere a horse will go, and there never is any jolting. The spring of the poles and the skin takes up all of the shocks.

When I was six years old I asked my father: "Will

5

you give me a horse?" "Yes, you may have any horse of mine that you want, but you must catch him," he replied. He gave me a rawhide lariat rope. He and my mother and some other older people laughed about it, but I took the matter seriously. With the lariat looped and coiled I went out among the herd to search for horses belonging to my father. I selected a small pony as being my choice. I maneuvered a long time before I could get the loop about its neck. It struggled, but I hung on. When it quieted down I followed carefully along the line, talking soothingly, until it allowed me to pat its neck. After a while I got into its mouth and around its lower jaw a loop of the rawhide, according to the old Indian way of making a bridle. When it had calmed after this new advance I began to make strokes upon its back. Then I tucked the long coil into my belt, the same as I had seen men do, and I climbed quickly upon the little animal. It shied, and I fell off. But I still had my rope, this uncoiling from my belt as the pony moved away. I seized the tether and followed again its guidance to the coveted mount. More petting and soothing talk. Another attempt at riding. Off again. Before making a third try I spent a long time at the gentle taming procedures. Nevertheless, the pony shied and then bucked after I had mounted it. But I grabbed its mane and stuck to my seat. Within a few minutes I had control. I rode to my father's lodge.

"Yes, that is your pony, to keep," he told me.

Bands of us boys went out at times on horseback to hunt wolves. We had only the bows and arrows. We killed many wolves with the arrows. My father had given me a good bow and a supply of arrows when I was nine or ten years old. We then were in the Black Hills country.

The only trading post I ever saw during those years was somewhere on the Geese river.* The trader was known to us as Big Nosed White Man. I was twelve years old the first time I went there, and I never was at any other trading place during those times. My father got me a rifle at this place. It used powder and bullets and caps, not cartridges. I learned how to make bullets for it.

I recollect very clearly one certain boyhood hunting experience. We were camped on Otter creek about two miles from the present white man town of Ashland, Montana, situated by the Tongue river. It was midwinter, the snow was deep, the weather was cold. My mother said to me: "We have no meat."

Another boy and I set off for a hunt. We were about the same age, fifteen years old. We each had on a shirt, leggings and moccasins, all of buckskin

* North Platte river.

or other skin. The leggings had no seat in them, as was the Indian way of clothing the lower limbs. We had no head coverings nor any mittens for our hands. Although we were accustomed to hardship, this was a cold day for us. We waded and wallowed through snow up to our knees and our thighs. I had my muzzle-loading rifle and a bow and arrows. My companion had only his bow and arrows.

A brush rabbit sat huddled under a shelter in a brier patch. I fumbled out an arrow and placed it upon the bow. My numb fingers scarcely could hold the arrow alone, surely could not draw the bow to a tensity enough for accurate shooting. The arrow missed. I rubbed and slapped together my hands to make them warm and mobile. Then I strung another pointed missile and took a careful aim. This time the rabbit's body was perforated. We laid it beside our trail and went on in pursuit of more game.

We saw four buffaloes on the land where now stand the Mennonite missionary houses. They also saw us, and they ran away. They crossed Tongue river on the ice, and soon afterward we got a view of them clambering up the hillside beyond the river and going on to the timbered benchland out of our sight. No chance to shoot at them. We trudged on, though, rubbing and pounding our hands and our bodies in order to keep from freezing. We crossed the river

8

on the ice and came out from the bordering timber near the present-day home of my friend Joe Crow.

A deer jumped out and stood looking at us. The first shot from my rifle brought it down. We rushed to it and cut its throat. We hurriedly cut open the body and jammed our hands inside, to get them warm. Many a time I have done that same thing in other instances. After this limbering of the fingers we skinned the animal and cut off all of the meat from the bones. The meat was wrapped into the skin, then we set off on the back trail for the home camp. We took turns at carrying the burden. As we plodded along we paused to pick up the dead rabbit. About dark we arrived at our lodges, very tired but contented.

On another winter hunt I went alone. My mother said, "We have no meat." So I took a packhorse and started out. The snow was deep. I led the horse as I walked, to keep warm. It was a long and tiresome day. I was becoming discouraged when I found the tracks of a buffalo. I followed them, and finally I got into the right position and killed the animal with a rifle. It was hard work, me alone skinning off the hide, cutting off the meat, rolling the bundle and packing my horse. I got through with it, though, and set out for the home lodge. My legs carried me there, but it was after dark when I gave

9

the horse's leading rope to my mother. All of our family laughed in joy, for we had plenty of meat.

But I was in great bodily distress. I was snow-blind and the soles of my feet were frozen. The fire-light dazzled my eyes to the utmost painfulness. My feet tortured me as they began to get warm in the comfortable lodge. My mother sent for the doctor, a medicine man named Red Bear. He got snow and rubbed the soles of my feet. He took snowflakes be-tween his lips, puffed flicks of them into my eyes, and also he flipped snowflakes from his fingertips into my eyes. Pretty soon I felt much better. Be-fore he went away that night I was entirely cured. He was a wise medicine man for sick people. Many of our doctors in the old times made wonderful cures.

One time when I was on a hunting trip with others in the Bighorn mountains I saw an eagle capture and carry away a buffalo calf. The big bird took the little animal far up to the top of a cliff, where there was an eagle nest. We sat on our horses and watched, to see what would happen. Ordinarily a capturing eagle would drop its prey from high in the air, so it would be killed by the fall to the ground. But this did not happen in this case. As long as we stayed there watching, we still could see the buffalo calf standing up there on the cliff and wig-gling its tail.

A band of soldiers fought our Cheyennes back and forth across a river one time when I was seven or eight years old. It was the Lodgepole river, near where it flows into Geese river. Members of our Crazy Dog warrior society did all of our fighting that day. The Elk warriors and the Fox warriors stayed back with the body of our people who were looking on. My father belonged to the Elk warriors, so he was an onlooker. Roman Nose and High-Backed Wolf were the specially brave Crazy Dogs on that day.

The Shoshones, the Crows and the Pawnees were the tribes we fought most during my time of growing up to manhood. The Pawnees, though, were too far away from the regions where I spent a large part of my early life—the Black Hills, the Powder, Tongue and Bighorn countries. So my own youthful warrior experiences were mostly in combat against the Crows and the Shoshones. One incident out of many in this kind of warfare will show how it was carried on.

A band of Shoshones came at night and stole some of our horses. We were camped on a divide between the upper part of Tongue river and the Little Bighorn. Deep snow and winter weather. I then was sixteen years old. I went with the party of Cheyennes who took the trail of the thieves. After travel-

11

ing all day and into the night we found a small camp of Shoshones. Most of them, alarmed by their dogs, had fled when we made our attack upon them. But repeated shots kept coming from one certain lodge. We concentrated our assault upon this lodge. Two Cheyennes were killed and another one mortally wounded before we could suppress this destructive defense. White Wolf, eleven years older than I was and yet living as my neighbor on Tongue river, was the brave warrior who dealt the fatal blow to that Shoshone. White Wolf crept along the ground and into the lodge. He had in his right hand a six-shooter. It was totally dark in there, and he fumbled about the interior, seeking whomsoever he might find. His gun bumped into somebody, and he pulled the trigger. Later developments revealed this was the only occupant of the lodge. The victim was an old man. He was the only Shoshone we killed in that fight, so far as we could learn. But we won the battle and got back our horses.

We cut up the body of the old Shoshone man. We cut off his hands, his feet, his head. We ripped open his breast and his belly. I stood there and looked at his heart and his liver. We tore down the lodge, built a bonfire of it and its contents and piled the remnants of the dead body upon this bonfire. We stayed there until nothing was left but ashes and coals.

12

The Cheyennes during my youth associated much with the Ogallala Sioux, the Arapahoes and the Minneconjoux Sioux. Many Cheyennes learned the speech of these other tribes, and in turn they had many members who used ours. Most of my outside mingling was with the Ogallalas. By the time I was grown to full stature I could talk Sioux about as well as I could talk Cheyenne. I still can use either language.

Forty army mules were brought into our camp on Rosebud creek when I was about nine years old. Three Cheyennes got them. These three were Wrapped Braids, Old Bear and Pipe, a half-man-and-half-woman Cheyenne. They had chased away a lone soldier herding the mules near a soldier fort on the Bighorn river.* There were many attacks on this and other forts by the Cheyennes and the Sioux, but I was too young to take part in them.

Some Crow chiefs visited our camp on Rosebud creek. The Crows were our enemies, but our people treated these visitors well, as was the Indian custom when enemies came peaceably. After a feast and a smoke had been given them they told our chiefs that the big chief of the soldiers at the Bighorn fort had sent them to make peace with us and invite us to join the Crows and the soldiers in warring against the

* Fort C. F. Smith.

13

Sioux. They said the soldiers would give us lots of presents if we would be friendly with them. All of our camp moved over there. We were given some blankets, many boxes of crackers, and our women received beads and other gifts. We then went back to the Rosebud valley. I do not know what was done about making peace, but I know that our young men warriors kept on doing as they had been doing.

Another soldier fort that was being fought by the Ogallala Sioux and some of the Cheyennes was on what we called Buffalo creek.* Little Wolf was then our most important old man chief. Crazy Head was next in importance among us. Red Cloud was the leading old man chief of the Ogallalas, with Crazy Horse as their principal warrior chief. At a time when our whole tribe were in camp on Rosebud creek, just below the mouth of Lame Deer creek, and when the Ogallalas were on Tongue river, just below where Birney, Montana, is now situated, some of their people came over the divide to us and asked the Cheyennes to join them in a great attack on the Buffalo creek fort. Our chiefs considered the matter. It was decided that whatever young men of us might wish to go would be allowed to do so. Our camp then was moved up Lame Deer creek to the base of the divide, a short day's ride from the Ogallalas

* Fort Phil Kearny, on Little Piney creek.

on Tongue river. Our great medicine man, Crazy
Mule, showed that he could cause bullets shot at him
to fall harmless at his feet. A hundred or more of
our young men said they could go to fight the soldiers
if Crazy Mule would go with them. He agreed to
go. Our second chief, Crazy Head, led the band of
warriors. Little Wolf stayed in our camp.

My oldest brother, named Strong Wind Blowing,
was killed in that midwinter battle with the soldiers.*
He was about sixteen years old. Chief Little Wolf's
younger brother also was killed. These two were the
only Cheyennes who fell that day. I do not know
how many Sioux may have been cut down by the
soldier bullets, but I believe there were not many.
Our returning warriors said that more than a hundred white men lost their lives, that Crazy Mule's
medicine caused them to fall down dead without need
for the Indians to kill them.** There was rejoicing
in our camp on account of the victory. But our
family and all relatives of the two dead Cheyennes
were in mourning. We wept and prayed for the
spirits of our lost ones.

Some time after that battle a half-breed Indian
came as a messenger from the soldier fort chief to
the Cheyennes. He said, "Come, friends, and let us

* Fort Phil Kearny fight, December, 1866.
** Suicidal acts, to avoid capture alive?—T. B. M.

15

have peace." Little Wolf told us we ought to go, so the whole tribe moved near to them. Little Wolf and others of our chiefs had a council with the soldier chiefs. The big chief of the soldiers said to Little Wolf: "We are going away from this country. I give to you all of these soldier houses. Your people may live in them and learn how to cultivate the land." A separate council of our chiefs was held. They replied, "Yes, we will take the houses."

The Cheyennes were pleased. "That one will be my house," some one of them would say, pointing out a certain building. "I want that one," another would claim, indicating some other structure. But Little Wolf was not satisfied. He meditated and expressed his disapproval. "We can not live here," he urged. "It is impossible for Indians to live in the same houses all the time and get enough buffalo and other meat to sustain them." The women especially implored him to change his mind. The question was settled fully one morning when Little Wolf set fire to the fort. He went from building to building, carrying his firebrands. He did not cease his efforts until the entire evidence of white man occupation was in ashes.*

Little Wolf had been a big tribal chief, the most influential one, for about two years before that time.

* Autumn, 1868.

In his earlier manhood years he was for a long time chosen over and over again as the leading chief of the Elk warrior society. If during his time any Cheyenne was looked upon as the bravest man of all, he was the man. He never was afraid to speak the truth. The people all believed him. He was a gentle and charitable man, but if insulted to anger he was likely to hurt somebody. In either disturbed or undisturbed mood everybody knew he meant just what he said. He was my uncle by marriage, one of his two wives being a sister of my father. He used to tell me many thrilling stories, both at his lodge and at my father's lodge. I recall one in particular, when he had a hand-to-hand combat with a Shoshone. Each had a sheathknife. They grappled and wrestled and slashed one another. Finally Little Wolf pinioned the arms of the Shoshone, threw him to the ground, plunged upon him and stabbed him to death. He gave me a great deal of good advice, both as to warfare and as to how to carry myself uprightly as a man among my own people. My conduct all throughout my life has been influenced by his teachings, more than by those of any other preceptor except my own father.

I think my body grew more rapidly than did my mind. By the time I was eighteen years old I was among the tallest men of the tribe. I believe there

17

were but two who stood a little above me. Both of these two were killed in the great battle against the soldiers of Custer. Then remained myself and Tall Bull as the two topmost in stature. We were the same in height, were about the same age, but he was distinctly the heavier. We were close associates during youth and manhood. He died at Lame Deer eight or ten years ago. I do not know by any measurement just what was my height when I was a young man. I think I have grown shorter as old age has crept upon me. My friend the white man doctor measures me now at six feet two inches and weighs me at 235 pounds.

Our tribe during my growing years moved here and there throughout the region between the Black Hills and the Bighorn mountains and Bighorn river. We never went north of the Elk river (the Yellowstone) except on two occasions when some of the tribe went across for only a few days each time. The places of crossing were just above and just below the mouth of the Bighorn. Only one time was the tribal camp circle made west of the Bighorn river. We considered that country as belonging to the Crows. Our war parties went there, but our campings were eastward from this stream. I do not know why we crossed to that side on this occasion. We had been having a series of ceremonial dances at

18

successive camping places, and it may be that this invasion of Crow land was intended as a challenge.

I was about fourteen years old, I believe. The season was what in later life I have come to know as June. It was the time for our usual early-summer religious devotions. A medicine dance had been led by White Horse, an old man, when we were just below where Greasy Grass creek flows into the Little Bighorn. We stayed there five sleeps. Then we moved a few miles down the Little Bighorn, where Crazy Mule led a buffalo dance. Camped there four sleeps. Moved again down the Little Bighorn, this time placing our camp circle on the exact spot where it was located four years later, at the time we killed all of the soldiers. Bear Sits Down gave a buffalo dance at this place. Four sleeps here. The movement was continued on down the Little Bighorn to its mouth, where we crossed the Bighorn and set up our camp circle on its west side. Here Brave Wolf led a Great Medicine or Great Spirit dance, the ceremony known to the white people as a sun dance. Four sleeps we stayed here, then we crossed back to the east side of the Bighorn. That was the only time our people as a tribe ever crossed that river.

II

Roamers in the Game Lands.

The first agency for our Northern Cheyennes that I heard anything about was said to have been at the mouth of the Cheyenne river, east of the Black Hills. But I never was there. Afterward it was located south of the Black Hills, near the present Pine Ridge agency for the Ogallala Sioux. I have been told the white people called this the Red Cloud agency, but the Cheyennes knew it as the White River agency. I was at this place two times, but only for a few days in each instance. My father's family was almost all of the time with other Cheyennes moving about over the country between the Black Hills and the Bighorn river. Here we hunted the game and the enemy Crows and Shoshones, and here we lived in every way the life of the plains Indians of those times. It was not an idle existence. We were busy much of the time, fighting our enemies or gathering food and clothing and sheltering skins.

As we were camped on lower Tongue river, when I was about nine years old, one morning a herald startled the people by his cry:

"Our horses all are gone!"

There followed a lively stir among the young men. A party of them, mounted on a few horses that had been overlooked by the raiders, hurried away on the trail. A thin snow helped them. In the late afternoon they caught up with the lost herd, apparently abandoned. But after a search of the vicinity they discovered that somebody was in a canyon cave there. One of the Cheyennes crawled into the cave, in an endeavor to verify the supposition. The verification came in the form of an arrow that hit him in the right eye. He quickly backed out. "Everybody bring wood," the Cheyenne leader ordered. They built a fire at the cave's opening. With blankets they fanned the flames and the smoke into the hole. The prisoners fanned outward and thrust sticks at the fire heap to push it away. "Bring more wood," the leader called. The one-sided contest went on until two Crow Indian men burst out from the cave almost suffocated and in desperation. The first one out was beaten and stabbed to death by the surrounding Cheyennes. The second one got past them, sprang upon one of their horses and dashed away. The Cheyennes pursued him. He happened to mount a slow animal, so it was not long before the chase developed into a beating by pony whip handles. The Crow suddenly jerked his mount to a

21

standstill. At the same moment he flashed out his sheathknife and made a vicious sidewise stab. The blade buried itself in the breast of a Cheyenne, who fell dead. The other Cheyennes rushed upon the Crow. In a twinkling he had received many death blows from various weapons. Somebody scalped him, and then they cut off his feet, hands and head. I was not with this party, but I was in the camp. I heard all about it when they returned.

I saw the killing of another Crow, though, when we were at this same camp on Tongue river. One morning a Cheyenne horse was discovered dragging a rawhide lariat looped about its lower jaw. This was peculiarly the Crow way of bridling a horse, the Sioux and Cheyennes ordinarily making a headstall and mouth bit with the rope. Evidently some Crow had captured our horse and it had escaped from him during the night. There was a scurrying out to inspect and count our herd. Apparently no others were missing. The inquiry was directed then toward an examination of the ground on the outskirts of the area where the ponies were grazing. Three strange horses had come from the hills to the westward and gone away in a gallop. Another trail was of human footprints, these imprinted as if the maker of them had been lame and had been using a stick for support. This trail led to a hillside cliff. There under the shelter of an overhanging stone roof lay a Crow Indian man apparently dead or sound asleep. A Cheyenne leveled his rifle at close range and fired. The Crow partly jumped up to a sitting attitude and then fell back dead. Investigation showed him to have a broken leg and a broken arm. The horse he had captured was not well tamed, and it had bucked him off. Perhaps it first had carried him away from his companions, and perhaps either he or the horse had made a noise that might have alarmed the camp, whereupon the two other marauders had abandoned him and fled. As I now reflect back sixty years, I pity that unfortunate Crow Indian. But at that time I felt no pity.

Nine Crows came and stole a band of our horses at a time when we were camped far up the Tongue river. I then was about sixteen years old. I joined the pursuing party of Cheyennes. We rode fast and far, following the trail over hills and valleys toward the Bighorn river. Some of our horses, including mine, played out. Four of us turned to go back while the others went on after the Crows. Porcupine was the oldest of my returning group of four. Night was coming upon us, so we stopped to sleep and to rest our horses. During the night a sound of moving horses awakened us. We kept quiet, listening and looking. Porcupine saw someone on horseback

23

about a hundred yards distant from us. He called out a challenge: "Cheyenne? Crow?" The rider lashed his mount to dash away. Porcupine fired his rifle in the direction of the fleeing prowler. We learned nothing then of the outcome of this incident. But several months later an Arapaho friend told us of the ending. He had been hunting in this region, and right where we had slept that night he found the dead body of a Crow shot through from back to front.

The others who had gone on after the Crows driving our herd caught up with them just below the old soldier fort on the Bighorn river. My older brother was with them, and he told me what happened there. The horse band was across on the west side, and four Crows were having a playful time at bathing in the river. They were swimming, splashing, joking, laughing. The dozen or more Cheyennes kept themselves hidden and hurriedly dressed themselves for a fight while their horses rested a few minutes. Then they burst into their war-songs and charged into the water upon the surprised and defenseless bathers. Three Crows were killed, one escaped. All of our horses were recovered and three of theirs were added to the band. The third Crow killed was an old man, but he was very active. He dodged, jumped, dived. But the Cheyennes had too many spears jabbing at

24

him and too many bullets flying toward him. My
brother's six-shooter put the fatal blow upon him.

The following year, when our tepees were assembled on the west side of Tongue river just across
from the mouth of Hanging Woman creek, my father
and I went out one day to get an antelope. He was
about to shoot at one when the animal and some
others with it suddenly ran away. We were hidden,
so it seemed certain their fright came from someone
else. We crept and peeped. Pretty soon we saw a
group of Indian hunters on horseback.

"They are Crows," my father excitedly whispered.

Oh, what clever dodging we did! We got to our
horses, mounted them, kept them moving through
gullies and brushy spots until we reached the home
camp. A band of Cheyennes joined us to attack the
Crows. At a long distance off we followed them
until our horses tired out. By this time we were
at the upper branches of the Rosebud. We gave up
the chase. Nobody hurt.

Great herds of buffalo west of the Bighorn used
to draw the Cheyennes over into that Crow country
for the hunt. We camped on the eastern side, but
our hunting parties crossed the river and went as
far as Shooting at the Bank creek.* Each hunter led
one or more pack horses to carry the meat and skins

* Pryor creek.

25

taken. Many times I have swam the Bighorn or some other river while holding in my teeth the leading rope of my riding pony. The pack horse rope would be held in the same way or might be tied to the tail of this leader. My clothing would be compressed into a bundle and strapped to the back of my head.

As we were camped on the east side of the Bighorn, about two years before the great Custer battle, three Crows were seen one day chasing antelope on our side of the river. Report of their presence there was brought to our camp. An old man herald mounted his pony and went about the camp circle calling out:

"Crows are after our antelope herds. They may steal our horses."

Six Cheyenne young men got their war clothing packs, mounted their war ponies and set out to find the bold Crows. I was not with them, but a special friend of mine was one of the pursuing party and he told me of their experience. They crossed the Bighorn river just below where had been the soldier fort. During the course of the pursuit they killed two Crows. The third one was followed on to the main Crow camp beside Shooting at the Bank creek. The six Cheyennes lingered there to spy upon the camp. The lingering was a little too extended, for soon they found themselves engaged in a fight with

26

a much larger band of Crows. A Cheyenne wearing a double tailed warbonnet had his horse shot down, then the man himself was shot through the thigh, this disability rendering him an easy mark for fatal blows that soon fell upon him. A second Cheyenne was killed by arrows or bullets. A third one met death by the same means. The other three escaped and made their way back to our side of the river and to the home camp circle.

During this same summer the Crows made a raid one night on our horse herd. Of course, when daylight revealed the situation a war party of Cheyennes went out for revengeful retaliation. I was not in camp at this time, being on a hunting trip toward the mountains, but Braid told me of what happened. He was one of the band of avenging Cheyennes. The Crows drove all of the horses to their camp on Shooting at the Bank creek. The Cheyennes hid themselves to watch for some opportunity for reprisal. But the crafty Crows evidently discovered them or had planned thus to entrap them. Notice came only when a horde of them charged out for a fight. Two of the Crows were killed and two Cheyennes also met death. Braid's horse was shot down and he himself was hit by a bullet that broke the bones in the lower part of one of his legs. A companion on horseback took Braid up behind him and the two got away into safety. All of the Cheyennes then fled from the field. Braid is yet alive, at the age of eighty-nine years, his home being on the Rosebud side of this Tongue River reservation. The white people call him Arthur Brady.

About a year before these events just related a big camp of Cheyennes was located on the Little Bighorn a short distance below where Greasy Grass creek empties into it. Fresh footprints of unknown horses near the camp site aroused suspicion. Crows? Shoshones? People conjectured. An old man herald rode about and notified everybody. That night all of the horses were brought into the camp circle and picketed among the lodges. Many watchful people slept lightly or awakened from time to time and peered out from the tepee flaps. Last Bull, asleep in a small tepee with his wife, was startled by the snorting of a mule he had picketed near by. The mule snorted again, then a third time. Last Bull saw a human form crawling along toward his mule. The aroused man had no gun, so he crept under his tepee wall and into the next one, there to borrow a six-shooter from an old woman.

Fire Wolf saw the wriggling form cut the rope and move off leading the mule. He bravely jumped out, without any weapon, and seized the intruder. They grappled and struggled. The stranger had a rifle.

During the scuffle it was discharged. The noise aroused the camp. Cheyennes came running. Cries rang out:

"Kill the Crow! Kill the Crow!"

The thief jerked out a sheathknife and stabbed Fire Wolf again and again until the Cheyenne had to let loose his hold. The freed man sprang to his feet and ran, leaving the mule. A shot from Last Bull's borrowed six-shooter brought him down. A dozen Cheyennes closed in upon him and beat him to death. Fire Wolf had some bad knife wounds, but he recovered. The clothing, the bodily decorations in general and the mode of hair dressing revealed the dead Indian as being not a Crow. He was a Flathead, perhaps a visitor among the Crows or a member of a band visiting and hunting with them.

A battle with the Shoshones was fought near the headwaters of Powder river when I was about fifteen years old (1873). A small band of Cheyennes had their lodges a day's journey farther up the river from the main body of the tribe. I was with the small band. Four or five Shoshones came at night to our little camp and stole our horses. We walked to the main camp and told of the raid. All were for immediate war against the whole Shoshone tribe. "Kill all of the Shoshones," was the common cry. The main camp moved on up the river to our small encampment. There preparations were made for the warfare. That very night thirty-two Shoshone warriors came into the view of our night sentinels. Evidently the enemies had planned to wipe out our little band, not knowing of the presence now of the whole tribe.

The sentinels raised an alarm. Yet the Shoshones did not offer to retreat until they found themselves overwhelmed by a great body of our warriors. Their horses were tired from the journey to our camp while ours were just taken from their picket ropes. Perhaps the raiders had been saying, "We shall kill all of the Cheyennes here," but now they plunged their horses into a long and deep canyon in their effort to get away from us. The Cheyennes strung themselves all along both sides of the canyon. Shooting was kept up during the balance of the night and until an hour or more after daylight. Two of the enemy escaped. Thirty of them were killed in the canyon. Seven of our Cheyennes also lost their lives. We recovered the horses the four had stolen. This fight was on a small creek flowing into the west side of Powder river from the mountains near by.

White Bull was leading a hunting party one time in the Elk river country. I was yet a small boy, so I was not with them. Their scouts observed the distant herds of buffalo excited. Crows? Shoshones? White soldiers? The Cheyennes hid themselves for the night. In the early morning they found moccasin tracks by a creek. The moccasin trail led to a Blackfeet camp. There the Cheyennes stirred up a fight, but I believe nobody was killed. The great warrior Roman Nose rode back and forth in front of the Blackfeet and defied them. All of them were said to have shot at him without a bullet or arrow having harmed him. He had a powerful spirit or medicine protection for himself. White Bull had taught him this medicine.

Soldiers got after a small band of mingled Cheyennes and Sioux near the Black Hills one time. We were running away when a Cheyenne was killed. Two Sioux, another Cheyenne and myself went back to recover his dead body. We got off our horses and crept over a hill. We four took our dead companion by his hands and feet and dragged him over the knoll. There we rolled him into a blanket and we took the four corners. Bullets were whistling all about us. The blanket ripped and the body fell through the opening. We again took hold of the hands and feet, and in this way we got him to our horses and delivered him to his own people.

Several months before the great battle with Long Hair (General Custer) and his soldiers, some Chey-

31

ennes coming from the agency on White river told us that the white men were going to come out and fight us. As parties went out for hunting, a lookout was kept for these white enemies. My brother, myself and two other Cheyenne young men went on a special scouting journey. We were camped then far up the Powder river. At night we four slept out in the open country. Early in the morning a fifth Cheyenne came to us. "Soldiers are near us," he said. We learned our horses were missing. The soldiers had taken them. We all ran away afoot. We scattered in different directions, except my brother and me, who went together into a canyon. Soldiers rode along on both sides of the canyon and shot at us. We shot back at them, first using up our bullets and then resorting to our arrows. We kept creeping along the canyon. The soldiers gradually dropped away. We were not harmed nor did we know of our having harmed any of them. When they left us we carefully worked our way on up the canyon and over a hill toward our camp. Breathing hard, almost exhausted, frightened to the verge of collapse, we stopped for a few minutes of rest. Then we hurried on. At the outskirts of the camp circle we paused to send a warning wolf howl. The people all gathered about us.

"What has happened?" they asked.

We told of our experience. At the same time the other returned young men were giving the same kind of information. The chiefs ordered everybody to pack up, and the camp was moved far on down the Powder river. Some of us stayed back to watch the soldiers. One night I saw them in their camp. Two sentinels were walking back and forth near their horses. I or any of my companions could have killed either or both of them. But this would have endangered our people, so we did nothing of that kind. We stole back our horses, though. I got the same horse they had taken from me a few nights before this. Our camp kept on moving, and the soldiers never found us on this hunt.

A great band of Southern Cheyennes came for a visit to us in the Black Hills about two years before the Custer battle on the Little Bighorn. All of us joined together then for a long hunting journey to the westward, to the Powder river, the Tongue and the Little Bighorn. Many thousands of buffalo, deer, antelope. Many skins, much meat, everybody happy and prosperous and in health. On the Little Bighorn river we had one day of Great Medicine thanksgiving dancing just below the mouth of Greasy Grass creek. Further down the valley the camp divided, half of the people going northwestward to trouble the Crows while the other half took a southwestward course toward the country of the Shoshones.

I went to the Shoshone country. We did not see any of those Indians, but a few of us saw their agency. We saw also the soldier houses there. We kept clear of the soldiers, and I think they never knew we were in that region until after we had gone. We rounded up and drove off a herd of white man cattle and killed every beef. Game was scarce there, and we needed the food.

We followed the mountains to upper Powder river, where we joined again with the Cheyennes who had separated from us on the Little Bighorn. After a few days of feasting in the great combined camp, there began to be departures in bands, bands, bands, for return to the agency south of the Black Hills. My small remaining group went to Otter creek, a tributary of the lower Tongue river. Good hunting, lots of game, on this creek. We followed it to its head and moved on eastward to Powder river. We went up that stream and diverted to the Little Powder river. Here other Cheyennes came to us. Then more arrived, and yet more. Again a great band of us were roaming together.

An early autumn snowstorm in the upper Powder river region put a check upon our great summer movements. Separations came again. Indians went back again to the agency for the winter. My band moved over to the upper Tongue river. Here, only a short distance down that stream from the present white man town of Sheridan, Wyoming, buffalo in great throngs were feeding. We had but to kill and eat. As I now think back upon those days, it seems that no people in the world ever were any richer than we were. That is all anybody actually needs—a good shelter, plenty of food, plenty of fuel, plenty of good water. We stayed all winter in this vicinity. My father and his family never cared to live at the agency.

In every herd of buffaloes the adult males were about equal in size and of the same dark brown color. All buffalo cows likewise were about equal in size, smaller than the bulls. The sucking calves were of yellow color. At the age of one year they began to change to the darker yellow and then to brown and dark brown or black.

A white buffalo was killed by the Cheyennes on a branch of the upper Powder river. That was when I was a boy, about the time the soldier fort was there. Many Cheyennes were after the animal, but Left Handed Shooter killed it. Such animal was regarded as a spirit being or a "medicine" animal. The assembled Cheyennes stood back from this one in respectful awe. Left Handed Shooter could not persuade anyone to help him in skinning it. He alone took the hide from the whole body, separating off the head and horns.

Four medicine women were called to Left Handed Shooter's lodge. They pegged down the sacred skin, dried it, scraped it with their elkhorn scrapers, did all of the work of tanning it as a robe with the hair left on it. An old medicine man then took it to his lodge. There he painted it. He put upon the smooth inside many black suns, many black moons, many stripes, all in groups of four, the Indian sacred number.

The painted skin then was hung upon a tall pole. The horned head was put upon another pole near by. All of the spirit men or medicine men came, all of the people assembled. There were many long prayers, to the Great Medicine above and to the spirits below. Finally an old man announced:

"We give this tanned white robe to the Great Medicine above. We give the head and horns to the spirits below."

The robe was taken down from the pole and was carefully folded. Medicine men and women then respectfully carried it with the head and horns to the top of a hill. There these revered objects were left as gifts to the unseen rulers of the Indian world. The meat of the animal was not considered as sacred. It was eaten, the same as if it were any other buffalo flesh.

After that time another white buffalo was seen and chased by Cheyennes on Tongue river below the present town of Sheridan, Wyoming. It was a fleet-footed and long-winded animal. All of the Cheyenne horses were exhausted in the chase. The coveted buffalo escaped us, and I never heard of anyone having seen it afterward.

I killed a buffalo cow having white hair covering the upper and inner thighs, the back part of the belly, the udder, and having white teats. My mother took great care in tanning it and made of it a fine robe for me. It either was taken or was burned by the soldiers who drove us from our camp on the Powder river a few months before the Custer soldiers came.

A black buffalo calf was killed by Exhausted Elk far up the Tongue river. It being black instead of the usual yellow color of the calves caused it to be treated as a spirit animal. Four medicine women tanned its skin, assembled medicine men held ceremonies, the congregated people looked upon it with veneration. The skin was painted and placed upon a hill as a sacrifice gift to the Great Medicine, the same as was done with the skin of the white buffalo. Also, its flesh was eaten as if it were only an ordinary buffalo calf.

A half-bull-half-cow buffalo was killed one time by the Cheyennes. My father helped in the killing of it. This animal was of enormous size. It was big, fat, had a tall back, long horns, and its hump was almost double the size of the average buffalo bull. My father called friends to his lodge for a feast upon this meat. It was not regarded as a medicine animal. The heart and the liver were cut into big slices to be eaten raw, as Indians usually ate these parts. Only the old medicine men ate of these slices at my father's feast.

There always was some danger mixed with the pleasures of wild game hunting. I remember a Cheyenne who was gored terribly by a buffalo bull. He recovered, though. After that he became known as Buffalo Not Kill Him. Walking Whirlwind, a young man about my age, had his shoulder torn by a bear. He also recovered.

A bear attacked three old Cheyenne women as they were picking berries on Tongue river. One of the women was badly clawed. The two companions put her upon a horse and took her to camp. She died just after her arrival there. At that same time one of our men was out hunting. He saw a bear, shot it and killed it. As he approached the dead animal he observed dried blood all about its nose and its cheeks. This strange condition puzzled him. In skinning the bear he carefully preserved the bloody muzzle. When he arrived in camp with his meat packed in the skin he learned of the killing of the old woman. Everybody agreed this must have been the bear that killed her.

Two Cheyenne men, Bear Dung and Sun Road, went buffalo hunting from a camp of ours on the lower Rosebud. As they were circling about a milling herd a bull sunk its horns into the belly of Bear Dung's horse, ripped it open, lifted and tossed aside the animal. Bear Dung went sprawling to the ground. The bull immediately plunged at the man and gored him to death. Sun Road hurried into camp and told of the sad occurrence. The dead man's women relatives took out a travois and brought him to camp. He was a brother of Buffalo Hump, an old Cheyenne now living on the Rosebud. Sun Road also is still alive, his home being on the Rosebud side of our reservation.

Competitive sports used to interest us. Horse races, foot races, wrestling matches, target shooting with guns or with arrows, tossing the arrows by hand, swimming, jumping and other like contests were entered upon. In the tribe such competition usually was between men representing the three warrior societies. These were the Elk warriors, the Crazy Dog warriors and the Fox warriors. If any Sioux tribe or big band camped jointly with us the matches were between representative members of the two tribes. Bets were made on every kind of contest. The stakes were of guns, ammunition, bows and arrows, blankets, horses, robes, jewelry, shirts, leggings, moccasins, everything in the line of personal property. The betting always was on even terms. Articles were piled upon a blanket, matched articles in apposition to each other. The winners took all and shouted over the victory.

The Elk warriors, the society to which I belonged, had the best runners. Our speediest man on foot was named Apache. He was almost as tall as I was and he was much heavier. He had remarkably big thighs. One time at a double camping with the Ogallalas on upper Powder river a foot race was arranged between the two tribal champions. The Ogallala fast man was tall and slender. His name was Black Legs. The distance they were to run was about a mile, I believe, although at that time we had no measurements for distance. Four friends of each man accompanied the two racers to the starting point. A revolver shot told them when to go. Near the finish the Sioux fell exhausted. Our man Apache was very tired, but he ran on to the end of the route. Of course, the Cheyennes took all of the stakes, let out a chorus of cheers and fired their guns into the air.

"The Cheyenne medicine broke his legs," the Sioux said when their man collapsed.

The old Chief Little Wolf had been a great runner when he was a young man. The longer the distance the better it suited him. As the Cheyennes and the Ogallalas were traveling together in moving camp there was much bantering such as, "I think the Sioux can travel faster than the Cheyennes can," or, "It appears the Cheyennes must go a little more slowly in order not to run away from their friends the Sioux." Finally a young Sioux jokingly challenged Little Wolf to a foot race.

"How," assented Little Wolf, "I'll run with you."

The caravan was stopped and arrangements were made for the race. Little Wolf then was past fifty years of age, while his Sioux challenger was just entering young manhood. Nevertheless, the Cheyennes backed their chief heavily. A great pile of bets were placed upon the containing blankets. Four Cheyennes and four Sioux went with the two men to the agreed starting point, which must have been three or four miles away. At the crack of a revolver shot the race began. Up to the last mile the young Sioux kept well in the lead. Then he began to move more slowly. It appeared Little Wolf never changed his pace. So he closed up toward the leader. In the last part of the last mile he went ahead, still running at what appeared to be his same rate while the other man's speed continued to lessen. By a broad hundred yards Little Wolf won the contest. Many of the Sioux, even some who had lost bets, joined the Cheyennes in cheering for the old man.

A good wrestler and general strong man was Little Hawk. He and Buffalo Hump and Brave Wolf made up a playful raiding group in the camp one time after a great hunting party had brought in lots of buffalo beef. All about the camp circle there were drying poles loaded with meat. The three young men had not been fortunate in the chase, so they decided to borrow from their friends. They went to a certain tepee.

"We need meat," they announced. "Your drying poles are too full, and we think our wants can be supplied there. But Little Hawk wants to wrestle for it. If anybody here can throw him we shall not take any food from this lodge."

Nobody there wanted to accept this challenge. The young men took some meat and went on to another tepee. There they made the same kind of announcement and proposition. There likewise all of the men present feared to grapple with Little Hawk, and there also the three joking robbers helped themselves from the bountiful store. At the next tepee the transaction was more complex. After some exchange of talk the spokesman of the lodge said:

"Big Thigh is here. He says he will wrestle you."

The conditions of the match were agreed upon. The two men stripped to their breechcloths. A group of onlookers assembled. The group soon became a great crowd. Big Thigh and Little Hawk appeared equally confident. Both of them rushed into the grapple. They tugged and shoved and tripped. The advantage seemed to shift back and forth. The throng of spectators whooped and danced. There was some partisan cheering, but most of it was merely the expression of delight at witnessing this tribal championship battle. After several minutes of fierce and continuous struggling Little Hawk began to weaken and wilt. Big Thigh pinioned the arms of his antagonist and bore him face downward to the ground. The victor sat astride the back of the vanquished and sprinkled handfuls of dirt upon him. He also picked up a folded blanket lying near by and used this as a soft club in pretense at beating into complete submission the defeated Little Hawk. Shouts of congratulation greeted the conqueror while jeers were heaped upon the under dog and his two confederates. Brave Wolf and Buffalo Hump, ridiculed to complete embarrassment and compelled to replace their looted buffalo meat, quickly took themselves into hiding.

Our target shooting was with rifles, revolvers and arrows. For the arrow contests an erect wooden figure of a man was the customary mark. Sometimes the arrows were shot from the bow, sometimes they were tossed by hand. Both accuracy and extent of penetration counted in either form of this archery. Shooting arrows for long distance was another test of capability. Here a strong bow and a powerful arm and hand were important elements for success. In all of these games the regular rule allowed four successive shots for each contestant. Fine points in the manipulation of arrows were brought out in the sidewise tossing of them at short distances, each toss being made in attempt at the exact crossing of another arrow thrown out by an opponent.

Most of our few rifles were muzzle loaders and our revolvers usually were of the kind using caps and moulded bullets. The target for practice with them ordinarily was a black ring as broad as a large hand marked upon an animal's dried shoulderblade or upon a barked tree. Teams of three or more men on each side often were arrayed against each other for either the arrow or gun contests. Usually the teams represented their respective warrior societies. On many occasions, though, there were personal engagements. In these there might be sought only an honorable distinction or there might be betting added as an incentive to achievement. An incident of this character that was much talked about among the Cheyennes came up at a time when we were camped on the Powder river.

Jules Seminole brought a keg of whisky to the camp. He got it at some white man trading post. He was a southern half-breed married to one of our Northern Cheyenne women and accounted as belonging to our tribe. One of our young men solicited him:

"Give me a drink of your whisky."

"No, but I'll bet a drink that I can beat you at shooting," Seminole proposed. "What have you to bet?"

The young man feared defeat. But he went canvassing here and there in an effort to find someone who would take up Seminole's challenge. One after another declined to contest. Finally, in jest rather than in earnest, he put the case before an old medicine man who was totally blind in one eye and partly blind in the other.

"I'll bet a good buffalo robe against the whole keg of whisky that I can beat you at shooting," the old man declared to Seminole.

Seminole evidently suspected some kind of trick.

45

He hesitated, but the urgings of the gathered crowd carried him into acceptance of this counter proposition.

A tree was barked and a black circle target drawn upon this clean surface. Seminole shot first. He had a cartridge rifle. The bullet imbedded itself an inch or so below the black circle.

"Get me a pin," the old medicine man requested of his young helper.

The pin was brought. The aged Cheyenne placed it point forward upon his right palm. He held this palm upward in front of his eyes. His squint wrinkles deepened and his lips formed themselves into a pucker. A sudden puff of his breath caused the pin to vanish. Nobody knew what had become of it.

"Examine the target," the performer told them.

There it was, buried to its head just inside the circle. The people all wondered. The keg of whisky was conceded to its new owner.

"I'll bet a horse against the whisky that you can't do anything like that again," Seminole dared him.

"How," came instantly a responsive agreement.

The target was placed more distant, this at the request of Seminole and by assent of his competitor. Onlookers became involved in the betting. The medicine man found many backers of his mysterious powers. The half-breed adjusted his sights. He took an unusually long and careful and steady aim. "Bang!" His bullet struck within an inch of the circle's center. His betting supporters were gleeful, the opposition were in doubt. They awaited anxiously the next move of their champion.

"Bring me a claw of a redbird," he calmly ordered.

A dozen young men put themselves into his service. They wanted to help him in drinking the whisky. Within a minute he had the required object.

The redbird claw was placed upon the same upturned palm where had been the pin. "The target is too far," came a complaint. Then: "Yes, I can see it now." Puff! The claw was gone. Where? Right into the central black spot of the black circle target!

All comers had a drink of the whisky. A tin cup was brought and the old medicine man dipped in and passed out hot liquid mouthfuls to hundreds of Cheyennes. Nobody got enough to make him drunk. I spat out my mouthful. It did not taste good.

Red Haired Bear and his wife were traveling with their lone lodge one time in the Black Hills. At their noon camp he saw deer tracks and set off to follow them. They led him up a dry coulee and into the timber. There a strong and disagreeable odor was wafted to him. He grasped his gun more firmly and went on. Just then a big snake stood up and flashed

47

its tongue at him. Its head was above his head and its body resembled a tree. It struck him—one, two, three, four times. It backed off and poised as if to strike again. He was sickened, but he aimed his gun.

"Great Medicine, help me," he prayed.

"Yes, be brave and I will help you," a reply came from above.

He bethought himself not to shoot at its head, since the bullet might glance off harmless. He shot it through the neck. The immense serpent threshed about in terrible fashion, crushing bushes and tearing up the earth. But it gradually quieted down, and finally it lay dead.

The faint and terrified man took the back trail for his camp. He had four gullies to cross. He got over the first one without much difficulty. The second one troubled him. Just before he started across the third one he almost fainted. But he braced up and went over it. He was dizzy and wobbling as he approached the fourth gully. "Be brave now," the Great Medicine said to him. He had dropped his gun, but the encouraging words led him to pick it up and go on. He staggered into and out of this fourth obstacle. At the camp he told his wife of what had occurred. She gave him a big dose of gunpowder in water. Then he vomited, the vomit having the same odor as had come from the snake.

48

A second dose of gunpowder brought up more of the poison. A third treatment had the same effect, but the odor now was almost gone. The fourth time he took the mixture it stayed down in his stomach. Then he felt all right. Red Haired Bear himself told me of this experience. But he was not a reliable man, so I never was sure whether it was true or not.

White Frog and Red Hat told a story of them having an adventure of this same kind. They had been to the trading post, where they had taken their pack horses loaded with skins of beaver, buffalo and antelope. While returning they arrived at Tongue river just above the mouth of Crow creek. The water was high. They dismounted, waded and led their horses to an island. For crossing the next channel they drove the horses ahead of them. The men were naked and were holding their clothing over their heads as they waded.

A monstrous snake rose up from the water and threatened them. "It will eat up both of us," they exclaimed together. They prayed the Great Medicine to pity them. At once there came a flood of rain and a whirling wind. The wind picked up the snake, dragged it along the water's surface for a short distance, then lifted it into the air. It went up, up, up, and soon it was gone from their sight. White Frog and Red Hat agreed in their stories to us that

49

the snake was so big it looked like a floating log. One Cheyenne who heard them said it might have been a floating log that looked like a snake.

When Black Wolf went one time on a deer hunt he saw two women sitting on the edge of a cliff. Both women were beautiful in face and form. As they sat there dangling their feet over the cliff they beckoned to him. He went to them and sat down beside them. Pretty soon his nostrils perceived a strong odor of deer. At the foot of the cliff, in a pool of clear water, he saw a reflection of himself with two deer beside him. "You are only two deer," he accused the women. At that they both jumped up. They changed instantly into deer and went bounding away into the timber.

A Southern Cheyenne out hunting saw a lovely woman by a grove of trees, braiding her hair. She looked at him and smiled. That was enough to draw him straight to her. But when he took hold of her he smelled her flesh.

"Oh, you deceitful deer!" he exclaimed.

She struggled then to free herself from him. But he held firm. He tied her hands together and tied her feet together. The deer woman declared:

"If you keep me thus tied you will die. If you let me go loose you will live to be old and always will be in good luck."

50

He decided to let her go free. She ran away as a doe deer. When the man arrived at his home lodge he was wildly insane. Medicine men were called. He told them the story of his meeting the deer woman. The medicine men prayed for him. His right mind soon came back to him.

I had one time a strange adventure with a deer. I shot it with my rifle, the bullet passing through it from the rump forward. It ran away, I followed. I shot again, this time the bullet going through its chest, right to left. It turned around. Another shot made another hole through its chest, left to right. A fourth and a fifth bullet likewise was sent into and out of its front body. It ran to a bushy grove. In this grove I found it lying down. It was facing me. It was not only alive, but it appeared not to have been hurt at all. I hesitated and trembled a little as I drew my six-shooter. At close range I aimed at the middle of its forehead. The bullet brought blood from the exact point where I had aimed. But the deer appeared unharmed. I fired again, aiming at the same spot, and a new trickle of blood flowed out. Still the animal gave no sign of having been injured. I stood there and thought about the case. I decided to shoot once more—an eighth effort. That is two times the Indian sacred number four. I moved up close and put my revolver's muzzle near the middle

51

of the ridge above the deer's right eye. Holding myself steady, I pulled the trigger. Instantly afterward the animal's body became limp. It was dead.

I do not entirely understand that. It may be I was dreaming, but it does not seem like a dream.* The Cheyennes consider all deer as having strong spirit powers. Medicine men like to get their medicine strength.

An old Cheyenne man and his wife told me a story, when I was a boy, about a big stone that stands near Antelope creek west of the Black Hills. They said that at some time, long ago, some Indian girls were at play there. They were poking a forked stick into a hole, in search for beaver. They touched something, twisted, pulled, and brought out some hair on the end of the stick. They supposed it to be the hair of a wolf, a coyote or a porcupine. As they talked of it, a bear of immense size came from the hole. It chased the girls, capturing many of them and tearing them to pieces. Two sisters escaped. The bear followed them, going to their home tepee, but it did not harm them. When night came, the two girls crept out. They met two young men and

* In telling all of these fanciful stories, Wooden Leg exhibited a queer mingling of belief and doubt. They show an odd mental streak in a man having a large stock of level-headed common sense, and whose statements of fact as to genuine occurrences are worthy of full credit. He is the kind of man who could not tell a lie without at once retracting and correcting his misstatement, if he knew it to be such.—T. B. M.

52

told them of the frightful animal. "It can not be killed by any shot in its head nor its heart nor in other parts of its body," they told the two young men, "but a shot through its foot, from the bottom upward, will kill it." The young men considered the case. Then they said to the two girls: "All of us will hide here and wait."

When the bear awakened in the morning it learned the two girls were gone. It moved about inside and then outside, smelling of the ground. Sniff, sniff, sniff, sniff. It set off on the trail of the girls, following to the base of the great stone. There it sat down upon its haunches and looked upward toward the stone's top. Pretty soon it began climbing up the steep side. A little distance up, its feet slipped and it slid down. It tried again, this time going higher, but it slid down again. Trials were made at many places. But always the effort was a failure.

The two young men and the two girls were hidden close by. One of the young men shot an arrow at the bottom of the bear's foot as it was clambering up the stone. When it went up again he shot another arrow. On another effort of the bear a third arrow was sent after it. The three arrows whizzed past the bear and went on high into the air. They came down without doing any damage. The fourth arrow flashed past very close to the bear's left hind foot.

53

The animal slid down and ran away. The arrow kept on going up, up, and it never came down.

I have seen many times the long upright marks of the bear's claws on this great column of stone. They are deep seams or furrows. It must have been a monster of a bear. As far back as I can remember, all of the Indians called this stone Bear Tepee or Bear Lodge.*

An old Cheyenne man and I were traveling together one time past the Bear Tepee. He told me a story about it. He said that a long time ago—nobody knew how long—an Indian man journeying alone chose to sleep at the base of this tall stone. A buffalo head was lying near him. He slept four nights. During that time the Great Medicine took both him and the buffalo head to the top of the high rock. When the man awakened he could find no way to get down. He was hungry and thirsty, but he had neither food nor water. He was greatly distressed in mind. He thought of his wife and his children. He wept and prayed all day. At night, exhausted, he slept again. During that night the Great Medicine gently took him down again to his leaf bed on the ground. The buffalo head was left at the top, near the edge. That Indian man was said by some people to have

* Modern whites know this as "Devil's Tower."

been an Apache, others said he was a Shoshone, yet others declared he was a Cheyenne.

I saw that buffalo head many times. The first time was when I was with the old man and he told me the story of it. He had a spyglass and we looked through it. We could see plainly that it was the head of a buffalo. I was a small boy at that time, eight or ten years old. The Bear Tepee is four or five hundred feet high, maybe higher, and its sides are straight up and down. How else could a buffalo head get up there except it be placed there by the Great Medicine?

I have heard many old Cheyennes say that a long time ago the Great Medicine used to come down to the earth and talk with people. They said He had camped and visited and smoked with the old-time Cheyennes. Lots of times I have heard them talk about Him having given to our people the Black Hills and all of the gold there.

III

Cheyenne Ways of Life.

The warrior societies were the foundation of tribal government among the Cheyennes. That is, the members of the warrior societies elected the chiefs who governed the people. Every ten years the whole tribe would get together for the special purpose of choosing forty big chiefs. These forty then would select four past chiefs, or "old men" chiefs, to serve as supreme advisers to them and to the tribe. There were not any hereditary chiefs among the Cheyennes.

The Elk warriors, the Crazy Dog warriors and the Fox warriors were the ruling societies of the Northern Cheyennes. Other like organizations had been in existence before my time, but during all of the period of my boyhood and manhood those three were the only active ones in our northern branch of the double tribe. Each warrior society had a leading war chief and nine little war chiefs. So, there were many men who might claim the title of chief. All together there were seventy-four such officials, counting both the tribal rulers and the warrior society rulers. There were four "old men" tribal chiefs, forty tribal big chiefs, three leading warrior chiefs and twenty-seven little warrior chiefs. Ordinarily they were ranked or held in respect in this order, the old men chiefs first, the little warrior chiefs last.

The warrior chiefs had original authority only in their societies, each in his own special organization. By alternation, though, the tribal chiefs delegated governmental power to the warrior chiefs. That is, one group or another of the warrior chiefs and their followers were called upon to serve as active subordinate officials to carry out the orders promulgated by the big chiefs. Such warrior society group, when on this duty, were like the white man's sheriffs, policemen, soldiers.

Promotion in public life followed the line from private member of a warrior society to little chief of the same, then to leading chief, then to big chief of the tribe, finally to old man chief. Of course, all of the tribal and old men chiefs were members of one or another of the warrior societies. It often occurred that in time of battle or in organized great hunting expeditions a tribal big chief or an old man chief had, during such time, the low standing of a mere private person subordinate to the rule of the warrior chiefs. And, in many instances some man might be at the same time both a warrior chief and a tribal big chief or even an old man chief. Little Wolf had this honor put upon him. Even after he had become one of

57

the four old men chiefs he was kept in office as leading chief of the Elk warriors.

Four unmarried and virtuous young women were chosen as honorary members of each warrior society. If one of these entered into marriage or became unchaste she lost her membership and some other young woman was chosen in her place. The young women took no active part in the proceedings. They were allowed merely to sit inside the lodge of assemblage, there quietly looking on. At the society dances no women were permitted to do any of the work. Two little chiefs were appointed on each occasion to do the cooking, to serve the feast or to perform any other menial service necessary. The meetings or dances were held in privately owned lodges of members. The coverings were lifted or were removed so that spectators might view the affair from the outside. The three different societies had the same character of organization, and their social and military operations were carried out on the same general lines. A man could join only one of them.

I joined the Elk warriors when I was fourteen years old. We were camped then at Antelope creek, near the Black Hills. Their herald chiefs were going about the camp circle calling, "All Elk warriors come for a dance and a feast." They were gathering at a large tepee made of two family lodges combined into one. Left Handed Shooter, at that time leading chief of the Elks, came to my father's lodge and said to me: "We want you to join the Elk warriors."

Oh, how important I felt at receiving this invitation! I had been longing for it, waiting to be asked, wishing I might grow older more rapidly in order to get this honorable standing already held by my father and my two older brothers. Seventy or more Elks were dancing. Occasionally one fired a gunshot into the air. As they danced they were scraping their "rattlesnake sticks," the special emblem of Elk membership. Each of these sticks was made of hard wood, in the form of a stubby rattlesnake seven or eight inches long. On each stick was cut forty notches. Another stick was used for scraping back and forth along the notches. The combined operation of many instruments made a noise resembling the rattlesnake's warning hum. Each member owned his personal wooden stick, but there was one made from an elk horn that was kept always by someone as a trustee for the society. No payment nor gift was necessary for admission into a warrior organization.

In the camp circles, in the tribal movings from place to place, in the great tribal hunts, in the times of Great Medicine or other general ceremonial dances —in fact, at all times of our lives some one or other warrior society was authorized or commanded by the tribal chiefs to take charge of the government. Ordinarily there was shift of the delegated authority by regular rotation, but such change in regular order was not always the case. The conclave of big chiefs decided which society should have it. A society might be appointed to act for one day, two days, three days, any stated length of time, or they might be appointed to serve during the continuation of some certain event. At any time their appointment might be revoked by the big chiefs and another society named in their stead. Anyhow, some one or other warrior band was on duty at all times to put into execution the will of the big chiefs.

Perhaps at some time the Crazy Dog warriors might be acting as the policemen at this particular place of camping. Perhaps the four old men chiefs might determine that a general buffalo hunt ought to be entered upon. A herald on horseback was sent about the camp to proclaim:

"All chiefs, open your ears and listen. Come to the council lodge."

There the matter was discussed. Perhaps it was decided first to move camp farther down the river, or up the river, or over to the next valley, or yet farther away. The big chiefs then considered which warrior society should conduct the camp movement. Perhaps they agreed upon the Fox warriors. The leading chief and the little chiefs of this society were notified there at the council. The old man herald went out to ride again about the camps and call out:

"All Cheyennes, open your ears and listen. Tomorrow morning we move to Tongue river. Have your lodges down and yourselves and your horses ready. The Fox warriors will lead us."

The next morning, as all were preparing for the move, the Fox warriors assembled out forward in the direction of the intended movement. The old man herald instructed them: "You are the leaders today. Make all of the people obey you. Make them stay in their proper places. If any of them disobey our ordinary rules of travel you may pony-whip them, you may shoot their horses, you may kill their dogs, you may break their guns or their bows, you may punish them in any way that seems to you best, except you are not allowed to kill any Cheyenne." The Crazy Dog warriors, who had been policemen in the camp, now went off duty and became merely Cheyenne individuals. The leading chief of the Fox warriors was the most important man of that day, his little chiefs and their subordinate warriors were his helpers. The tribal old men chiefs and big chiefs led the camp movement, the Fox warrior band immediately following them or sending their members from time to time back along the caravan to keep order. The big chiefs in front decided when it was time to stop for a rest, when to move on again, when and where to camp. The Fox soldiers transmitted and enforced their orders. When the big chiefs chose a spot for the camp their herald stationed himself where he could tell all of the oncoming people, "Camp here." If there were any disputes about special location of lodges the Fox warriors settled the disputes. In fact, though, there rarely were any such disputes. Every camp circle of the Cheyennes was arranged very much like their preceding circles. Families or related families or clans set up their lodges at all times in about the same location with regard to each other. Always the horseshoe incomplete circle opened to the east. Always every individual lodge in the camp likewise had its entrance opening toward the east—toward the rising sun.

To organize for the tribal buffalo hunt another council was called. This or any other council usually was held at and after darkness, by the light of a great bonfire. The big chiefs regularly would tell the leading warrior chiefs, "We want four good and reliable warriors to scout and discover the location of a buffalo herd." When the warrior leaders had nominated these four the old man herald moved on horseback through the camp calling out their names and the duty put upon them. They went to the council and there received their instructions through their warrior chiefs. They performed the scout duty according to their orders—nobody ever dared refuse to go —and upon their return a report was made to the old man herald. Meantime, perhaps the big chiefs decided that the Elk warriors should conduct the buffalo hunting party. The herald went out and proclaimed:

"All Cheyennes, open your ears and listen. Many buffalo have been discovered by our scouts. Sharpen your knives and your arrow points. See that your guns are in good order. Have your riding horses and your pack horses ready. Tomorrow morning we go. The Elk warriors will lead and conduct the hunt."

The Elks then actually led the party. Nobody but big chiefs were allowed to go in front of them. The Elk warriors did all of the scouting for game and watching for enemies while the party was on the move. Any non-Elk intruder would be ponywhipped, or worse. If any Elk himself disobeyed the orders of his warrior chiefs this disobedient one was punished, either by his fellow Elks upon their own initiative or by command of the warrior chiefs. The effort at all times was to carry out well whatever governmental task was placed upon the warriors, either on the hunts, at the camps, during a journey, in time of battle or under any conditions where they were vested with authority. The three societies competed against each other for efficiency in governmental action as well as in all other affairs appertaining to respectable manhood. There was competition also within each society, every ambitious member trying to outdo his fellows in all worthy activities.

The Fox warriors were leading a buffalo hunt one time when I was about sixteen years old. We then were on Crow creek, northeast of where Sheridan, Wyoming, now stands. Last Bull was the leading chief of the Fox soldiers. I was riding with three other youths about my age.

"Oh, lots of buffalo!" one boy suddenly exclaimed.

We skirted around the band of hunters and got forward. A Fox warrior saw us crowding ahead. We also saw him, and we whirled our horses to go back. Two or three of the Foxes followed us. We scattered. I made a dash for Tongue river. It was frozen solid. My horse slipped and slid, but I got across. My pursuers stopped at the stream, but I kept on going away from them. I did not know what became of the other three boys. I was scared. My heart was thumping, thumping, pounding my breast. I expected to be pony-whipped, to have my horse killed and my clothing torn to pieces. But it appeared they never found out our identity.

Another time, about a year later, I got into the same kind of trouble. This time we were moving camp. The Crazy Dog warriors were in the lead and conducting the movement. We were traveling up the Tongue river, far up, above the present Sheridan, and were about to go over the divide to the upper Powder river. Two other youths and myself forgot the rules. We rode forward from our proper place in the procession and went on out to a hilltop, there to have a look over the country, as every Indian naturally likes to do.

Four Crazy Dog warriors were right after us. They were riding fast. The other two boys got away, but my pony played out on me. I had to stop and dismount. I was frightened to distraction, but my mind was made up to take bravely whatever punishment they might inflict. Nevertheless, I became mentally upset when four determined-looking Fox warrior policemen dashed up to me.

"Do not whip me," I begged. "Kill my horse. You may have all of my clothing. Here—take my gun and break it into pieces."

But after a talk among themselves they decided not to do any of these penal acts. They scolded me

65

and said I was a foolish little boy. They asked my name, and I told them. That was the last time I ever flagrantly violated any of the laws of travel or the hunt.

A guard line usually was thrown out by the warrior policemen when any buffalo herd was about to be attacked. It was required that all of the hunters remain behind this line until every preparation was made and until the appointed managers gave the word for a general advance. Of course, all were excited, anxious to get at the game. Or, somebody might think the policemen were too slow in completing the preparatory steps. So, occasionally an impatient hunter became obtrusive. This one was pretty sure to bring upon himself a lashing with pony whip thongs or a clubbing with the reversed heavy handle. Finally would come the signal:

"Go!" Then the wild Indian chase was on.

Special warrior society hunts often were engaged upon. For these only the members of the one particular organization were eligible. The societies contested against each other in this regard, each trying to beat the others in quantity of meat and skins brought back to camp. Left Handed Shooter, leading chief of the Elk warriors, one time appointed me as one of the four preliminary scouts to locate buffalo for an exclusively Elk warrior hunt. We went out

66

at night. Winter weather, snow on the ground. Early in the morning we found a big herd. We returned to camp and reported the discovery. An old man herald called the Elk warriors and shouted out information of our report and of the proposed hunting party.

Old Bear, a big chief, got four or five other Cheyennes to slip out with him for a premature raid upon the herd we had located for our Elk warrior adventure. Little Wolf, at that time a little warrior chief, took with him a band of Elks and followed the lawbreakers. Little Wolf opened the attack upon them by sending an arrow that killed Old Bear's horse. The Elk band pony-whipped all of the Old Bear group, including the big chief himself, and made them go back and stay in camp.

Feathered Wolf, an Elk warrior, one time attached himself uninvited to a hunting party of Crazy Dog warriors. He was leading two pack horses for carrying the meat he expected to get. Some Crazy Dogs warned him:

"You do not belong with us. You ought to go back."

"But I am badly in need of meat," he pleaded.

Others came and urged him to return. They talked of punishing him by whipping, but they did nothing. They ended merely by telling him:

"You are crazy."

He mingled with the hunters and shot away all of his arrows as they chased the herd. When the killing was done he said:

"I killed one buffalo and helped in the killing of another. You should give me plenty of meat."

"Yes, we'll give you some of it," different ones promised him.

But nobody gave him any. He had to go back to his home lodge with his two pack horses empty and himself hungry.

At his lodge that evening he announced a smoking circle. He stood out in front of his tepee and called invitations to many members of the Crazy Dog society. It was supposed he hoped thus to lead them into making gifts of the appetizing food. But all of the invited ones were busy at something else, so he had to smoke alone and the drying poles beside his tepee remained bare. His wife brought him the smoking outfit. "Ah, kinnikinick," he chuckled contentedly. He filled his pipe and smoked it to the last ashes. Pretty soon he became pale, weak, sick, then he vomited. His wife too had punished him. She had given him the strongest tobacco she could find in the camp.

Two certain men were observed one time to have a big supply of buffalo meat hanging on the drying

poles by their tepees. There had been a special warrior society hunt that day, but these men did not belong to that society. Investigation showed they had
obtained their store from one of the animals killed
in a side coulee and overlooked by the lawful hunters.
The meat was taken from the two men, their guns
were broken, their pack saddles were cut up, their
lodges were torn down and burned.

Half a dozen Sioux pushed themselves one time
into an Elk warrior hunt. We always were friendly
with the Sioux, about the same as if they were Cheyennes, but these were out of place at this particular
time, and they knew it. Little Wolf led a party of
his Elks in whipping them away. Two or three of
the uninvited guests had blood running from head
cuts made by the heavy handles of the pony whips.
The Sioux—the plains Indians generally—had laws
and customs similar to ours, so it was considered
they had incurred our penalty. Often a disobedient
Cheyenne or an intruding hunter might gain im-
munity from a whipping by prompt confession of
guilt and by voluntary yielding of horses to be killed
or of other property to be destroyed.

The arrow was the preferred weapon when on a
tribal hunt in a buffalo herd or when a large party
were joined in the pursuit. Each rider shot arrow
after arrow into whatever animal was convenient to

him during the tumult of the running chase. When it was ended he had one or more arrows in various dead buffalo scattered over the area covered by the flight of the herd. Every man kept his own arrows always marked in some peculiar manner whereby they could be identified, so when the field was reviewed after the termination of the killing he could find out which buffalo he had killed or had helped to kill. It could be learned in each instance which arrow was the fatal one and which were of little or no importance. Thus the claims to skin and meat could be settled. In case of disagreement, the chiefs decided the question. Gun bullets could not be distinguished the one from the other, so the guns were used only when one man was hunting alone or when a small party of special friends hunted together. The guns also had to have powder and lead and caps, which we did not always have on hand. We could make the arrows, or we often recovered them from the dead animal.

Different tribes had different ways of making their arrows. All arrows belonging to members of any certain tribe were made according to a certain general plan, so that by examination of any arrow it could be learned to what tribe the owner belonged. I used to be able to distinguish several different tribal forms from one another. I can recollect now the distinguishing features of four of them: The Crow, Sioux, Pawnee and Cheyenne.

The Crow butt end was whittled to a sharp ridge and the notch was cut across this ridge, the same as was done by the Cheyennes. Their metal or stone point was a long triangle with its shortest side at the arrow's shaft and with all three sides formed in exactly straight lines, these features likewise the same as in the Cheyenne arrows. Both of these had the slender neck whittled from the notch end in a long taper to the main shaft. But the distinction was in the size of the shaft. The Crow shaft always was fat and heavy. The Cheyenne shaft was slender.

The Sioux arrow had its notch extremity cut flat across the end, in this respect differing from all of the others, which were beveled on two sides to make a sharp ridge for the notch. The neck of the Sioux arrow was begun just below the notch by a circular cut straight into the wood. Then, beginning further down, the neck was shaved and tapered carefully up to this straight cut. The Sioux metal or stone points differed from all others. The form in general was the same long triangle, but the short side at the arrow's shaft had a deep concave curve. Thus it had two horns or barbs. Here was the particular brand of the Sioux arrow.

The Pawnees had the flat butt end and its notch

71

the same as the Sioux. But the neck below the notch was tapered like a Crow or a Cheyenne arrow. The triangle points were also the same as on the Crow and Cheyenne arrows, having no horns or barbs.

The Cheyenne arrow was distinguished from the Pawnee by its notch cut into a sharp ridge instead of into a flat surface butt end. Its tapering neck, its sharp ridge butt end and its straight line point separated it from the Sioux. The diameter of the shaft rendered it readily distinguishable from the Crow. Moreover, the Cheyennes had one peculiar brand that plainly indicated their arrows. This characteristic was in the three wavy lines symmetrically spaced around the shaft and painted all the way along it from the feathers to the base of the hard point. These special wavy stripes were designed as having a spirit or medicine influence, to help in killing the buffalo. Communication with the Great Medicine above us is supposed to be made in wavy lines, not straight lines.

All Indian arrows I ever saw have three rows of clipped feathers set symmetrically into slots in the neck and upper shaft for a distance of five or six inches. Between these feather rows are three straight lines painted in color, usually red. The shaft may be painted according to the fancy of the individual, or according to his personal mode of branding it. Old Cheyennes told me that in past times all Cheyenne arrows were painted blue. This was done by way of respectful regard for the blue waters of a certain highly revered lake in the Black Hills. During my days most arrow points were metal, although a few men, especially the older men, continued to make them of stone. All Indian arrows were of the same length—that is, every man made his own arrows to measure exactly from his armpit to the tips of his fingers.

Other weapons differed in the different tribes, and sometimes a certain form of weapon was characteristic of a certain tribe. The Sioux were the only Indians I knew who made regular use of the stone warclub made by attaching an oval stone to the end of a stick wrapped with rawhide. The Cheyennes rarely carried one of these, while a Sioux appeared not fully equipped unless he had one tucked into his belt. Instead, the Cheyenne counterpart implement was a hatchet or small ax. Sometimes the hatchet was transformed into a fancy pipe for ceremonial smoking. The metal head was drilled for the bowl and a little round canal was burned through the central length of the handle to serve as a pipestem.

Spears were used by the Cheyennes. The long and slender points might be of metal or they might be of stone or of bone, the rib of a buffalo or a bone from some other animal serving well for such pur-

73

pose. The shaft was decorated, of course. Great care often was taken in its coloring and general design. A regular feature of the plan was the eagle feather attachments. One eagle feather having a black tip dangled from the shaft near the hard point's base. Two eagle feathers floated from a slender buckskin thong tied to the upper end of the shaft.

The Sioux had knife sticks for fighting. These had long shafts, the same as a spear. But instead of the attached point at the end there were three blades at the shaft's side and near its end. The blades were in a row, close together, and were tied there by rawhide after having been set into a slot. They projected out three or four inches from the heavy shaft. Sometimes the edges were straight, sometimes they were pointed so that they resembled a section of sickle bar for a mowing machine. Always they were kept sharpened to a keen edge.

The earrings of an Indian often indicated his tribal stock. A Cheyenne ear had but one piercing, only one ring, and this ring was looped directly through or close up to the ear. The Crow likewise had but one piercing and only one ring or shell disc, but this was suspended below the ear by an intervening strand. The one piercing of the Sioux ear had a long loop directly through it, and from the bottom of this long loop dangled another loop of the same kind.

The Pawnees, Kiowas and Apaches had various piercings around the edge of the ear lobe, each piercing having in it a small ring. The Arapahoes and the Utes had ear decorations resembling the Cheyennes. The Sioux wore necklaces, regularly in single strands. The Crow necklaces ordinarily were in multiple strands. In the old times the Cheyennes did not wear decorative necklaces, but later they adopted the fashion to some extent. Mostly they designed them in single strands, like the Sioux standard plan. But the multiple curved loops of the Crows became also fashionable among us. Eagle feathers stuck up from the back hair of many a Sioux. The number of such feathers worn by any one man was supposed to denote the number of enemies he had killed. The Cheyennes never adopted this custom.

All Indian lodges coming under my observation were built on the same general lines. The conical tepee was the standard form. Buffalo skin was the standard material for covering the poles. The size was regulated according to the quantity of skins available or according to the number of persons in the household or according to some other special condition. But there were tribal differences that enabled an informed observer to distinguish camps or even to classify a lone tepee.

The Sioux lodge was unusually tall and was narrow at the base. Its flap opening at the top was large and long. The Pawnee lodge was the opposite of the Sioux. It was remarkably low and broad, and it had a short and small top flap opening. The Cheyennes and the Arapahoes had tepee plans alike, in general form midway between the Sioux and the Pawnee structure. The camp circle as a whole was in all cases the same—a horseshoe with its opening to the east. All Indians had also the same custom of placing each tepee with its entrance opening facing the rising sun.

Inside the Cheyenne lodge an old woman slept just at the left side of the entrance. Next past her, still on the left side, the lodge's owner and his wife had their bed. If the family was large the girls slept near the father and mother while the boys were located across on the opposite side of the earth floor. Other adults, or whatever guests might be there, were placed between the spaces allotted to the boys and the girls or were put between the boys and the right hand side of the entrance opening.

An old woman was an important part of every household organization. This was the custom among all of the plains Indians, especially in families where girls were growing up. This old woman saw that each occupant of the lodge used only his or her own proper bed or place of waking repose. She compelled each to keep his or her personal belongings beside or at the head of the owner's assigned space. She was at the same time the household policeman, the night watchman and the drudge. Ordinarily her badge of office was a club. She was conceded the authority to use this club in enforcing the rules of the lodge.

From fifteen to seventeen buffalo skins were united to make a covering for the usual Cheyenne lodge. When skins were plentiful not many lodges had less than fifteen, regardless of the condition that some of the tepees might have in each only a young married couple, with perhaps an old woman or some other one or two added people. On the other hand, rarely was a lodge larger than seventeen skins, even if twenty people were sheltered there. The larger lodges had to have heavier poles, and, in moving, these with the skins had to be transported by the horses. Too much of such burden hindered the progress of the camp movement. Big lodges made pleasant abodes, but they were troublesome in traveling. The average and usual Cheyenne tepee was twelve to fifteen feet in diameter across its earth floor. The height from the floor's center to the tepee's peak was the same as the diameter of the floor. That was the regular standard architectural plan of a Cheyenne lodge.

The camp circle of the Northern Cheyenne tribe, all assembled, enclosed a space about one-fourth or one-third of a mile in diameter. It usually straddled a small stream of water. If the location permitted, a position was taken near to a larger stream into which the small one emptied. Hunting parties or war parties of men made themselves temporary night shelters of willow wands stuck into the ground, bent over and tied together for a dome roof, then covered with robes. Or, such parties crept into caves or sought the protection of heavy brush and thick foliage. The main camp never went into high mountains during the winter. Too much snow. Mountain campings were made during the summer season.

For moving the village, the usual time for leaving the old site was about nine o'clock in the morning, I believe. Not much if any preparation was made until that morning came. The arrival at the next stop would be about the middle of the afternoon. Long before dark the whole village would be set up and everybody would be at home, as if this had been the dwelling place for many months. A thousand or several thousand people might travel along that way from day to day, actually moving their towns or cities, taking all of their property, their wives and children and old people, their horses and their dogs, everything that made up a full home life. I think that is better than the white people can do.

The women did all of the work of moving. They took down the lodges, packed and attended to the transportation of them and all of the household effects, set up the lodges at the new location and put all of the furnishing and personal baggage in the right places in each lodge. The whole removal was accomplished during a part of one day. In such traveling we sometimes could outrun the soldiers, notwithstanding they had only themselves and their horses to care for. We often got our homes and all of our people and their belongings across rivers where the soldiers could not or did not follow us.

The women brought wood, cut it, kept the fires burning, cooked the food, cared for the children, did all of the home work. The men took care of the horses, guarded against enemies and fought them when necessary or when desirable, hunted the wild game, brought in the meat and the skins. Ordinarily a man did not toil at domestic tasks nor did a woman hunt or fight. In emergency, though, either a man or a woman might aid or take the place of the other.

Women used saddles for riding. They sat astride. The saddles were made by them, the tree of elkhorn or of hard wood, this wrapped with buffalo rawhide

79

sewed in place with shredded tendon sinew thread. They also made pack saddles of the same material, but having a different form. Old men likewise used saddles. But young men always rode bareback. I learned to use a saddle as a scout at Fort Keogh after our Indian roaming and fighting days were past. The white people say we mount a horse from the wrong side, but I never changed that. They say too that we do not know how to sharpen a knife. In doing this we grind only one side of the knife's edge. But we make them keen by that method. I see no need for grinding both sides of a knife's blade.

I did not smoke during my boyhood. As a youth I took occasional tastes, but the habit was not formed. The Cheyennes of those days did not chew tobacco. My father gave me a medicine pipe, for devotional or ceremonial smoking, when I was seventeen years old. He himself made it. The bowl was of red stone. My mother made me a long buckskin pouch and beaded it, this to contain my pipe and tobacco—or, the mixture that commonly is known as kinnikinick. This mixture was half tobacco—plug tobacco shaved off and dried—and half dried inner bark of the red willow. In the South our people used some other kind of bark, as our northern red willow did not grow there.

Old-time pipes, before my days, were made of deer leg bone. The bone was wrapped with rawhide strips taken from the back of a buffalo's head. This wrapping was partly for the spirit influence and partly to keep the bone from breaking when heated by the smoking.

We wore clothing, winter and summer. We had light summer moccasins and heavy winter moccasins. These always were cut low and had but one string, whereas the Sioux moccasins were cut high, to lap around the legs, and had two or more strings. One time I saw some white children barefooted. I pitied them, supposing them to be very poor. When I was a small boy, a soldier at the fort on Buffalo creek gave me a hat. Not long afterward I lost it. I was eighteen years old before I got another one. It was not customary for men, except old men, to wear any special head covering. Women all went bareheaded or covered the head with a shawl or a blanket or a robe.

The buffalo hat was worn by old men. It was made of buffalo rawhide. A broad oval segment of the skin was used. An irregular circle was marked on this surface, the drawing made to accord with the shape of the head. From the center to the outer rim of this circle several cuts were made. The cut flaps were lifted to stand upright. This left the crown wide open and its rim surrounded by the upstanding diamond points. A leather thong under the chin held the hat in place.

Our people learned from the Crows this way of making hats. That is, we discovered the idea from them. One time, when the Cheyennes were camped on Tongue river above the present Sheridan, the Crows stole some horses from us. As the Cheyennes pursued them the Crows abandoned the horses and fled. They lost two hats, and the Cheyennes found these. They were used as patterns. My father used to wear a cloth over his open-top hat, to shield his head from the sun's heat. Every old man made his own hat.

Buffalo robes from adult animals served as overcoats for men or women. Buffalo calf or deer robes were used by the children. Buffalo hair sometimes was stuffed into the moccasins to keep the feet warm. Grease paint was used on the face for the principal purpose of shielding the skin from cold during the winter and from sunburn during the summer. The most common color was a brownish red, but personal fancy might choose some other color or some combination. Each warrior also had his particular mode of painting himself, his spirit or medicine ornamentation, when preparing for battle or for death or for social mingling.

All of the best clothing was taken along with him when any warrior set out upon a search for conflict. The articles were put into a special bag—ordinarily a beautifully beaded buckskin pouch, but perhaps a rawhide one—and this was slung at one side of his horse. The bag also contained extra moccasins— beaded moccasins—warbonnet, paints, a mirror, special medicine objects, or anything else of this nature. If a battle seemed about to occur, the warrior's first important preparatory act was to jerk off all his ordinary clothing. He then hurriedly got out his fine garments. If he had time to do so he rebraided his hair, painted his face in his own peculiar way, did everything needful to prepare himself for presenting his most splendid personal appearance. That is, he got himself ready to die.

The idea of full dress in preparation for a battle comes not from a belief that it will add to the fighting ability. The preparation is for death, in case that should be the result of the conflict. Every Indian wants to look his best when he goes to meet the Great Spirit, so the dressing up is done whether the imminent danger is an oncoming battle or a sickness or injury at times of peace. Some Indian tribes did not pay full attention to this matter, some of them seeming not to care whether they took life risks while naked or while only partly clad or shabbily clad. But the Cheyennes and the Sioux were careful in following out the procedure. When any of them got into a fight not expected, with no opportunity to dress properly, they usually ran away and avoided close contact and its consequent risks. Enemy people not understanding their ways might suppose them to be cowards because of such flight. In fact, these same apparent cowards might be the bravest of the brave when they have on their good clothing and feel that they may present a respectable appearance if called from this life to meet the Great Spirit.

The naked fighters, among the Cheyennes and the Sioux, were such warriors as specially fortified themselves by prayer and other devotional exercises. They had special instruction from medicine men. Their naked bodies were painted in peculiar ways, each according to the direction of his favorite spiritual guide, and each had his own medicine charms given to him by this guide. A warrior thus made ready for battle was supposed to be proof against the weapons of the enemy. He placed himself in the forefront of the attack or the defense. His thought was: "I am so protected by my medicine that I do not need to dress for death. No bullet nor arrow can harm me now." On the other hand, a warrior not made ready by special religious exercise and appliances had in his heart the thought: "A bullet or an arrow may hit me and kill me. I must dress myself so as to please the Great Spirit if I should go now to Him."

Warbonnets were not worn by all warriors. In fact, there were only a few such distinguished men in each warrior society of our tribe. It was expected that one should be a student of the fighting art for several years, or else that he be an unusually apt learner, before he should put on the crown of eagle feathers. He then did so upon his own initiative, or perhaps because of the commendatory urgings of his seniors. The act meant a profession of fully acquired ability in warfare, a claim of special accomplishment in using cunning and common sense and cool calculation coupled with the bravery attributed to all warriors. The wearer was supposed never to ask mercy in battle. If some immature young man pretended to such high standing before it seemed to his companions that he ought to do so, he was twitted and shamed into awaiting his proper time. I first put on my warbonnet when I was thirty-three years old, fourteen years after I had quit the roaming life. After a man had been accepted as a warbonnet man he remained so throughout his lifetime. War chiefs and tribal chiefs ordinarily were warbonnet men, but this was not a requirement for these positions. Pure modesty might keep the bravest and most capable fighter from making the claim. Also, an admittedly worthy wearer of the warbonnet might not be chosen for or might refuse all official positions. The feathered headpiece, then, was not a sign of public office. It was a token of individual and personal feeling as to his own fighting capabilities.

The warbonnet was made by the man who was to wear it. His wife, mother or sister made only the beaded band for the forehead. The man made also whatever spirit charm objects he might use, or he got a medicine man to make them for him. The women made all of the war shirts, leggings, moccasins and such clothing for the men. They also made all of the common clothing for the men, for themselves, and for all members of the household. The men made their own pipes, weapons, lariat ropes and such other articles as were used by men only.

Our hand mirrors were not used entirely for dressing and painting. We made use of them for signaling. Two persons who understood each other could exchange thoughts in this way over long distances, and even when they could not see each other. Some kinds of such signals were understood by all of our people. The little glass was often useful in approaching a camp when the traveler was in doubt whether it was an assemblage of his own people or of an enemy or unknown people. In such cases, flashes of inquiry and flashes of response, or lack of responses, settled the doubt.

My father bought me a rifle and a six-shooter when I was about sixteen years old. He got them at a trader's store somewhere, when he went away on a journey to the place. He exchanged buffalo robes for them. The rifle was a muzzle loader, using powder, bullet and caps. The six-shooter also was loaded in the same way. Before that time I had learned to shoot with other people's guns, but these were the first ones I ever owned.

Some Indians used to cut off the rifle barrels, to make them lighter for carrying on horseback. It was supposed they would shoot just as well with the short barrel. We never cut off the stock. The shortened rifles were used in chasing buffalo on horseback. Such weapons could be handled with one hand while the horse was controlled with the other. They were known to us as the "buffalo gun."

An old-time way of killing buffalo was by chasing them in winter over a steep bluff into a deep snowdrift. As they floundered there they could be speared or beaten to death. A few times I was in that kind of hunt. I heard old people tell of having used snowshoes to go after buffalo, but I never saw any of that kind of hunting. We always stripped the meat from the bones while butchering. The only bones we took were the ribs. We sometimes used the legs as mauls to break up the ribs. Oh, how good was buffalo rib roast!

Four arrows was the regular allowance for the killing of one buffalo during a horseback chase. The need of more than that number was discreditable to the skill of the bowman. Less than that was a matter for boasting. If one killed a buffalo with only one arrow, that was wonderful.

I have helped in the chasing of antelope bands over a cliff. In the Black Hills was one special place where we worked for our meat in that manner. The creek near by was called Antelope creek. The first time I went there an old man accompanied me. We located ourselves in hiding near the base of the cliff, with women and old people and children. Two young men rounded up a herd and drove them over for us. Many of them were killed or got broken legs. We clubbed to death the injured ones.

We could get food, clothing and shelter from the buffalo only. Saddles and harness, halters and bridles, were made by using their rawhide. Stout thongs for all purposes were cut from them. For a rawhide lariat rope, long strands were cut by following around the outside of a buffalo rawhide. Three or four of these strands were plaited together. Buffalo hair, particularly from the neck of a bull, also was spun into long strands and plaited to make a lariat. The buffalo, then, was very important to us in our mode of life. When any man went out specially hunting them he usually led two or three pack horses to bring in his gathered supply of food and skins.

Fishing lines were made of horsehair. The hairs were tied to make long threads, and these were plaited together. We got metal hooks from the white men traders. I have caught rabbits also with baited hooks on the horsehair lines. I heard of eagles having been captured in that way. But I never tried it on an eagle. The Arapahoes used to be great eagle hunters. Old men told me the Cheyennes in past times had caught them from pits. The pit was covered with sticks, and a dead rabbit or some other tempting flesh bait was placed upon the sticks over the center of the pit. The hunter hid himself below the bait. When an eagle alighted he seized its legs, jerked it down, grabbed its head and wrung its neck.

Twisting rabbits out of a hollow log, using a forked stick to get the hold for pulling them, was a boyhood game. I set my muzzle loader rifle one time on the upper Rosebud as a trap and caught a fox. I have caught coyotes by that same means. The taking of the bait pulled the trigger and shot the animal. A piece of fat meat was the best lure for them. I have poisoned lots of wolves and got their pelts. A good way is to put the poisoned meat upon the top of a stick stuck into the snow, the meat being about on a level with a wolf's body. The trapper goes back next day and follows the trial of whatever wolf might have gone away from the stick.

My first choice of meat was antelope. Buffalo was a close second choice. Deer and elk came next. It appeared, though, that no Indian ever got actually turned against buffalo flesh. Beaver, rabbit, prairie chickens, bear, fish and turtles are good. Otter or wolf are not good, except wolf pups taste good if one be hungry. Dogs are the same as wolves. An old dog or an old wolf being boiled sickens me. Boiling pups give out almost as bad an odor.

Salt was in use by the Cheyennes before I was born. We used it when we had it, but we did not always have it. There was a stream known to the Indians as Salt creek somewhere in the South. From there the Southern Cheyennes used to bring to us great chunks of salt. We sometimes smoked our meat, partly to help in preserving it and partly because the flavor was an agreeable change at times.

Steel and flint was the usual source of fire. Neither my older brother nor myself had these, but my father had a good pair. We used to borrow from

90

him. In the usual personal traveling pack was a small box or bag containing steel, flint and kindling. Dried buffalo dung, usually known as "buffalo chips," makes good kindling when it is pulverized. Spark, kindle, blow, spark, kindle, blow, until a small blaze is started. Then put on twigs or grass, then small wood, then large wood. Buffalo chips in their natural chunks made good wood.

The Crows used to have a custom of making a pile of buffalo chips to be kicked to pieces by whoever might come to camp pretending to bear an important message. This was by way of oath that he would tell the truth. There was no such custom among the Cheyennes. Our way was to build a bonfire and call the chiefs. No oath of any kind was taken. It was supposed the truth would be told without special promise. Perhaps that was not the case with the Crows.

I have heard of another Crow custom different from the Cheyenne way. I have been told that when a Crow stole a horse or found any article it was expected of him that he give it away. It was considered not right for him to keep it. A Cheyenne might present a stolen horse or a found article to a relative or a friend, but it was regarded as entirely fair and proper for him to keep it for himself if he chose to do so. Ordinarily he kept it. I admire the old Crow way of acting in that respect. Such conduct makes a good and unselfish heart.

The Sioux often buried their dead on scaffolds, but I never saw any Cheyenne burials in that way. Sometimes our dead were put upon platforms on tree branches. Mostly, though, they were placed in small hillside rocky caves if these were convenient. In later times, and in many instances at the present day on our reservation, the dead body was deposited on the surface of the ground on a rocky hill or in some place out of the way of usual travel. The body was well wrapped in blankets or skins, and it may or may not have been put into a wooden box. In either case a heap of stones was piled over it to shield it from animals.

Our women used to cut their legs and arms, usually in crosswise slashes, as an act of mourning. Some of them—the older ones—yet do this. A married woman cut off her hair, in ragged form, if her husband died. In mourning for other relatives the hair might be worn loose and uncombed for a long or a short time. Men did not cut the flesh in mourning. They let loose the hair or cut off their braids. Men who had lost relatives often cut off also the manes and the tails of their horses as a sign of mourning.

There was no marriage ceremony among the Cheyennes. Such union was mainly a simple agreement between the two principal parties. In far back old times young men purchased their brides, but during my days this was not the custom among us. In our later practice presents might be given by the young man, these ordinarily to the girl's brothers. But these were given after the marriage, as an indication of good will, not as a purchase price. Reciprocal gifts often were made to the newly married couple.

The older way of entering upon the preliminary steps toward marriage was for the young man first to consult his own father. An old woman relative was enlisted as an emissary. "Tell the girl's father I will give him four horses (or some other number of horses) for his daughter as a wife for my son." The old woman went and negotiated with the father and his daughter. If the offer or some modification of it were agreed upon, the initiative father gathered together or borrowed from relatives such horses or blankets or other gifts as were required. These were taken to the lodge of the girl's father. The prospective bride was put upon a blanket. Her personal belongings were put there with her or were wrapped in another package. She and her property were carried to the lodge of the young man's father and placed inside, the carriers leaving her there and going elsewhere. The young man seized her as his wife.

All of the supposed purchase gifts often were bestowed upon the young couple. Relatives of the two parties exchanged presents and compliments. The old woman emissary got a horse. Gifts all around were made in accordance with the ability of the people interested and in accordance with the degree of satisfaction felt because of the event.

Our most common custom was for the young man to do all of his own managing of the affair. In the night time he crept stealthily to the vicinity of the loved one's parental tepee. He looked and listened —listened long and intently. He crept closer, still closer, until he was at the outside wall of that side of the lodge where slept the one he was seeking. He whispered, perhaps had to whisper more loudly, to awaken her. They conversed in whispers, possibly the first time they ever had spoken directly to each other, although all their lives they had lived in the same camps.

"Will—will—will you marry me?"

"Y-y-yes."

She crept out and joined him. They went together to the lodge of the young man's brother or sister or to a place where dwelt elder relatives of his.

The next morning two intruders were discovered there, a young man and his young wife. The discovery was announced, all parties interested were informed. Not often was the information displeasing. Ordinarily all concerned were contented and manifested their contentment in the usual exchange of gifts.

The newly married couple lived temporarily at the lodge of relatives on one or the other side, preferably with a brother or a sister of the husband. This was but a fleeting residence. The first important duty of the husband was to get skins for a tepee, either by borrowing them or by taking them in the hunt. Then it was the duty of the young wife to tan and sew together these skins and set up a home lodge.

Plural wives were kept by many of the old Cheyennes. The one family lodge sheltered the entire combined family. Commonly the two or more wives were born sisters. This condition checked or prevented the jealous quarreling likely to occur were they from different families. Two wives ordinarily was the limit. But in my time I knew two different men who each had three wives living with him. In each of these instances the three wives were sisters. The two men were named Red Arms and Plum Tree. Both of them and their entire families were in the Cheyenne camp on the Little Bighorn when we had the great battle there. Plum Tree was the father of

95

Sun Bear and Two Feathers. Both of these sons of his fought the soldiers at that time, and Two Feathers is yet living here on the Tongue river.

Captive women from other tribes were made wives of our men. There were many of such among us. Spotted Hawk's mother was a Ute woman captured by our people when she was a small girl. The old Chief Dull Knife, or Rabbit, or Morning Star, had as his wife a Pawnee captive woman. At the time she came to us, two other Pawnee women were brought and were taken into marriage for bringing up Cheyenne children. Crow women stolen long ago by our warriors in raids were mothers of some important Cheyennes, including Big Foot, Big Thigh and the Chiefs Crazy Head and Little Horse. I do not know of any Cheyenne women having been captured from us by the Crows. The Pawnees and the Shoshones got away with some of them.

An unfaithful wife did not incur any public penalty, according to the laws of the Cheyennes and the Sioux. Her husband might inflict some penalty. That was permissible, but he was not conceded the right to kill her. I knew one man who cut a great gash in his wife's forehead because of her going with another man. Ordinarily, though, the loss of his wife's affection was looked upon as a joke on the husband, and he kept quiet about it or pretended that he did not bewail the loss. The Arapahoes had a tribal punishment for a wife's unfaithfulness. They cut off the end of the woman's nose. Then any future observer might have notice of her frailty when contemplating the taking of her as his wife.

Fighting between Cheyennes, either men or women, was forbidden by the tribal laws. In case of a fight some chief near at hand would call out: "Warriors, separate these fighters and whip them." The warrior policemen then on duty would respond to the call. A band of them would give such punishment as seemed to them fitting. If the fighters renewed their strife they might have punishment added, might have their tepees torn down, their horses killed, property damage done to them in some other way, any suitable and sufficient punishment—except, no policeman warrior nor anyone else lawfully could kill a Cheyenne.

Pony whips, either the lashes or the heavy stick handles, were the customary attacking weapons in a personal fight. Cheyennes did not use fists as the white people do. Not often did any two women fight. If they did, they merely scratched and pulled hair. It was more of a comic show than an alarming sight to see two women clawing each other. I never heard of any Cheyenne woman killing another nor maliciously killing a man. Nor did the men kill

97

women. I used to hear old people talk about a Cheyenne named Wounded Elk who had beaten his wife and then shot her, killing her. I never heard of any other like case. That incident happened before I was born.

Suicides were not uncommon among us. Men shot themselves, women hung themselves. Foolish ones yet do such acts. Several years ago my neighbor and friend Whirlwind shot himself to death. Five or six years ago a woman hanged herself at Lame Deer. Many of these sad occurrences, particularly among the women, have come to pass during my lifetime.

A sister of Bobtail Horse and Hollow Wood hung herself when I was yet a small boy and our people were camped on a branch of the Tongue river. Her mother had scolded and threatened her, but had not struck her, as the striking of any child was not customary among the Cheyennes. But the girl was ashamed and crestfallen because of the scolding. She brooded a while, then she disappeared. Searchers failed to find her. Two years later, a Cheyenne young man hunting deer in that vicinity found the remains of her body suspended by the neck from a tree limb. Several years before that time another young woman had done this same act near there on this same stream. From this first incident, and confirmed by the later one, the creek got a permanent name. It became known as Hanging Woman creek. It flows into Tongue river from the east side, just above the present white man village of Birney, Montana.

As we were in camp one time on the Rosebud, below Lame Deer creek, another boy and I went rambling afoot among the timber by the stream. We suddenly came upon a woman dangling and strangling. I had no knife. The other boy had one.

"Cut the rope," I urged him.

He already was about to do this. We let the woman down upon the ground. I ran to the creek near by, got a mouthful of water, hurried back and squirted the water into her face. I stayed beside her while my companion rushed into the camp to tell her people. A band of women came, bringing a blanket. They put the disabled one upon the blanket and carried her to her home lodge. A medicine man was called. The next day I saw the woman. She gave no indication then of having had any unusual experience.

A widow Cheyenne woman was living in our camp at a time when we had stopped on the east side of the upper Little Bighorn river. Her husband had been killed three or four years before then, in the battle where Cheyennes and Sioux had won a great victory over the soldiers. (Fort Phil Kearny, 1866.) From this Little Bighorn camp my older brother and another boy and myself went out riding. I then was about twelve years old. Ahead of us, on a branching creek, we saw a woman walking rapidly afoot. She had a blanket over her head and shoulders. She turned into a thickly wooded gulch beside the creek and disappeared into the timber. We wondered a little at her strange actions, but we felt it not proper to follow her. Pretty soon three other boys came galloping their horses.

"Did you see any lone woman around here?" they asked anxiously.

"Yes, she went there," and we indicated the wooded gulch.

My two companions followed them. I went to a plum patch. As I stood there eating plums I saw a man and a woman hurrying up toward the gulch. Both of them were crying. I followed them.

The five boys were trying to revive the woman being sought, who had hanged herself. But she now was dead. The body was rolled into the blanket she had been wearing and she was taken into camp.

This widow had been dependent upon friends for her support since her husband's death. She had a daughter eight or nine years old. One day the young widow asked her mother for a certain fine robe. The mother refused. The request was urged. Still the mother for some reason said, "No." The aggrieved and disconsolate young woman was so downcast by this apparent coldness of her mother that she went out and hanged herself.

My mother's sister hung herself in their family lodge when we were in camp one time on Powder river. I was nine years old. Our family lodge was right beside the one where dwelt this aunt of mine. My mother heard the noise of the struggling and strangling. The sister's tepee entrance flap was tied shut, but my mother burst through it. She found my aunt suspended by a rawhide rope tied high upon a pole of the lodge. She hastily cut the rope and cut it again from her sister's neck. White Bull, a medicine man, was called. His medicine then was the tusks of a bear. He held these over and around my aunt while he got down upon his hands and knees and grunted like a bear. He kept this up until she suddenly had a hard coughing spell and brought up a chunk of something that had been choking her. She soon stood up and was all right. White Bull was a good medicine man. He saved the lives of lots of Cheyennes.

Only one wildly insane Cheyenne person did I ever see. As I was out on a hill beside the camp one day I heard a woman screaming. I looked in the direction of the sound and saw a woman outside a lodge

101

charging about here and there and tearing off her clothing. People were running to the scene. I hastened down there. A chief called out:

"Warriors, come."

Warrior policemen rushed there from all parts of the camp. They seized the woman and held her while medicine men were summoned. I stood there among the surrounding crowd and watched the proceedings. Finally the medicine men caused her to gag and choke and cough out the tail of a deer. At once she came into her right mind. Our medicine men always could cure that kind of sickness.

This woman had another attack of this same kind some months after that first one. The medicine men gave her the same kind of treatment. Again she spat out the tail of a deer and instantly became sane. Not long after that she got married. She had a third attack a month or so after the marriage. Her husband did not send for any medicine man this time. He himself tied her and whipped her. He beat and lashed his wife until she spat out a deer tail. This cured her right away. I never heard of her going insane after that time.

The killing of any Cheyenne was the most serious offense against our tribal laws. The punishment was prompt. A council of the big chiefs and the warrior chiefs was called at once. The case was inquired into. If guilt was evident, the offender began without delay the payment of his penalty. Sometimes action was taken without the council being assembled, the situation being so clear that unanimity of feeling was expressed either for or against the person charged with the crime. The defendant was not permitted to be present at the trial council. When the decision was rendered he was notified at his lodge by the warrior policemen. If found guilty they proceeded at once to put into effect the regular fixed and standard punishment.

"Get ready to go," they ordered him.

Banishment for four years was the main penalty. It had to be entered upon that same day. If the offender protested or dallied, he might suffer the additional infliction of being whipped, of having his horses killed or his tepee destroyed. If he acceded willingly, he was allowed to take along his possessions. In any case, he had to go. His wife or his children might go with him or remain with the tribe, as they might choose. If he had a medicine pipe, that sacred object regularly possessed by every adult male Cheyenne, his very first act of entrance upon the banishment was the smashing to fragments of this most revered talisman. Everything else he owned he might take along with him. But he must not have the devotional medicine pipe.

103

Two or three miles from the main camp was considered a sufficient distance for the banished one. Relatives might visit him there or take food to him, but it was not allowable for them to remain long, and in no case should they remain after sundown. The chief spiritual guide or medicine man of the tribe withdrew the sacred protection, so the outlawed one was altogether out of touch with the Great Medicine. He kept watch of the camp movements, and he could follow at a distance with his lone tepee and set it up at a distance within sight of but out of convenient hearing of the new camp location. He hunted alone. If in the course of his hunting he accidentally came close to other Cheyennes, it was expected he should hasten away from them. The warrior policemen would whip him, or they might kill him, if he should offer to intrude himself. It was not permissible for anyone to speak to him nor in any other manner extend to him a friendly recognition. He was entirely avoided—or, it was required of him that he entirely avoid all other Cheyennes. Day after day, month after month, summer and winter, fair or foul weather, for four complete years he lived altogether the life of a scorned hermit. He was conceded the right to join some other tribe, but he did not do this. The great obstacle was, the people of the other tribe surely would ask: "Whence came you, and why?"

When the four years ended, the absolved man came back and took temporary abode in the lodge of relatives. Soon he set up his own lodge. He was admitted then to the principal rights, privileges and immunities of a recognized member of the tribe. But to this rehabilitation there were some important exceptions. For one, he never thereafter was allowed to have a medicine pipe nor to take part in any smoking circle. He was tolerated in personal presence there, if he chose thus to place himself, but as the pipe was being moved along from one to another it always went on past him, just as if he were not there at all. Nobody abused him. They simply ignored him. Hence, he ordinarily kept entirely away from such gatherings.

An insignificant little pipe having a short stem was conceded to him as an individual comfort. But he had to smoke always alone. Such little pipes were made of stone or of the leg bone of a deer or of some other material not used for making the venerated pipe used in formal smoking. When I was a little boy I used to see one certain very old man who smoked one of these little short-stemmed pipes. I did not understand why he should do this. I asked my father about it. He told me: "He killed a Cheyenne."

Social ostracism in various ways haunted the subsequent life of the murderer otherwise cleansed from his stain. If he came hungry to any lodge he was fed. But when he was gone, the spoon or dish he had used was destroyed. If he sat upon a robe, nobody else ever afterward would sit upon it. If he became needy, gifts were taken to his lodge, but this was done by way of pity rather than by way of friendly feeling. By exemplary conduct he might partly restore his standing, but it never was fully restored.

One time, when I was a boy five or six years old, all of the Northern Cheyennes and all of the Southern Cheyennes were camped together by the Giving White Medal river.* Each of the tribes had its sacred medicine tepee, the Northern Cheyennes for their Buffalo Head and the Southern Cheyennes for their Medicine Arrows. The great double camps remained together several days. There were many ceremonies, many social dances and other affairs, much going back and forth between the two camps in the renewal of old acquaintance and the making of new acquaintance.

Chief of Many Buffalo and Rolling Wheel were two men belonging then to our Northern Cheyenne tribe. Chief of Many Buffalo was not married. Rolling Wheel had a wife and a small boy. This wife was tempted by the single man, and she took her boy and went to live with him. Rolling Wheel complained to

* Smoky Hill river (?).

106

the chiefs. He asked that Chief of Many Buffalo be compelled to give him a certain running horse, the swiftest animal in the whole tribal herd.

"Yes, he must give you that horse," the chiefs decided.

An old man was sent to notify Chief of Many Buffalo. The owner of the racer announced that he would keep it, that he had concluded he did not want the woman. He sent her away to her father's lodge. "That makes no difference," the old man said. "Rolling Wheel now owns that horse."

He went and informed the aggrieved husband of the situation. He told him:

"The horse belongs to you. Go and get it."

"I go now," Rolling Wheel replied.

He took his lariat rope and went out among the herd. There on a little knoll stood Chief of Many Buffalo, armed with a rifle.

"Go away," the armed man commanded.

But Rolling Wheel kept on after the horse. The rifle flashed and barked. The man with the lariat tumbled forward dead. Chief of Many Buffalo was a murderer.

This banished man was not allowed to have any tepee. For four years he slept in caves or in other natural shelters he might find in the neighborhood of our camping places. At the end of his term of isolation he left us and went to the Southern Cheyennes. There he married a widow of that tribe. Soon afterward he brought her and her two children to join us. They made their permanent home with our people. I remember clearly the time of their arrival at our camp. I was ten years old. We were on Crow creek, a stream that flows into Tongue river just north of the present Sheridan.

The misguided wife of the dead Rolling Wheel remained for several years an inhabitant of her father's lodge. Finally she was married to another Cheyenne. She was my aunt, a sister of my father, White Buffalo Shaking Off the Dust.

A Cheyenne named Hawk came to us when I was a small boy. I heard people talk of him. They said he had been away four years, in consequence of his having killed Sharp Nose. From the repeated stories I learned the details.

The two men had been out together capturing wild horses or on a raid upon an enemy herd. They brought home three horses, one of them considered a specially good animal and the other two of inferior grade. Each one wanted to keep the first choice and give the two others to his companion. They quarreled. It appeared that Sharp Nose had the better claim to preference, but Hawk had possession of the disputed animal. He had it picketed beside his lodge.

Sharp Nose on horseback and his father afoot went there to argue further about the matter. Hawk sat just outside his tepee entrance. He had his bow and arrows. As the two approached, he stood up and declared:

"I am going to kill you right now."

His arrow went through the body of the young man on horseback. Sharp Nose plunged forward and fell dead to the ground. His father shouted imprecations upon the hot-headed killer. The father of Hawk intervened to take a part in the affair. This old man went into their tepee and came out with a muzzle loading rifle in his hands. The father of the dead Sharp Nose turned and walked away toward the camp boundaries. The rifle was leveled and fired at him. He staggered, evidently wounded, but he did not fall. The shooter reloaded his rifle with powder, bullet and cap. By that time the retreating victim was far off and still walking away. A second shot was sent after him. This time the result was fatal.

Hawk and his father were banished at once, not being allowed to take with them any property whatever. I used to gaze upon the returned Hawk with awe-stricken feelings. People whispered, "He killed a Cheyenne." I do not remember ever having seen his father. I believe the old man died while they were in exile. The killing had been done somewhere between Cherry creek and the Arickaree river (northeastern Colorado). When Hawk joined the tribe again we were near the agency south of the Black Hills.

No property indemnity payment nor any other substitute penalty could take the place of the four years of banishment put upon a willful killer. If a killing were accidental, the survivor might be compelled to give horses and other presents to the relatives of the deceased, or he voluntarily and promptly might do his best to make amends to them in that manner. If no blame whatever rested upon him, he need pay nothing. Yet, it was customary for him to show in some such way his sadness of heart because of the occurrence.

Two youths, brothers, found one time a wolf's den. One of them took his lariat and crawled into the hillside cave to get pups. He felt about in the darkness, got the rope about a pup's hind feet and dragged it out. They knocked it in the head and he went back after another one. This time, either a pup or an old wolf bit his hand. He retreated. Outside he got a forked stick. With this projecting out in front of him, he returned to the attack upon the wolves. The forked end got engaged in the hair and skin of the wolf. The youth twisted and tugged, backing out and dragging after him the snarling and snapping

110

animal. The brother stood with his rifle poised and ready to shoot. Limbs of brush diverted his aim, and the bullet crashed into the head of the other boy. The shocked and weeping brother put the dead body upon a horse and took it to their home lodge. People flocked there to see and to hear.

"You killed him in anger," somebody accused.

"No, it was an accident," he sobbed out. And he explained how it had occurred.

A group of warrior policemen went with him out to the wolf's den. There he rehearsed for their observation all of the incidents of the happening. They became fully satisfied that he had no intention to kill his brother, that it truly was entirely accidental. The youth was released with no penalty whatever.

As we were camped one time on the upper Powder river, when I was about thirteen years old, Wolf Medicine and other men loaded their pack horses with buffalo robes and other skins and went to the trader post at the southward (Fort Laramie) for buying some supplies. They got tobacco, caps, powder, lead, sugar, and goods of that character. Wolf Medicine brought a sack of flour. Our women were just then learning how to make bread. Wolf Medicine's wife knew how to make it so it tasted good. He was a little chief of the Elk warriors, and he wanted to give them a feast. He said to his wife:

"Make plenty of bread. I shall invite all Elks to come."

"How," she assented, and she went immediately at mixing flour and water. Then: "Oh, I have no soda."

A young woman there said: "My mother has soda. I will go and get some." She went to her home lodge and told her mother. This woman rummaged among her packages, looking into one after another. "Here it is," she finally announced. The young woman took the white powder to the wife of Wolf Medicine. As the good cook proceeded with her work, her proud husband went out to the front of his lodge and stood there calling:

"All Elk warriors, come. Wolf Medicine has a feast of bread."

That brought them in droves. The wife engaged some helpers. They fried many slices of bacon and they boiled a great potful of coffee. When the food was being eaten everybody said: "Wolf Medicine's wife can make good bread." The hearts of the husband and the wife were made glad by the compliments showered upon them.

After the feast, Wolf Medicine brought a supply of tobacco. The assemblage was converted into a grand smoking party. They passed the pipe and chatted and told stories. After a while somebody said: "I feel sick. My stomach pains me." Just then the neighbor woman came running and screaming:

"I gave you the wrong powder! It is the wolf poison!"

The commotion aroused and brought the whole population of the camp. The victims were wallowing and groaning. An old man herald went among them calling out: "Make yourselves vomit." Some already had done this, others began at once to gag their throats with fingers poked into them. Two men, Old Bear and White Elk, did not do this. Instead, they took doses of gunpowder in water. Both of these men had convulsions and were sick a long time, but they finally recovered full health. All of the others got relief soon after the gagging and vomiting. One of them was my father. As a test, some remnants of bread was given to two dogs. Both of the dogs went into convulsions and died. The woman who had provided the supposed soda was not punished. On the contrary, she was for a long time afterward so distressed in mind that people sympathized with and tried to console her.

A certain half-Sioux-half-Cheyenne man was married to a Cheyenne woman and they lived with our tribe. He killed one of our Cheyennes, served his exile term of four years and returned to a small

113

village of Cheyennes where were his relatives. That was considered right, but his next movement was considered not right. He went to visit another Cheyenne village where were many relatives of the man he had killed. Warning was sent to him not to come there, that he would be killed, but he heeded not the notice, or he designed to show special bravery that might win a good standing. Two Cheyenne men accompanied him to the visited camp.

The three companions went from lodge to lodge, being received courteously and fed at the various stopping places. A brother of the man who had been killed sat in his own lodge, there meditating and saying nothing to anybody. He kept beside him a loaded rifle. From time to time, as the three men moved among the lodges he watched them from the interior of his tepee. People began to taunt him:

"You are afraid."

"No, I will kill him today."

The Sioux-Cheyenne walked at all times between the two Cheyenne companions when the three went from any one lodge to another. But as they were passing across one open area the middle man stopped and bent himself forward to tie a loose moccasin string. In a moment the bang of a rifle shot rang out from the watcher's tepee. The half-Sioux pitched headfirst to the ground. His death was regarded by all as an earned infliction. The chiefs agreed: "He ought not to have come so soon to this place where are his victim's relatives. His slayer did right."

An Ogallala Sioux man had one of our women as his wife. They lived with our people. The couple had much domestic trouble. It was said the husband grossly abused his wife. The matter came to a climax as our Cheyennes were camped on the Giving White Medal river. I was a baby or a small child, and my knowledge of it comes only from hearsay stories. But in later times I knew the people involved.

The maltreated wife had two brothers, Dirty Moccasins and Tall White Man—not the present old man Tall White Man, but another Cheyenne dead many years ago. These two brothers decided to end the continual humiliation of their sister. They got their bows and arrows and went man-hunting. Each of them sent an arrow through the body of the offending Sioux and put out the lights of his life. They were not banished. Besides their having the natural sympathy of the people, the dead man was a Sioux, not a Cheyenne. Nevertheless, ever after that, Dirty Moccasins smoked only a deer bone pipe and Tall White Man used always a little stone one. For many years I saw him as a scrawny and feeble old man smoking the tiny short-stemmed stone pipe.

The Sioux and his wife had a ten-year-old daughter. When she grew to womanhood she married a Cheyenne man named Elk Creek. This couple had three daughters, grandchildren of the Sioux killed by the two brothers. One of these grandchildren married Round Stone, another married a Fort Keogh soldier named Thompson, the third is the wife of Willis Rowland, our present interpreter at the Lame Deer agency.

I heard a story about two Sioux in a Sioux camp who quarreled concerning the ownership of a horse. One of them had possession of the animal. The other sat in his lodge and brooded over what he regarded as a wrong done to him. He planned an unusual mode of carrying out revenge. He went to a Cheyenne camp near by and inquired there for a medicine man. A Cheyenne led him to a certain lodge.

"I have important business," the Sioux announced. "Come out where nobody can hear us."

The three went out of the camp, to a hilltop. The young Cheyenne served as negotiator between the Sioux and the medicine man.

"I want him to kill a Sioux," the visitor proposed.

There was some exchange of talk about the compensation to the medicine man. Finally, an agreement was reached. The medicine man received a blanket, some moccasins and clothing, some food and a keen-bladed and sharp-pointed sheathknife. A day was consumed in settling the conditions. While this was going on, the Sioux camp moved away and was set up elsewhere. The angry Sioux and the medicine man followed them. The lodge of the enemy was pointed out. The medicine man drew the figure of a man upon the outside wall of the lodge. At the right place he made a special picture of the heart. Then he told the angry Sioux:

"Take this knife. At dawn tomorrow morning you must stab the heart picture I have drawn. Then bring to me the knife."

The commanded procedure was carried out. The wielder of the weapon was astonished when blood flowed freely from the stabbed picture heart. He ran away and told the medicine man, told him of the blood and returned to him the knife.

"Good. He will die tonight," came the assuring declaration.

As the medicine man went back to the Cheyennes he congratulated himself on the clever trick he had played upon his confiding employer. "Good knife, good blanket, good clothing, all for me," he chuckled. But: That same night the enemy Sioux man actually became ill. He vomited blood, and before morning he was dead. I do not like that kind of medicine actions. Such use of the powers makes bad Indians.

The warrior days of a Cheyenne man began at the age of about sixteen or seventeen, or sometimes a little earlier for such activities as were not very difficult or risky. They ended somewhere between thirty-five and forty, according to particular circumstances. The regular rule was, every man was classed as a warrior and expected to serve as such until he had a son old enough to take his place. Then the father retired from aggressive fighting and the son took up the weapons for that family. If a man came into early middle age without any son, he adopted one. If he had more than one son, he might allow the additional one or more to be adopted by another man who had none. By following this system, all of the offensive fighting was done by young men, mostly the unmarried young men. The fathers and the older men ordinarily stayed in the background, to help or to shield the women and children. Or, if it was practicable, the fathers and old men and women followed out the young warriors and stayed at a safe distance behind, there to sing cheering songs and to call out advice and encouragement. If a warrior's father or some other old person put himself unnecessarily forward in a battle he was likely to be criticised for his needless risk, and also the young warriors felt aggrieved at his taking from them whatever of honors might be gained in the combat. In general, the young men were supposed to be more valuable as fighters and less valuable as wise counselors, while the older men were estimated in the opposite way. It was considered as being not right for an important older man to place himself as a target for the missiles of the enemy, if he could avoid such exposure. Even in a surprise attack upon us, it was expected the seniors should run away, if they could get away, while the more lively and supposedly more ambitious young men met the attack.

Our war chiefs—that is, the three leading chiefs and the twenty-seven little chiefs of our three warrior societies—were more useful as instructors in quiet assemblage than as directors of operation in times of battle. There were frequent gatherings of the warrior societies, each in its own gathering, where the chiefs exchanged ideas about methods of combat and about daily care of the personal self, and where the listening young warriors learned their lessons. If some aggressive war was contemplated, these chiefs agreed upon the plans. But when any battle actually began it was a case of every man for himself. There were then no ordered groupings, no systematic movements in concert, no compulsory goings and comings. Warriors of all societies mingled indiscriminately, every individual went where and when he chose, every one looked out for himself only, or each helped a friend if such help were needed and if the able one's personal inclination just then was toward friendly helpfulness. The warrior chiefs called out advice, perhaps a reminder of some rule of action theretofore discussed in the gatherings, or perhaps some special suggestion that exactly fitted the immediate situation, such as, "Yonder is one whose horse is down; go right in after him." Ordinarily the advice of the chiefs was heeded. But the obedience was a voluntary one. In battle, the chiefs had not authority to issue commands that must be obeyed.

Special war parties made up of members of some certain warrior society often went out seeking conflict with the enemy. The warrior societies competed with each other for effectiveness in this kind of activity, as well as in all other activities regarded as commendable. At times, the members of some certain warrior society would be selected by the tribal chiefs to do all of the tribal fighting in some case where the opposition was looked upon as being not great enough to make necessary the use of the entire tribal military forces. If this appointed segment of our fighters did well they were acclaimed. If they did not do well, especially if other warriors had to go to their assistance, the original combatants were discredited. Ordinarily, whatever warrior society was on duty as camp policemen had also the duty as special camp defenders. It was their business to be the first ones out to meet any attack upon the camp. Members of the other societies added their help if necessary, refrained from doing so if they were not needed. If the enemy onset was sufficient to render needful the resistance of all of the warriors in the camp, all of them were called by the heralds of the tribal chiefs. In cases of extreme danger, even the old men and some of the women might use whatever weapons they could seize and wield.

The Sioux tribes had ways closely resembling those of the Cheyennes. We traveled and visited much with them, particularly with the Ogallalas, sometimes with the Minneconjoux. The Sioux tribal governments were almost the same as ours. Each of them had numerous tribal chiefs, each had various warrior societies and chiefs of them. Their warriors dressed for death in battle, all of their people dressed for death in time of peace, according to the same customs among us. Their warrior training by precept and by discipline was similar to our system. They fought their battles as a band of individuals, the same as we fought ours, and the same as was the way of

121

all Indians I ever knew. They had war dances and medicine dances differing only a little from our ceremonies of this kind. So when white people learn the ways of the Cheyennes they have learned also a great deal of the ways of the Sioux and of other Indians in this part of the world.

IV

Worshiping The Great Medicine.

I made medicine the first time when I was seventeen years old (1875). It was during the month of May, I believe, although we did not divide the years into months or weeks as the white people later taught us to divide them. Our family was in a camp of fourteen or fifteen lodges of Cheyennes in the hills at the head of Otter creek, a stream flowing into the eastern side of Tongue river. The main camp of the tribe was on Powder river, east of our location.

To "make medicine" is to engage upon a special period of fasting, thanksgiving, prayer and self denial, even of self torture. The procedure is entirely a devotional exercise. The purpose is to subdue the passions of the flesh and to improve the spiritual self. The bodily abstinence and the mental concentration upon lofty thoughts cleanses both the body and the soul and puts them into or keeps them in health. Then the individual mind gets closer toward conformity with the mind of the Great Medicine above us.

I said to my father: "All during my boyhood and youth the Great Medicine has been good to me. I have fond parents and kind brothers and sisters. I have had plenty of food and have had no bad sickness. No bullet nor arrow has hit me. No serious injury of any kind has fallen upon me. I ought to do something to show my gratitude for all of these favors."

"Yes, my son, you owe a debt for them," my father agreed.

Red Haired Bear, a good medicine man or spiritual adviser, was in our small camp. His wife was my mother's sister. I went to him.

"I want to make medicine," I told him. "I think I have lived in a way good enough to render me worthy. I want to become still better. I want to thank the Great Medicine and ask His continued favor. I want to become able to kill all enemies I may meet and to be shielded from their assaults upon me. I do not want to die in any manner until I reach old age. I wish you would help me."

"How," he responded encouragingly. "What number of days do you think you can endure?"

"The whole four days," I replied confidently.

"How," he glowed. "I will help you."

He warned me it was a difficult undertaking for any young man. He urged me to be brave. He said the bravest ones always got the greatest spiritual benefit. I asserted myself as feeling equal to any distress that might come to me.

"That is good," he cheered me on. "You shall have the strongest of trials. You shall stay out one night without any shelter, the next night you may have a little cone tepee, the third night you may build for yourself a willow dome lodge."

This proposition put a check upon my eagerness. I had not thought of being unprotected from bad weather during any part of the time. It occurred to my mind that a rainstorm might interfere with the devotions. Even with a little cone tepee over me, a strong wind might upset the entire programme. My medicine might be broken by accidents like these. I asked if a willow dome lodge could be used during the entire procedure.

"How. It shall be as you desire."

He started me out to cut willow wands for making the medicine lodge. He told me I must get seventeen of them, each a clean and strong and long piece of pliable green wood. I carefully gathered them, selecting and rejecting. I tied them into a pack bundle. Throwing the bundle upon my back and taking a crowbar in my hands, I carried the burden far up a gulch and into the timber at the hilltop. I chose a spot for the lodge and put down my load. With the crowbar I punched in the ground sixteen holes around a circle about eight feet in diameter. Into these holes I set upright sixteen of the wands. I then bent their tops across, pairing them and tying together the pairs. The skeleton dome was completed by weaving through the coupled tops the seventeenth strand, this running from east to west. I returned then to Red Haired Bear for further instructions.

"Get a buffalo head," he ordered me.

I searched the neighborhood until I found one. Under his directions I heaped up dirt into a low mound about eight feet due east from where was to be the eastern entrance opening of the lodge. Upon this mound was placed the buffalo head, it being set to face toward the lodge. I cleared off all grass and twigs to make a clean path between the buffalo head and the lodge opening. I gathered armfuls of sweet sagegrass and spread it as a carpet upon the floor of the enclosed circle. The two of us returned then to Red Haired Bear's lodge.

The medicine man painted my whole body. Red clay mixed into water, in a dish, was used for most of the painting. Four times he took portions of the powdered red earth, each separate time casting the portion upon the water's surface and uttering low prayers as he stirred it into solution. After having put the red coloring upon the entire surface of my skin he got out from his medicine bag a package of pulverized black earth. Four different casts and

four separate stirrings into water were made likewise
with this coloring material. With the black paint he
made first a circle about my face, including the forehead, the chin and the cheeks. Black wristlets and
black anklets were next formed. On the middle of
my breast he painted a black sun. On my left
shoulderblade he put a black moon.

My director then offered a prayer:

"Great Medicine Above: You see Wooden Leg.
He wants to be a good man. Look upon him and
favor him. Make him brave and wise and kind.
Make him generous to his people, to all Indians,
even to his enemies if they come peaceably and in
need. Help him to defeat all enemies who may
beset him, and shield him from their efforts to take
his life. Guide him so that he may be rich in food
and skins and horses. Help him to find a good wife.
Give to them many children. Keep them all in good
health and make them live a long time."

He prayed also to the ground spirits. As he
prayed to the Great Medicine he looked upward, and
as he addressed the spirits below he looked down
toward the ground. When the prayers were ended
we walked together to the medicine lodge I had built
in the hilltop forest. We sat down there beside the
slender path I had made to connect the buffalo head
and the entrance to the lodge. He talked to me:

127

"This is going to be a hard trial for you, the hardest trial you ever have had. Throughout four days you will have neither food nor water. Your desires will distress you. Other distresses may be piled upon these. You may retreat now and postpone it to another time if you want to do so. What say you?"

"I dread it," I confessed, "but I know it will not kill me. I do not want to wait. I want to go on right now. I shall keep my courage from failing by fixing my thoughts upon being a good man."

"That is good," he cheered me. Then he added: "Be brave."

The medicine man prayed again for me. He looked again upward and again downward, going through the same prayer for the below spirits as he had made to the Above Spirit. The praying was of the same kind as he had uttered just after the painting preparations, but he added some other solicitations for my welfare.

After this prayer had ended I crept in upon the sagegrass floor of the skeleton willow dome. He covered the frame all over with many buffalo robes we had brought. Not even a faint ray of light could get inside. He then went away to our camp.

I now was alone. For a little while I just sat there in the darkness—complete darkness, although it was about the middle of the afternoon. I was naked, except for the breechcloth and a buffalo robe. I had a supply of kinnikinick, some matches, and my medicine pipe that had been given to me by my father. I loaded and lit the pipe for a thoughtful smoke. The flash of the match dazzled my eyes. Time dragged along. I could not smoke continuously, so I just sat there and meditated, or tried to do so. I did not know when the sun went down nor when darkness came. It began to seem rather lonely. I grew sleepy, so I stretched myself out with the robe about me and drifted into a doze. But every little sound startled me. I sat up and had another smoke. Soon I had another, and then another. I slept again, this time more soundly. I had not the least notion as to how long I remained asleep. It seemed I had been there more than a day and night, that the medicine man had forgotten me. I listened intently to every slight rustle in the surrounding forest. My prayers all had been in thoughts, not in spoken words. I almost wished for some disturbing intrusion to break up the entire proceeding. Noise of a horse's footsteps fell into my ears. Closer, closer, very close.

"Hey, Wooden Leg!" It was the voice of Red Haired Bear. "One day has passed. It now is noon."

He dismounted and opened slightly the entrance covering. The light blinded me for a moment. Gradually he opened it wider, finally throwing it altogether aside. He allowed me to go outside for a few minutes, then I had to return to the interior.

"Let us smoke together," he invited.

He sat just outside and I sat just inside. My smoking equipment was brought into use. He pointed the stem and sent a puff to each of the four principal directions, then to the above, to the below and to the buffalo head. We passed the pipe back and forth in many exchanges, until one loading of it was exhausted. He prayed again for me. Then he admonished me:

"The next day will be more difficult. But, be not afraid. The Great Medicine sees you."

He shut up the lodge, mounted his horse and went away.

Fitful slumbers, prayers, smoking, efforts at meditation, these alternated in my quiet activities. I was hungry and thirsty, especially thirsty. My body was hot. My heart was heavy. My ears constantly were listening, listening, to every faint whisper of Nature. All of the time appeared to be night, the blackest of night. Suddenly there came a stamp—stamp—stamp. Then:

"Boo-o-o-o! Boo-o-o-o!"

130

A buffalo bull! The animal snorted, stamped and bellowed again. It surely would charge upon my lodge and tear it to pieces, I thought. I did not move, but I prayed earnestly: "Great Medicine, shield me. I have tried to be a good young man. You have been kind to me in past times. Be kind to me now." I heard the threatening beast move away. It did not return.

Hours, hours, hours. I did not know whether it was day or night. I heard a horse coming. That was a welcome sound. I was all attention.

"Hey, Wooden Leg!"

"Hey!"

"Two days have passed," Red Haired Bear informed me. "The sun now is far toward the west on your third day."

Again he opened my dark retreat, gradually letting in more and more light. Again we smoked together. I told him of the buffalo bull. He listened with evident great interest.

"That is a good sign," he comforted me. "No buffalo ever will harm you. You and all other Cheyennes will get plenty of meat and skins from them. The bull was your friend, telling you all this."

Another prayer went from the medicine man to the Above and to the below. After a short allowance of time for me outside, he put me again

131

into the enclosure and shut tightly the small hole.
"Be brave," were his parting words.

"Yes," I replied. But I was not sure.

Hot, thirsty, yet more hot and more thirsty. I
prayed particularly for strength of body and firm-
ness of heart to carry me through to the end of the
trial. I loaded my pipe for a solacing smoke. But
it was not a solace. The heat burned my already
parching tongue. I tried to sleep. Maybe I did
sleep. I do not know. I made attempts to meditate
quietly. I do not know whether I actually was thinking or was following dreams racing through my mind.
All I could be sure about was that I either was
sitting down or lying down all the time. I heard
something that cleared my mind at once. My mother
brought wood and stones and placed them out by the
buffalo head. She did not speak nor make any sign
of recognition, but I knew it was my mother. It
seemed I could look right through the robes and
see her there. After she had deposited her burden
she went away.

Oh, how lonely I was! I loaded and lit my pipe.
No, it was not good. My mouth and throat were
burning. Water! Water! But: "The Great Medicine sees me," I kept thinking. My thoughts whirled
and chased each other rapidly in circles. I dreamt
that I heard the footsteps of a horse.

"Hey, Wooden Leg!"

"Hey!"

"This is the day."

Happiness almost filled my heart. The only hindrance was in the thirst and the hot body. After I had been let out we smoked together. It was a torture to my tongue, but I did not complain. We went then to my father's lodge in the camp. My father called out invitations to old men friends. They came and sat in a circle upon the robes spread over the lodge's floor. I sat with them, by the side of my father. My mother brought a bucketful of water and set it off a little distance in front of me. I suppressed a strong desire to plunge my face into it, but I could not keep my eyes from staring at it. The medicine man sprinkled red powder upon the surface of the water, four small scatterings in four separate places. He passed his hands to and fro over it and prayed. It seemed I never in my life had heard so long a prayer. When it was ended he said to me:

"Wooden Leg, you have been four days without water. Now you may drink four sups."

I seized the sides of the bucket. The four sups were four long-drawn mouthfuls. The water rumbled through my bowels. After a few minutes I was told, "Now you may have more, but do not take all you want." I drank slowly, but I drew in big mouth-

133

fuls and took many of them. Not long afterward I was allowed to apply myself a third time at the bucket.

My mother brought a potful of buffalo meat she had been boiling. All of the guests were given portions of it. A piece was put upon a tin plate and set before me. It looked good enough to grab and swallow immediately. But I waited for advice. My adviser did not long detain me.

"Wooden Leg, you have been four days without meat. Take four sliced-off bites, one for each day of the fast."

I selected a long chunk from the plate. I stuck the end of it far into my mouth, and with a sheath-knife I cut it off. The chewing was vigorous, and I soon had it swallowed. The chunk was pushed a second time into my mouth and its end cut off there. A third and a fourth mouthful were taken in the same manner. After a few minutes, more meat was allowed to me. Then still more, all I cared to eat. It was the best meat I ever tasted.

The old men joined in asking me:

"Tell us of your experience."

I told them—told them particularly of the coming of the buffalo bull. They complimented me, said I was brave, said the Great Medicine was my friend, assured me that no buffalo ever would harm me.

Their approval and their assurances made me glad. My heart was like the sun coming up on a summer morning.

All of these old men, some of their wives, my father and mother and the medicine man went with me to my medicine lodge. We were to have a sweat bath worship together. My mother carried a bucketful of water for sprinkling upon the hot stones inside the lodge. The medicine man piled the stones into a cone heap. He leaned sticks of wood up the sides of this stone structure and set a fire to going among them. The other men stripped themselves to breechcloth and crept into the lodge. When the stones had become well heated by the wood fire over them the medicine man passed them to one of the men inside. They were handled with forked sticks and were piled into a pit some of the men had made in the center of the lodge's earth floor. When the pit was filled with the hot stones the medicine man set inside the bucketful of water. He himself then crept in, on hands and knees as we all had done. One man remained outside to close the opening, to ventilate temporarily when we might require, to wait upon us in whatever way our needs might demand. Not any of the women went into the lodge. Twelve men were in there.

At the left inside of the entrance sat the medicine

man. I was next at his left side. My father was third, at my left. The other men were seated on beyond, the row extending around the circle. All had backs to the wall. We had smoked together while the stones were being heated, but the pipe now had been placed outside. Its bowl rested on the ground beside the buffalo head and its stem projected upward past the nose and eyes of the hallowed object. A good spirit influence was coming from the nostrils of the head straight along the clean path and into the lodge. No knowing and worshipful Indian ever crossed that path. Such act would cut off the steady flow of healing virtue.

The medicine man opened the interior proceedings with another prayer for my welfare. Once more he pleaded with the Great Medicine to make me good and generous, to give me success in hunting, to protect me from enemies and to enable me to kill them. Once more he asked that I might get a good wife, might have many children, and that myself and all of my family might keep good health and live to advanced years. He beseeched again that I might gather together many horses and not lose any of them. I believed his prayers would be heard. My hopes were high. My trust in the Being Above was strong.

Water was squirted upon the hot stones in the central pit. The medicine man first gave each one in the lodge a drink of water. He took into his own mouth a chew of herb. After its mastication he supped and squirted four successive mouthfuls of water. Between the acts were short prayers. Thus he released from the stones the vitality put into them by the burning wood that had got it from the sun, the material representative of the Great Medicine. The stones hissed their protests as the water compelled them to release into the air the spiritual curative forces. Our bodies were enveloped by the steam wherein floated the vital energy. The vivifying and purifying influence soaked into our skins. Bad spirits were driven out of us and drowned in the water that dripped from us. The medicine man repeated from time to time the sprinkling of water upon the protesting stones.

The soft whisperings of an eagle wing bone flute came into my ears. The sound seemed to come from the roof and from other points in the utterly dark interior of the lodge. After a few of the gentle blasts, I felt the instrument being placed in my hands. My father put it there. It now was mine, to keep. It was to be worn about my neck, suspended at the midbreast by a buckskin thong, during all times of danger. If I were threatened with imminent harm I had but to put it to my lips and cause it to send out its soothing notes. That would ward off every evil design upon me. It was my mystic protector. It was my medicine.

After an hour or more together in the devotional dome, all of us went to our respective lodge homes. There my father presented me also with a shield of rawhide taken from the rump of a buffalo bull. The hair had been removed and the piece of skin had been dried rapidly before a fire, to make it extremely tough. It was covered with antelope buckskin sewed in place. The cover had medicine designs drawn in color upon its surface. This shield would turn off any bullet or arrow or other missile coming toward me. My father made it. He delivered it into my left hand.

My second medicine experience took place a month or so after that first one. Black White Man, a medicine man, took me through it. This time the plan was for but two days of self denial and worship. I made the dome lodge according to the same rules as had governed in making the first one, which was the regular way of making them. Black White Man painted me in the same way and with the same ceremony used by Red Haired Bear. I had the same kind of harassing sensations while alone, but they covered only two days instead of four. The resumption of water and food was carried out in a manner exactly like had been done in the previous proceedings. The

sweat bath devotions had a like preparatory programme and followed a course like that of the other
one and of all such affairs entered upon among the
Cheyennes. But during this second time of spiritual
upbuilding there was one intervening incident that
marked it as different from all others.

During the last part of my lonely vigil—I learned
afterward it was during my second night—my
quietude was broken by the tread of horses, many
horses. I heard men talking. Gabble-gabble-gabble.
It was not Cheyenne talk. It was not Sioux. This
being the case, the horsemen necessarily must be
enemies, either whites or Indians. It seemed now
that the bellowing buffalo bull of my previous experience had been but a tame threat. It appeared
I surely would be discovered or already had been
discovered, by the gabbling strangers. It seemed
that death threatened me. My hair raised itself and
I could feel it standing upright. My heart thumped.
It throbbed and pounded the inner wall of my breast.
To my senses its noise was so boisterous as to notify
the intruders and all the rest of the world that a
human being frozen by fright awaited the fatal blow.
I did not move—perhaps was not able to move. But
I could think. I centered my thoughts upon whis-
pering over and over, "The Great Medicine sees me."

"Hi-ye-e-e-e!" The war-cry!

"Bang! Bang! Bang-bang!" Rifle shots.

The horses near me clattered away. One of them bawled as if wounded by a bullet. The strange voices went out of my hearing. Other voices shouted. These were Cheyennes. I heard Cheyenne women and children crying as they ran past my retreat. But I could do nothing but just sit there with my buffalo robe over my head. The commotion gradually died down. My pious meditations were much disturbed by the alarming turmoil. I could not keep myself from wondering what had happened. I wondered if the Cheyennes had been driven from their camp and had left me there alone. This thought chilled me. But I stayed, waiting, waiting. Many hours later Black White Man came.

"They were Crows trying to steal our horses," he explained. The raiders had been repulsed, but one of our Cheyennes had been killed. "It shows that the Crows never can hurt you," the medicine man assured me.

For a third season of warrior discipline I went one morning at dawn to the top of a hill. There I fasted, prayed, meditated and dreamed all day. During the day I saw the lodges taken down and the whole camp move away down the valley. But I had to stay. When the sun had set I started out afoot to follow the trail of my people. I drank water along the way, but I got no food until my arrival at the home lodge at the end of my journey of ten or twelve miles.

Another disciplinary means for subduing the flesh was to stand upright all day, from sunrise to sunset, on a hill. The devotee did not move during that time except to keep his face turned at all times toward the sun. He might keep his eyes closed or shaded, but his countenance had to be presented ever toward the venerated token of the Great Medicine's existence. He prayed or otherwise kept his thoughts fixed on a high plane. This system of self denial was varied by the attitude taken. One might stand all day or sit in one position all day or lie down during all of the time. But the attitude assumed at the beginning must be kept to the end. My all-day supplications were made while sitting down.

Standing upright in water from sunrise to sunset was one way of putting the body under the rule of the spirit. The water had to be up to the neck or the upper breast. Not any drink of it was taken. It was not permissible to move the body except for keeping the face toward the sun. The bodily torture incident to the full standard Great Medicine dance —what the white people call the sun dance—was the most severe test of hardihood, so it was looked

141

upon as the highest form of self scourging. I never undertook this extreme step.

Women did not make medicine by feats of endurance. Such was for men only. Sometimes two men would go together for the all-day hilltop fast or for some other similar performance. Ordinarily, though, only one man made up the vigil. I like best the solitary way. I think it is better to be alone at such times. At any of the occasions observable it was permissible for onlookers to view the act. Such scrutiny might aid greatly in spurring on to full compliance with the rules. Payment to any medicine man helper was due. This might be such as was agreed upon in advance—often paid in advance —or it might be in the form of subsequent free gifts to him. The standard fee was a horse.

Our tribal Great Medicine dance was a ceremony of one, two or three days, the period depending upon immediate conditions. In times before mine the full period had been four days, but in my time three days was the maximum. It was not held at any regular time. Once every two or three years was the usual custom. It would be held, though, in successive years if the tribe was having misfortune or if enough special devotees wanted to undergo the trials. The summer season was the special time. The prime purpose was to ask the Great Medicine's favorable attention to the tribe as a whole, not to any particular persons. The prayers were for good grass, new colts in the horse herds, plenty of berries and roots, many children, success in hunting game and in repelling enemies.

The Cheyennes and the Arapahoes had their two Great Medicine ceremony dances together on one occasion when I was about twelve years old (1870). We were south of the mountains beyond the headwaters of Powder river. The two tribes camped as one, in one great camp circle, but all of the Cheyenne lodges were at one side of the camp and all of the Arapaho lodges at the opposite side. Each tribe had its Great Medicine lodge at its own side of the combined camp. I went back and forth looking on at both of them. The other people of both tribes did the same. I was not quite old enough during our free roaming days to take a part in the important tribal affairs. I merely looked, listened, kept quiet and thought about them. This double sacred dance of the Cheyennes and Arapahoes was for only one day. During that one day all of the participants and many other people took neither food nor water. After sunset they had a great feast. That was the regular way—the participants took neither food nor water while the ceremonies were being carried out, one, two, three or four days.

143

Special invocation dances were held irregularly, often several times during one season. One or several or many persons would perform the rites. At a buffalo dance the intent was to obtain the aid of the Great Medicine in our efforts at getting the meat and skins of these animals. Deer dances, elk dances, antelope dances, were engaged upon by individuals, by parties or by the tribe. The object was to enlist spiritual forces to help us in gathering meat and skins. Berry dances, by few or by many people, had a like incentive. Always the dances were in summer, none of them in winter. Always there was self denial in various forms, sacrifices were made in various ways. At times the self denial was carried to the point of bodily torture. That was our way of paying in advance for the favors asked. That was all we could do by way of payment.

The spirits of animals joined themselves often to assist or to hinder human beings. Sometimes one would give its medicine to a man, at other times some animal would break a man's medicine, or would try to do so. At my father's lodge an old man, Pockmarked Nose, told of a certain experience that came to him. My father afterward told me.

Pockmarked Nose went one time with a young man to hunt buffalo. They were on horseback and were leading pack horses to bring back the meat and skins. They traveled up and down hills and over the level plains. Finally they found a band of buffalo. They got themselves ready and charged into the band. The young man had a bow and arrows, Pockmarked Nose had a flintlock gun. He killed a buffalo. Just afterward a shot came from somewhere aside and another buffalo went down. That shot from aside puzzled the two hunters, but they rode on. Each time the old man or the young man killed a buffalo the shot from aside brought down another to match it. But, who was doing this shooting? Was it a friend or an enemy? They could not see anybody. When six buffalo lay dead on the plain the old man applied himself at discovering the identity of the third hunter. Far off, on a slight elevation of the land, stood a dimly outlined human figure. Pockmarked Nose rode toward it.

Was it the Above Spirit, the Great Medicine? Or was it a below spirit? Or was some powerful medicine man playing tricks? Pockmarked Nose did not know, and he never did find out to his satisfaction. The stranger had a wooden gun. He said: "Come, I give you this medicine gun. It never fails to kill." Pockmarked Nose took and kept the offered gun. I do not know what use he may have made of it.

My father himself saw a marvelous example of the spirit powers regularly belonging to the deer tribe. When he was a young man he and a companion were hunting near the medicine water * not far from the present town of Sheridan, Wyoming. They saw bubbles coming up and bursting upon the water's surface. They went up close, to learn what was causing this agitation. As they peered down into the deep but clear lake they saw there a deer moving about and quietly grazing along the bottom. While they were watching the animal it stopped grazing and floated slowly up to the water's surface. My father killed it with an arrow. He skinned it, cut the meat from the bones, wrapped the skin about the meat and loaded the bundle upon his packhorse. At his home lodge he stood out and called the names of various friends. He invited them:

"Come, feast with me. Good deer meat."

But when he shouted these words the flesh and the skin all jumped together and formed again the same live deer he had killed. The animal went running away. It ran back to the medicine water, plunged into it and disappeared. My father searched for it, but he could not see it. He told me he did not understand how a deer could do such things except it were by the help of the Great Medicine.

Three of our medicine men invited some of us young men into a tepee on one certain occasion when

* Lake DeSmet.

I was about fourteen or fifteen years old. They said, "We will show you how to make the winter go away so that the grass may grow, for the good of the young colts coming to our herds." Just at that time there was a big snowstorm making the people and the horses shiver. But the three medicine men went confidently at their ceremonies.

They sent a young woman out to gather some certain kind of sprigs of vegetation. It was not tobacco, but pretty soon the medicine men had it changed into tobacco. They formed a circle with us, loaded the pipe, and soon it was passing from one to another. To each of us in turn they said: "Draw in only a little of the smoke, but draw it in slowly and deeply. Hold it there a short time, then let it flow out from wide-open lips, not in puffs from firm lips." We did as they directed. While the smoking was being done the three old men made prayers. After a while one of them said: "Look outside." We looked. The storm had quit, the sky had cleared, the ground was wet but bare of snow, green grass was peeping up everywhere.

Every Indian had, or tried to have, some special medicine or spirit power of his own, to bring him good fortune or to shield him from harm. He had some object or objects that held this helpful influence, or he had certain ways of doing certain acts, or he had both of these aids. I had my special protective possessions and my particular methods of using them. It was considered not prudent to reveal these things, and I never have done so, except in some features that I could not keep secret.

A powerful spirit man during my boyhood was one whose name originally was Walks Above the Earth. He was known as a man whose mind was at all times on spiritual things, who gave little or no thought to ordinary earthly matters. His name got changed, though, in his later life. This came about because of his choice of a mule for his riding animal. One time when he and Little Chief were approaching a Sioux camp somebody remarked, in derision, "Here comes that crazy Cheyenne on his mule." That fixed upon him the name Crazy Cheyenne on a Mule. This afterward was shortened to Crazy Mule.

He had a variety of medicine powers. He put himself through many trials, so the spirits helped him. One time, when we were in camp far up the Powder river, he had four Cheyennes go up close to him and shoot at him, each in successive turn. They sent four bullets directly at his body. He was standing with his back against a tree. After the four shots had been fired he stooped forward and pulled off his moccasins. From them he poured out the four bullets. I saw this. I was eight years old. I saw him do the same feat at a time when our tribal camp was pitched on the Rosebud valley, just below where the present Forsythe road forks to go to Lame Deer and to Ashland. At another time he showed his powers when the tribe were on upper Lame Deer creek. This was just before our warriors joined the Ogallala Sioux to fight the soldiers in the fort * at the south of us.

Roman Nose was, I believe, the most admired of all warriors I ever saw. He was killed when I yet was a boy, but I remember him, and as I grew older I heard much talk of him as an example for the young men. The water spirits told him not to marry, so he lived a single and pure life. At various Great Medicine dances he went bravely through the bodily tortures as a sacrifice of self for the good of the tribe. White Bull, sometimes known also as Ice, was his usual medicine man adviser. In later years White Bull and others told me a great many stories illustrative of the admirable qualities of Roman Nose.

He made medicine one time when we were camped on Goose creek, a stream flowing into the upper Tongue river. The medicine water lake was not far away. At dawn Roman Nose stripped himself, made a raft of logs and went out upon the lake. He took

* Fort Phil Kearny.

with him his medicine pipe. He had a large buffalo robe for a bed and a small one for a pillow. No food, no water for drinking. He spent the day on his robe bed. He prayed, "Great Medicine, let me conquer all enemies," and other prayers of this kind. He meditated upon the Above.

That night a storm came. Lightning flashed and thunder shook the earth. Waves washed upon the raft and tossed it over the surface of the water. His friends were fearful he would be drowned. Early in the morning two men went to look for him. They saw him on the raft, floating safely. They told the people, "He was not harmed."

The second day he likewise prayed and meditated all day. His fast was continued. When that night arrived another storm came. The thunder and lightning were more active than they had been during the previous night. The waves lifted themselves higher. But when the calm morning dawned his watchers learned that nothing harmful had fallen upon him. The third day and night passed in the same manner, but the storm during the hours of darkness was yet more furious. "He surely will be killed by the water spirits tonight," the people said. But he was not.

The fourth night the storm was a terrible one, the worst any of the Cheyennes ever had seen. They were fearful for themselves as well as for the young man on the raft. Hailstones pelted our lodges and scattered our pony herds. "He will be beaten to death," everybody agreed. When the quiet twilight of morning came, two men went upon a hill to search over the waters. There was Roman Nose still floating on his raft. They helped him to land it and to put himself upon the shore. Not a hailstone had hit him. The water had been angry, crazy, reaching for his body, but not a drop of it had touched him. The water spirits failed to devour him. The Great Medicine prevented them. At the camp all of the old men sat themselves in a circle and listened to his rehearsal of the events of his great devotional adventure.

At a battle with soldiers on Powder river (1865) Roman Nose showed the people that he had special protection against enemies. He rode his horse several times back and forth in front of the white men. He rode slowly, not fast. The soldiers shot at him, but not a bullet went into him. They either missed him or fell back harmless. He had a strong medicine warbonnet. I did not see him defy the soldiers, but I heard a great deal of talk about it. Our camp was above the forks of Powder river and Little Powder river. The battle was down below, on Powder river. Both the Northern and the Southern Chey-

enne tribes were in the upper valley, camping side
by side. Both of the Great Medicine tribal lodges
were in the camps, the one for our sacred Buffalo
Head, and the other for the Medicine Arrows of the
Southern Cheyennes.

White Bull made many medicine fasts. He told
me about them. He said that one time when he was
fasting and praying on a hill, not in a lodge, on the
third day a doe antelope came near to him. She
lay down there on the ground and gave birth to twin
fawns. White Bull reached out and seized the doe's
hind feet. She struggled, but he did not release
her. She promised that if he would let her go free
she would give to him the two fawns. But he told
her he did not want the fawns, he wanted her medicine, her spirit powers. The doe groaned and protested, but finally she agreed:

"Yes, I give you my medicine."

He got the bear medicine also in a manner like
that. When he was fasting and praying on a hill
the bear came sniffing, sniffing, on his trail. It
stopped suddenly as it came into his view. Both
of them were startled and frightened. White Bull
trusted the Great Medicine, but the bear was altogether afraid. It said, "If you will not harm me I
will give you my medicine, and then you can speak
fire from your mouth." It gave him then its power

over spirits. He got also the medicine of a wild hog. Perhaps he had other medicines. I do not know. He had a good reputation for doctoring sick people. I have heard him "Blaa-a-a-a," like a doe antelope, when he was making medicine for them. I have heard him, lots of times, grunting like a hog or whoofing like a bear. I never knew how much to believe of his stories. Lots of people said he told big lies.

My father taught me some medicine practices for myself. He showed me where to gather the seed of certain grass that had power to shield me. A quantity of the seed was put into a buckskin pouch, and this I carried tied to my back hair. In the pouch was also a piece of loose buckskin. To prepare the medicine, a few seeds were pulverized between the fingers and the powder was allowed to fall upon the piece of buckskin spread out. A little saliva was mixed with it by the stirring of a finger. A slight spray of saliva then was put into the palms, after which the mixed seed and saliva medicine was taken into the palms and they were rubbed together. When they had been well rubbed they were passed all about my body or clothing, near the skin or clothing but not touching. Bullets then would be diverted and slip aside from me.

My horse was protected by the same medicine. In

the same way the palms were passed all over the body of the horse, close but not touching. This would turn aside bullets from him. The hoofs were lifted and the bottom of the feet treated by the palm passing. He then would be not easily tired, would be surefooted, would not step into a hole and fall down. The palms were passed across the front of the horse's nose. The medicine made him have a keen sense of smell and a clear eyesight. This helped him to find his way without difficulty during darkness or at any time when running.

The face painting as it was done for me by Red Haired Bear at my first medicine making was adopted as my fixed mode of battle preparation in this regard. It was a black ring about my face, including lower forehead, chin and cheeks in its circle. All of the surface enclosed in the circle was painted yellow. I kept at all times right at hand a supply of charcoal and yellow clay paint. It did not take long for me to apply them when an occasion for their need might come. With this preparation, with my best clothing, my shield, my eagle wing bone whistle, myself and my horse protected by the grass seed medicine, I was almost fearless. I was not entirely so, but almost. In every time of danger I tried to keep myself thinking:

"The Great Medicine sees me."

154

V

Off the Reservation.

After we had been driven from the Black Hills and that country was given to the white people my father would not stay on any reservation. He said it was no use trying to make farms as the white people did. In the first place, that was not the Indian way of living. All of our teachings and beliefs were that land was not made to be owned in separate pieces by persons and that the plowing up and destruction of vegetation placed by the Great Medicine and the planting of other vegetation according to the ideas of men was an interference with the plans of the Above. In the second place, it seemed that if the white people could take away from us the Black Hills after that country had been given to us and accepted by us as ours forever, they might take away from us any other lands we should occupy whenever they might want these other lands. In the third place, the last great treaty had allowed us to use all of the country between the Black Hills and the Bighorn river and mountains as hunting grounds so long as we did not resist the traveling of white people through it on their way to or from their lands beyond its

155

borders. My father decided to act upon this agreement to us. He decided we should spend all of our time in the hunting region. We could do this, gaining our own living in this way, or we could be supported by rations given to us at the agency. He chose to stay away from all white people. His family all agreed with him. So, for more than a year before the great battle at the Little Bighorn we were all the time in the hunting lands.

Not all of the dissatisfied Indians stayed away from the reservations. Bands were moving to and from the hunting grounds at all times, even during the winter, but only a few remained here throughout the year. The Indians involved were both Sioux and Cheyennes, but there were many more Sioux than Cheyennes. A band of Uncpapas, led by Sitting Bull, remained entirely away from Dakota. There were at all times a big camp and some smaller camps of Ogallalas. Families or small bands of other Sioux came and went. The Cheyenne camps varied from thirty or forty lodges to two hundred or more. During the winter before the soldiers came after us the Cheyennes and Ogallalas kept near each other much of the time. We spent the earlier part of the cold weather season on Otter creek. Then we moved together over to Tongue river, setting our two camp circles near each other on the west side of the river where now is the home place of John Bigheadman, known also as All See Him.

Sugar, coffee, tobacco, ammunition, everything of that kind, were scarce with us. We were not greatly distressed because of this, but we had learned to use and to like these additions to our old ways, so we were pleased when such things came to us. We liked to get ammunition, as that helped us to kill more game. But, best of all, we liked to get tobacco. We used the plug tobacco that most white people use for chewing. We shaved it off in thin layers, using a board to lay it upon while cutting it. It was mixed with willow bark. This bark we called kinnikinick. It was the dried inside layer.

Red Haired Bear had some tobacco, just a little piece, at one time when a certain very old man came to visit him. The old man was feeble and shaky. He was a good man, so Red Haired Bear determined to give him a treat. The host got out his pipe. "Give me a knife," he said to his woman. Then, "Get me the tobacco board." She did as he had asked. He cut off only a little of the tobacco and mixed it with plenty of kinnikinick. He loaded his pipe and lit it. When he had sent puffs to the four directions, to the Above and to the below spirits, he handed the pipe to the guest. The old man drew in and let out one draft. He stopped a moment as if thinking in-

157

tently about something. Then he drew in another draft. He let out a cloud through his nose.

"Oh, tobacco!" he exclaimed in delight.

He took deep and slow inhalations. He let them out slowly, by the mouth and by the nose. As Red Haired Bear took his turn at the pipe the old man grasped handfuls of the smoke, rubbed together his palms, sniffed them over and over, rubbed his face and his clothing. "Good, good," he kept saying. When the pipeful had been burned he had Red Haired Bear empty very carefully the ashes, mix some more kinnikinick willow bark with them and fill the pipe with this mixture. They had a third smoke of this kind.

Four men went to the lodge of a certain medicine man. He told them he had some tobacco, and that made their hearts glad. He had a chunk of wood that looked like a plug of tobacco. He put this piece of wood upon the tobacco board and pretended to shave off slices from it to mix with kinnikinick. Even while he was shaving the stick the men were sniffing and saying, "Oh, good tobacco." They smoked four pipefuls. The ashes were saved carefully. They were mixed then with other kinnikinick and four more pipefuls were smoked. The four men went away praising their host for having given them such fine entertainment.

As Cheyennes came to us from the agency they brought coffee, sugar and tobacco. Other articles were brought, but these were the most desired. The luxuries were distributed among friends, small quantities here and there. Someone and another then would go to the front of his tepee, call out the names of special friends and invite: "I have tobacco. Come and smoke with me." Or: "I have coffee and sugar. Come and feast with me." Sioux might make such gifts to Cheyennes or Cheyennes might provide them to the Sioux. Or, members of the two sets of Indians might invite each other to smoke or to eat. Usually, though, the givings and the invitings were within tribal bounds. Yet every Indian who might prosper in any way was expected to hold himself always willing to share and desirous of sharing his prosperity with his fellows, with all friendly people, even with avowed enemies if such should come peaceably and should be in want. A first principle of Indian conduct was: Be generous to all Indians.

Last Bull, leading chief of the Fox warriors, came to us with his family at the last end of the winter.* He was the first one to disturb our peace of mind with the announcement:

"Soldiers are coming to fight you."

He said that the whites would fight all Cheyennes

* February, 1876.

159

and Sioux who were off the reservations. He did not know from what forts the soldiers would come. He had not heard who would be their chiefs. But this did not matter. He and his family stayed with us. Other Cheyennes came.

We did not believe Last Bull's report. We thought somebody had told him what was not true. The treaty allowed us to hunt here as we might wish, so long as we did not make war upon the whites. We were not making war upon them. I had not seen any white man for many months. We were not looking for them. We were trying to stay away from all white people, and we wanted them to stay away from us. Our old men said that the reason the white people wanted us to leave off the roaming and hunting was that we should stay near them, so they could sell us more of their goods and their whisky. Our old men ever were urging the young men not to drink the whisky. The advice often was disregarded, but it appeared to be given serious consideration. Up to that time in my life I never had swallowed a drink of it.

Lots of buffalo were feeding on the grass at the upper Tongue and Powder rivers, on all of their branches and on the other lands in this whole region. Lots of elk, deer and antelope could be found almost anywhere the hunter might go to seek them. Lots of colts were being born in our horse herds this spring. We were rich, contented, at peace with the whites so far as we knew. Why should soldiers come out to seek for us and fight us? No, the report seemingly was a mistake.

Spotted Wolf, Medicine Wolf and Twin, three Cheyenne chiefs, came to us as we camped on Powder river. They advised us to go to our agency. "Soldiers will come to fight you," they assured us. We now believed this to be true. The chiefs in our band had a council. The next day they had another council.

"No, we shall stay here," they decided. "If soldiers come we shall steal their horses. Then they can not fight us."

Forty lodges of Cheyennes now were in camp on the west side of Powder river, forty or fifty miles above where Little Powder river flows into it. The report brought by the three chiefs aroused us into watchful activity. Every hunting party was on the lookout for white soldiers or for their trails. The women and old people in the camp kept themselves ever ready for immediate flight.

My older brother Yellow Hair and I went scouting. We mounted our horses at night and went up the Powder river valley. As we were creeping and peeping over a hill our horses got away from us. But

161

we kept on afoot. We saw camp fires in a dry gulch on the east side of Powder river. Some other groups of Cheyennes were scouting in the same vicinity. A figure on horseback showed for a moment on a ridge. White Man? Cheyenne? Other Indian? Must be a white man, a soldier. Somebody off aside from us acted quickly.

"Bang!"

The horse and rider went at once out of sight. My brother and I dropped down and lay quiet a long time. We talked of stealing soldier horses. Our own were gone, and we needed mounts. We crawled along further until we could see a soldier walking to and fro along the line of their horses, between us and the animals. He had a rifle. As we conferred together about what to do, other soldiers came to the horses. They were getting ready to move. Within a few minutes the entire body of them were gone. We went then close to the abandoned camp. We began to poke up the smoldering fires. Suddenly:

"Bang!" The bullet whistled past us.

We ran. Other shots were fired at us. We hurried into a narrow gulch or canyon. As we dodged from hiding place to hiding place up the gulch we could see soldiers on horseback following along the high sides. They were shooting down toward us.

162

But they could not see us. There was a high wind blowing, the weather was of the blustering kind usual at that time of year. We hastened on to where the gulch led to the high bench land. Our pursuers had left us before we reached this broad area. We were tired, very tired. We wanted to stop and rest, but we feared our legs might grow stiff, so we trudged on. At dawn we heard barking of dogs at our camp. That was a welcome sound.

"Waoo-oo-oo-oo," we wolf-howled from a hilltop before we went into the camp. Our alarm brought out the people. They flocked to our lodge. A council of the old men was called. My brother and I were brought before it. Other young men who had been out also were at the council. "Young men, what do you know?" the chiefs asked us. We told them. We learned that the lone horseman shot during the night before was a Cheyenne. Another Cheyenne had sent the bullet. It had gone in at the wrist and out just below the elbow. The affair was entirely a case of mistaken identity.

The council of old men decided we should keep away from the soldiers, not try to fight them. They sent out an old man herald to proclaim:

"Soldiers have been seen. We think they are looking for us. Today we move camp far down the river."

163

Our hunters and scouts kept a lookout for the soldiers. Our camp was moved to a point just above where Little Powder river flows into Powder river and on the west side of the larger stream. The soldiers went over the hills to the headwaters of Hanging Woman creek. They followed this stream down to Tongue river. We felt safe then. Many of our people thought they were not seeking us at all.

But one day some Cheyennes hunting antelope at the head of Otter creek, just over the hills west from our camp, saw the soldiers camped there. The hunters urged their horses back to warn us. Some of the horses became exhausted in the run, so their riders had to come on afoot. A herald notified the people. All was excitement. The council of old men appointed ten young men to go out that night and watch the movements of the soldiers. Others were out scouting or were awake and watching, but these ten had the special duty. Most of the people slept, feeling secure under the protection of the appointed outer sentinels. Early in the morning an old man arose and went to the top of a nearby knoll to observe or to pray, as old men were in the habit of doing. He had been there only a few moments when he began shouting toward the camp:

"The soldiers are right here! The soldiers are right here!"

Already the attacking white men were between the horse herd and the camp. The ten scouts during the hours of darkness and storm had missed meeting the soldiers. They found a trail, this trail going up the creek valley. They turned their horses and whipped them in the effort to get ahead of the invaders. But the tired horses played out. They did not catch up with the soldiers until these had arrived at the camp, or afterward.

Women screamed. Children cried for their mothers. Old people tottered and hobbled away to get out of reach of the bullets singing among the lodges. Braves seized whatever weapons they had and tried to meet the attack. I owned a muzzle-loading rifle, but I had no bullets for it. I owned also a cap-and-ball six shooter, but I had loaned it to Star, a cousin who was one of the ten special scouts of the night before. In turn, he had let me have bow and arrows he had borrowed from Puffed Cheek. My armament then consisted of this bow and arrows belonging to Puffed Cheek.

I skirted around afoot to get at our horse herd. I looped my lariat rope over the neck of the first convenient one. It belonged to Old Bear, the old man chief of our band. But just now it became my war pony. I quickly made a lariat bridle and mounted the recovered animal. A few other Cheyennes did

165

the same as I had done. But most of them remained afoot. I shot arrows at the soldiers. Our people had not much else to shoot. Only a few had guns and also ammunition for them.

All of the soldiers who first appeared had white horses. Another band of them who charged soon afterward from another direction had only bay horses. I started back to try to get to my home lodge. I wanted my shield, my other medicine objects and whatever else I might be able to carry away. Women were struggling along burdened with packs of precious belongings. Some were dragging or carrying their children. All were shrieking in fright. I came upon one woman who had a pack on her back, one little girl under an arm and an older girl clinging to her free right hand. She was crying, both of the girls were crying, and all three of them were almost exhausted. They had just dived into a thicket for a rest when I rode up to them. It was Last Bull's wife and their two daughters.

"Let me take one of the children," I proposed.

The older girl, age about ten years, was lifted up behind me. A little further on I picked up also an eight-year-old boy who was trudging along behind a mother carrying on her back a baby and under her arms two other children. The girl behind me clasped her arms about my waist. I wrapped an arm about the boy in front of me. With my free arm and hand I guided my horse as best I could. The animal too was excited by the tumult. It shied and plunged. But I got the two children out of danger. Then I went back to help in the fight.

Two Moons, Bear Walks on a Ridge and myself were together. We centered an attack upon one certain soldier. Two Moons had a repeating rifle. As we stood in concealment he stood it upon end in front of him and passed his hands up and down the barrel, not touching it, while making medicine. Then he said: "My medicine is good; watch me kill that soldier." He fired, but his bullet missed. Bear Walks on a Ridge then fired his muzzle-loading rifle. His bullet hit the soldier in the back of the head. We rushed upon the man and beat and stabbed him to death. Another Cheyenne joined us to help in the killing. He took the soldier's rifle. I stripped off the blue coat and kept it. Two Moons and Bear Walks on a Ridge took whatever else he had and they wanted.

One Cheyenne was killed by the soldiers. Another had his forearm badly shattered. Braided Locks, who is yet living, had the skin of one cheek furrowed by a bullet. The Cheyennes were beaten away from the camp. From a distance we saw the destruction of our village. Our tepees were burned,

167

with everything in them except what the soldiers may have taken. Extra flares at times showed the explosion of powder, and there was the occasional pop of a cartridge from the fires. The Cheyennes were rendered very poor. I had nothing left but the clothing I had on, with the soldier coat added. My eagle wing bone flute, my medicine pipe, my rifle, everything else of mine, were gone.

This was in the last part of the winter.* Melted snow water was running everywhere. We waded across the Powder river and set off to the eastward. All of the people except some of the warriors were afoot. The few young men on horseback stayed behind to guard the other people as they got away. One old woman, a blind person, was missing. All others were present except the Cheyenne who had been killed.

The soldiers did not follow us. That night we who had horses went back to see what had become of them. At the destroyed camp we saw one lodge still standing. We went to it. There was the missing old blind woman. Her tepee and herself had been left entirely unharmed. We talked about this matter, all agreeing that the act showed the soldiers had good hearts.

* March 17th, 1876. Gen. J. J. Reynolds in command of soldiers. Historians mistakenly mention this incident as a victory over "Crazy Horse's village."—T. B. M.

We found the soldier camp. We found also our horses they had taken. We crept toward the herd, out a little distance from the camp. One Cheyenne would whisper, "I see my horse." Another would say, "There is mine." Some could not see their own, but they took whichever ones they could get. I got my own favorite animal. We made some effort then to steal some of the horses of the white men. But they shot at us, so we went away with the part of our own herd that we could manage. When we returned with them and caught up with our people we let the women and some of the old people ride. I gave then to Chief Old Bear his horse I had captured when the soldiers first attacked us. He said, "Thank you, my friend," and he gave the horse to his woman while he kept on afoot.

We kept going eastward and northward. We forded the Little Powder river and went upon the benches beyond. Three nights we slept out. Only a few had robes. There was but little food, only a few women having little chunks of dry meat in their small packs. There was hard freezing at night and there was mud and water by day. But nobody appeared to become ill from the exposure. Early on the fourth day we arrived at where we had aimed, a camp of Ogallala Sioux far up a creek east of Powder river. Three or four Ogallala lodges had been

169

beside our Cheyenne camp when the soldiers came. These people traveling with us led us to their main camp.

The Ogallalas received us hospitably, as we knew they would do. Crazy Horse was their principal chief. Heads of lodges all about the camp were calling out to us:

"Cheyennes, come and eat here."

They fed us to fullness and gave us temporary shelter and robes. At night a council was held by the chiefs of the two bands. At the council our people told about the soldier attack. It was decided that the Ogallalas and the Cheyennes should go together to the Uncpapa Sioux, located northeastward from us. The next forenoon all of us set out in that direction. Horses were loaned to the Cheyennes by the Ogallalas, so none of us had to walk.

Buffalo Bull Sitting Down, known to the white people as Sitting Bull, was the principal chief of the Uncpapas in that camp. There were more of them than of Cheyennes and Ogallalas combined. When we arrived there they set up at once two big special lodges in the center of their camp circle. Our men were placed in one of these lodges, our women in the other. In each lodge sat a circle of Cheyennes about the inner wall. Uncpapa women had set their pots to boiling when first we had been seen. Now they came with meat. They kept on coming, coming, with more and more meat. We were filled up, and we had plenty extra to keep for another day. An Uncpapa herald went riding about the camp and calling out:

"The Cheyennes are very poor. All who have blankets or robes or tepees to spare should give to them."

Crowds of women and girls came with gifts. A ten-year-old Uncpapa girl put a buffalo robe in front of me and left it there. It was mine now. An Uncpapa man gave my father a medicine pipe to replace his lost one. I did not receive that kind of present, but I was provided with every important comfort. Whoever needed any kind of clothing got it immediately. They flooded us with gifts of everything needful. Crowds of their men and women were going among us to find out and to supply our wants.

"Who needs a blanket?"

"I do."

"Take this one."

"Who wants this tepee?"

"Give it to me."

"It is yours."

They brought horses—lots of horses.

"Who wants a horse?"

171

"I."

"You may have this one."

Oh, what good hearts they had! I never can forget the generosity of Sitting Bull's Uncpapa Sioux on that day.

Our women's backs were burdened and our gift horses were loaded as we went to the nearby place assigned to us for the setting up of our own camp circle. Every household had a lodge, the same as had been the case at our lost camp. Some of the new tepees were small, but they served all necessary purposes until we could get buffalo skins for making larger ones.

This triple camp was fifty or more miles east of Powder river, on east from a big and tall white stone which the white people call Chalk Butte. It was at the headwaters of a stream flowing westward into Powder river. The Cheyennes had been three sleeps on the way to the Ogallalas. One sleep there. Three sleeps of travel by Cheyennes and Ogallalas to the Uncpapa camp. Five or six sleeps the three tribes stayed together at this place.

Various scouting parties went out to find out where were the soldiers. Eight or ten of us Cheyennes went to Tongue river and beyond. At Tongue river we stopped for a daytime rest. Our horses were picketed out to graze. After a while they began to show signs of alarm. A Cheyenne went out to look. He saw a lone white man afoot among the herd. Indian horses were afraid of white people, so they were snorting. The Cheyenne approached the white man and called out:

"How!"

"How," the white man responded.

They shook hands. The Cheyenne got his own horse, mounted it, and asked the white man to go with him to the other Indians. They set off, the Cheyenne on horseback, the white man afoot. The stranger had a six shooter in a scabbard at his belt, but he made no offer to use it. He appeared friendly. He was thin and hungry-looking. His clothing was very ragged. The other Cheyennes got their horses, and they all gathered about the newcomer. Some of them mounted their horses, others stood afoot holding them.

"Who are you?" a Cheyenne signed.

The white man could make signs, but not very well. He made us understand him, though. He said he had been a soldier, but he got lost from them. He told us he had not fought us, as he had been lost before that time. He said the ragged clothing he had on was taken from a dead Sioux, as he did not want to be seen with soldier clothing. One Cheyenne kept saying, in our language, "Let's kill him."

173

But nobody agreed with him. Finally he jerked up his rifle and fired. The white man fell dead. Others then cut him and beat him, so that no one man could have the blame nor receive the honor.

Robbing the body was the next step. About all he had was the six shooter, some cartridges for it, and a little package tied to his belt. It had meat in it. It was horse meat and had been cooked in an open blazing fire. We threw it away.

This man was killed not many miles down the Tongue river from my present home place. The exact spot is on a ranch where now lives a white man named Wolf. The place is on Tongue river below the present town of Ashland, Montana.

HISTORICAL NOTE

A sketch of the military campaign of 1876 against the roaming Sioux and Cheyennes is interposed here for the enlightenment of such readers as may not be familiar with the frontier history of that period. There is nothing new in this sketch; it is simply a synopsis of what heretofore has been accepted and published.

After the Indian troubles during and immediately following our civil war, in 1868 a treaty was made with the Sioux and Cheyenne tribes of the northern plains country. A few of the Sioux, mainly a band of Uncpapas led by Sitting Bull, refused to go into the treaty council. Various reservations in the Dakotas were agreed upon as belonging exclusively to the various tribes of Indians involved. All lands lying westward of these reservations, as far as the Bighorn river and Bighorn mountains, in Montana, were to be hunting grounds for the Indians as long as wild game in abundance remained there.

OFF THE RESERVATION

Bands of these Dakota red people were going out to the hunting grounds and returning again from time to time. Some of them elected to remain most of the time, or all of the time, in the Montana open country. Sitting Bull and a few others like him stayed entirely away from the agencies. They were actuated partly by resentment and partly by a sincere desire to avoid conflict that regularly resulted from prolonged contiguity of Indians and whites.

The Cheyennes and the Ogallala Sioux were assigned to the Black Hills country as their reservation—forever, according to the terms of the treaty. Soon afterward it became apparent that rich gold fields were hidden away somewhere in the lands conceded to them. In 1874, obedient to orders from Washington, General George A. Custer led his Seventh cavalry from Fort Lincoln, Dakota, on an exploratory expedition into the Cheyenne-Ogallala country. They found ample verification of the rumors as to the presence of gold there. The news spread rapidly, and there was a rush of white men fortune-seekers into the midst of these Indian possessions.

The government made a weak effort to restrain the intruders. But the eager migrants flooded in and burst through the flimsy military barriers. The vexing problem was dodged by moving the Indians to other lands. But not all of them went to the designated new reservations. Many of them, angered at what they deemed a wrongful ousting, took their tepees and their families and went to live altogether in the open hunting regions. Indians from other reservations did likewise. That was the beginning of the "Indian uprising" of 1876.

In December, 1875, pursuant to our governmental policy, General Sherman, then commander-in-chief of the United States army, issued an important general order. He proclaimed that all Indians found off their reservations after the last day of January, 1876, would be regarded as hostiles to be fought by the military forces. It being evident that not many of the Dakota roamers in Montana would return to the reservations until they were forced to do so, bodies of soldiers were set in

175

motion for seeking out and driving these wanderers back within their assigned territorial bounds.

The active military field leaders in this campaign were Brigadier-General Terry, Brigadier-General Crook, Colonel Gibbon and Lieutenant-Colonel Custer. Each of these four officers had been brevetted Major-General of Volunteers during the civil war, but the contracting of the army after the war set each of them back to a lower ranking. Terry had infantry from Fort Rice and Custer's Seventh cavalry, from Fort Lincoln, Dakota. Crook had a force of cavalry and infantry at Fort Fetterman, Wyoming. Gibbon had infantry from Fort Shaw and cavalry from Fort Ellis, Montana.

From their three basic points—in Dakota, in Wyoming and in Montana—the three bodies of soldiers moved toward a common central area between the Powder and Bighorn rivers, in Montana, where the Indians being sought were roaming. Details of these military movements are too extensive for review here. The most thrilling phase of the campaign began when Custer and his Seventh cavalry set off up the Rosebud valley to follow a recent Indian trail. The result of this subsidiary proceeding was the supreme tragedy in the annals of our American frontier warfare.

The first fight of that 1876 struggle was this attack upon the Cheyenne camp on Powder river, March 17th. There have been published many worthy books recounting the military operations of that year. Reliable edification on this subject may be found in General Godfrey's magazine articles, in Colonel Graham's "The Story of the Little Bighorn," in Grinnell's "The Fighting Cheyennes," in Brininstool's "A Trooper with Custer," in the diaries of Lieutenants Bradley and McClernand, and in some other published writings.* These tell the stirring story of where our soldiers went and what they did during that eventful summer. Wooden Leg tells the equally stirring story of where the Indians went and what they did during that same time.

THOMAS B. MARQUIS.

* EDITOR'S NOTE: The interested reader will find also much enlightenment in Dr. Marquis' "Soldiering in the Old West," to be published soon by The Midwest Company.

176

VI

Swarming of Angered Indians

A band of Minneconjoux Sioux arrived at the Uncpapa camp either just before or just after we got there. They had not been troubled by the soldiers, but they wanted to keep out of trouble. Lame Deer was their principal chief. The Cheyennes were well acquainted with the Minneconjoux. We had camped and hunted with them many times. There were some intermarriages with them, so there were a few Cheyennes among them and a few of their people belonging to our tribe. We had mingled with them almost as much as we had with the Ogallalas. We never had associated closely with the Uncpapas. They were almost strangers to us. We knew of them only by hearsay from the Ogallalas and the Minneconjoux.

The movement to the Uncpapas was because they had a much larger band in the hunting grounds than had any of the other tribes. Some of them, with Sitting Bull as their leader, had been out all of the time for several years. At this first assembling, the Ogallala band was in number next to the Uncpapas. The Minneconjoux had not quite as many as had the

Ogallalas. The Cheyenne band was the smallest. During past times, when the Cheyennes and the Ogallalas and the Burned Thighs (Brûlé Sioux) had fought the white soldiers many times in the country farther southward, not many of the Uncpapas had been with them. These people kept mostly at peace by staying away from all white settlements. Now it was becoming generally believed among Indians that this was the best plan.

Sitting Bull had come into notice as the most consistent advocate of the idea of living out of all touch with white people. He would not go to the reservation nor would he accept any rations or other gifts coming from the white man government. He rarely went to the trading posts. Himself and his followers were wealthy in food and clothing and lodges, in everything needful to an Indian. They did not lose any horses nor other property in warfare, because they had not any warfare. He had come now into admiration by all Indians as a man whose medicine was good—that is, as a man having a kind heart and good judgment as to the best course of conduct. He was considered as being altogether brave, but peaceable. He was strong in religion—the Indian religion. He made medicine many times. He prayed and fasted and whipped his flesh into submission to the will of the Great Medicine. So, in attaching ourselves to the Uncpapas we other tribes were not moved by a desire to fight. They had not invited us. They simply welcomed us. We supposed that the combined camps would frighten off the soldiers. We hoped thus to be freed from their annoyance. Then we could separate again into the tribal bands and resume our quiet wandering and hunting.

The four camps could not remain long together in any one location. The food game would become scarce there and the feed for our horses would be eaten away. We had to move on. A council of all of the tribal chiefs decided we should go northward to the head of the next stream flowing into the east side of Powder river. The next morning after the decision had been made, the four different bands set off in procession toward the appointed place.

The Cheyennes were in the lead. The Ogallalas came next. Following them were the Minneconjoux. The Uncpapas were last. The order of movement was the result of an agreed plan. The Cheyennes and the Uncpapas had the specially dangerful positions. I do not know on just what grounds this was the arrangement, but I know that this was the intention. The Cheyennes kept scouts out in front looking forward from high points. The Uncpapas had always some of their young men staying back to observe if any enemies were following. The Ogallalas and the Minneconjoux sent guardians off to the hill points at the sides.

Three sleeps, I believe, our four camp circles stood in this new location. The Cheyennes in advance had been allowed to choose first the spot for the encampment. The Ogallalas and the Minneconjoux then located themselves only a little distance from us and from each other. The Uncpapas placed their circle on whatever good ground was left and on ground most suitable for guarding that side of the combined body of Indians. In the camping as well as in the traveling, the Cheyennes and the Uncpapas occupied the specially exposed positions.

The scarcity of feed for our horses led the council into a decision to move on yet farther northward. As I remember it, we spent one sleep in temporary camp during this movement as well as in the first combined shift of base. Our horses were weak for lack of food, so we had to travel slowly. We stopped at the upper regions of the next creek tributary to Powder river. I believe we stayed there three sleeps.

The Arrows All Gone Sioux (the Sans Arcs) came to us at this camping place. Five camp circles now were in close communion. The number of people in this added band was about the same as in the Ogallalla or the Minneconjoux organizations. In the case of each of the five tribes, only a part of their

180

members were here. But in each case more were
coming from time to time while few or none were
going back to the reservations. I believe the number of Cheyenne lodges now must have been increased
to fifty. The Ogallalas, Minneconjoux and Arrows
All Gone each had more, perhaps sixty or seventy.
The comparative size of the Uncpapa circle indicated
they might have had as many as a hundred and fifty
lodges.

After three or four sleeps the five camps moved
again. This time we swerved to the northwestward.
Our stopping place now was lower down on the next
creek flowing into Powder river. New grass was
beginning to peep up here. Our hungry horses
searched greedily for it. The herder boys were kept
busy at keeping them from rambling too far. The
tribal herds were kept separate, boys or youths from
each tribe guarding their own bands.

The Blackfeet Sioux joined us here, I believe. I
am not sure of the exact place where they came, but
I can not recollect any other point where they might
have come. I recall clearly, though, that when we
got to Powder river there were six camp circles, the
Blackfeet Sioux making up the sixth one. Theirs
was not a very large circle, but it was a separate one.
They camped close to the Uncpapas.

Many extra horses were brought in by some of the

181

newly arriving Indians. I think most of them were brought by the Blackfeet Sioux, or perhaps by the Arrows All Gone. But wherever they were needed by members of other tribes they were distributed out as gifts.

A few Waist and Skirt Indians * attached themselves to us. They were known also as No Clothing people, because their men had no clothing. They were extremely poor, having but little property and no horses. They had plenty of dogs—big dogs—to drag or to carry their tepees and other scant property. Their tribal name, as known to us, arose from their women having dresses made up in two parts. Other Indian women made up their dresses in one piece. I heard Cheyennes talk about Sitting Bull's father being with these people. He may have been there, but I do not remember having seen him. These Indians had small tepees, and their lodge poles were placed with the butt ends up. They camped all the time in a little group beside the Uncpapa circle. Some Assiniboines also were mingled with the Uncpapas, and others of them were with the Blackfeet Sioux. A few Burned Thigh tepees were with the Ogallalas and the Blackfeet Sioux. Many of the incoming Indians talked of having been north of Elk

* Santee Sioux, Wahpeton group, refugees from Minnesota, dwelling in Canada.

river.* Some of the talk I had heard was that they had been searching there for us. As I remember it, the extra horse bands were brought from the north side of that stream.

Chief Lame White Man and a big band of other Cheyennes came to us at Powder river. They had made a long journey out from the White River agency. They had been looking for us all about the heads of the Powder, Tongue and Rosebud rivers. They doubled back and found our trail east of Powder river. They had not learned of the soldier attack upon our Cheyenne camp.

Lame White Man did not belong to the Northern Cheyenne tribe, but he had been much of the time with us. He was a big chief or an old man chief of the Southern Cheyennes. He was not a chief with us, but he was a wise and good man. For this reason he had much influence among us, even as an adviser to our chiefs. His wife and family were with him, and their lodge became a part of our growing camp circle.

From Powder river our course was directed westward. We went over the hill country. The grass was coming up everywhere, and our horses were growing stronger. I believe we camped in two or three places between there and the Tongue river, one sleep at each place. Individual hunters and small

* The universal Indian name for the Yellowstone river.

hunting parties were gathering meat for their families. Even when we stopped for but one sleep at any place, all of the camp circles were formed and all of the lodges set up. It was the taking down, moving and setting up again every day of a little city.

A big band of additional Cheyennes came to us on Tongue river. They were led by Dirty Moccasins, an old man chief. They had crossed Powder river, journeyed over the divide west of it to Otter creek and followed this stream down to Tongue river. Our camp was thirty or forty miles down from where Otter creek flows into the river. Straggling lodges had been reaching us, but this was the largest annexation in any one group. Our Cheyenne circle now was double what it had been when we first joined the Uncpapas. The other circles likewise were growing in the same way. These Cheyennes brought extra ammunition, sugar, coffee and tobacco.

Going on west from Tongue river, we stopped several days, perhaps four or five sleeps, at the upper part of a stream we knew as Wood creek. It is the first creek of importance west of Tongue river and flowing, I believe, into Elk river. Our horses now were getting much grass. As the main part of the herds grazed, the men were hunting. Big parties of Indians killed lots of buffalo in this neighborhood.

There were many thousands of these animals here. The Cheyennes made a special effort to get a plentiful supply of robes for making larger lodges. The smaller ones given to our people by the Uncpapas had been comfortable, but larger ones were more comfortable. We also got skins for robes. Men and women all were busy, the men at hunting and the women at tanning the skins.

Councils of the chiefs of the six tribes assembled together were held at each place of camping. They talked of whatever might be of general interest. Particularly, a council settled where we should go next, at each move. We had not set out to go into any special region. The moves depended upon reports of hunting parties or scouts. They learned and reported where was most of such game as we were seeking.

Many young men were anxious to go for fighting the soldiers. But the chiefs and old men all urged us to keep away from the white men. They said that fighting wasted energy that ought to be applied in looking only for food and clothing, trying only to feed and make comfortable ourselves and our families. Our combination of camps was simply for defense. We were within our treaty rights as hunters. We must keep ourselves so.

From Wood creek we went yet westward to the

185

upper part of what we called Sioux creek. Here we stayed but one sleep and followed the same direction the next day. All of the people were on horses or on lodge-pole travois dragged by horses. All of the personal or family belongings were in travois baskets or on the backs of special pack horses. We had not any wagons. Such vehicles could not have been used in most of the country that Indians inhabited then.

We arrived at the Rosebud river or large creek about the middle of May, I believe. I did not know then anything about a calendar, but judging from my recollection of the condition of the grass and the trees, about the weather and other natural conditions, that must have been about the time.* Many times during the later years of peace I have been up and down that valley, on my way to and fro between the reservation and the town of Forsythe, so I with other Cheyennes have kept exactly in mind all of the old camping places along this stream.

The first Rosebud camping place of the six great circles of Indians was about seven or eight miles up from Elk river. The Uncpapa circle at that time was partly on the land where now is a ranch house

* Thomas H. Leforge and his Crow scouts learned that the hostile Indians arrived on the Rosebud about May 19th, 1876. They observed a great camp there on May 26th. A few days later this camp was gone. Lieutenant Bradley's diary records these facts. Bradley, Leforge and the Crow scouts were of the Gibbon forces, located then on the north side of the Yellowstone river.—T. B. M.

occupied by white people. The place now is known as the James Kennedy place, as a white man having that name lived there during many years. The Uncpapa circle extended from the present location of this house out across the present highway road and upon the bench eastward. The Cheyennes were camped about a mile and a half up the valley from Sitting Bull's Uncpapas. Our location included a line of trees such as yet are there extending from the creek across the road east of it. An old white man named Eugene Noyes was living there a few years ago, in a house just off a short distance southwest from that old Cheyenne camp site. The other four circles were at four different places between the Uncpapas and the Cheyennes. All of them were on the east side of the creek.

Charcoal Bear, chief medicine man of the Northern Cheyennes, came to us at this first Rosebud camp. Lots of our people were with him. He brought the tribal medicine lodge and our sacred Buffalo Head and all other of our tribal medicine objects. The lodge was set up in the midst of our camp circle. It put good thoughts and good feeling into the hearts of all Cheyennes.

I have heard in later years that soldiers from north of Elk river came across and saw our camp here. But I never knew of any soldiers having been seen by

187

any of the Indians in this region. We did lots of buffalo hunting all across from Tongue river and continued to kill many of them on the hills west of the Rosebud. I did not hear any talk of the buffalo or other game showing signs of having been alarmed by any other people. Six or seven sleeps, I believe, we stayed here. Then we moved up the valley about twelve miles.

At this second Rosebud camp the Uncpapa circle was on land just across the present highway road westward from and almost in front of a school house now standing east of the road. A mile and a half or more on up the valley was the Cheyenne circle. Between them, all on the east side of the creek, were the other four tribal circles. On this Cheyenne camping ground I had been in a camp of our people ten years before this, when I was a boy. Here Crazy Mule had made medicine and had done some wonderful acts. Here also at that past time a Cheyenne woman had gone out eastward up a wooded gulch and had hanged herself.

While we now were at this second Rosebud combined camp a report was brought in that Crows had been seen in our vicinity. A herald rode about our camp circle making the announcement. It was agreed our Crazy Dog warriors should go out to find them. The Crazy Dogs built a bonfire and had a preparatory dance. All of them stripped naked and painted their bodies. All of them danced barefooted. It was considered wonderful that they could do this without getting cactus thorns into their feet. As the dance was going on it began to become known that the report of Crows was a mistake, that nobody had seen them. The war dance was ended and the bonfire died down. It may have been that Crows actually had been seen, as I have learned in later times that some of them were scouting as helpers for soldiers north of Elk river.

After one sleep at the second Rosebud camp we traveled on up the valley another twelve or fifteen miles. This time the Uncpapas occupied land now on both sides of the highway road and to the west and south of a painted peak the white people now call Teat butte. The other camps were scattered irregularly on up the valley, all yet on the east side of the creek. It was about a mile and a half from the lower or last Uncpapa site to the upper or advanced Cheyenne site. Only one sleep here. The next forenoon the Cheyennes headed again a procession up the Rosebud valley.

The fourth Rosebud camp was at and above the place where now the main highway from Forsythe forks to go toward Lame Deer and toward Ashland. The lower or northern end of the group, the site of

189

Sitting Bull's people, was on the benchland by the present roadside east and northeast from the forks. Four camp circles were, as usual, somewhere between them and the Cheyennes in front and the Uncpapas at the rear. One of the Sioux camps was on the west side of the creek, the first time any of the circles had been set up on that side. The Cheyennes were about a mile east of where a roadside trading store in late years has been managed by a white man named Parkins. We were at the mouth of a stream flowing into the Rosebud and known now as Greenleaf creek. Our circle was only about a mile southward from the Uncpapas. The others were in an irregular curve between us. All of the Indians had been using the dirty yellow water of Rosebud creek, but now the Cheyennes had better water from Greenleaf creek. While we were here, some more Cheyennes arrived from the reservation. They told us:

"Lots of soldiers are being sent to fight the Indians."

Three sleeps I remained with our people at this camp. Great bands of Sioux went buffalo hunting among the hills and small mountains west of the Rosebud. I went hunting also, but I did not go there. Eleven Cheyennes, including myself, got our pack horses and set out over the low pass to Tongue river. We were on the lookout for soldiers or signs of them, but we did not want to fight them. We had our war bags, of course, but Indians did not take pack horses when going out to fight.

Two or three days after we had left our people they moved on up the Rosebud. This time the camp circles extended from just above the present Toohey ranch to a point about a mile and a half up the valley from that place. As usual, the Uncpapas were at the last end while the Cheyennes were at the first or upper end. The Uncpapas were on the east side of the creek, just west of the present main highway. The Cheyennes at the upper end of the group were on the west side of the creek, on a bench, a mile or so across west from the road. I was not there at the time, but this place is only ten or twelve miles north of our present reservation, so I have learned all about it from other Cheyennes as we have traveled up and down the road now there.

At this camp the Uncpapas had a Great Medicine dance. No other Indians took part in it, but great throngs of people from the other camp circles assembled to look on. This Great Medicine dance, or sun dance, as the white people call it, was held about a quarter of a mile west of the present highway that extends along the valley. The medicine lodge was pitched just north from the Uncpapa camp circle. Its exact site was on a flat bottom by the creek about

191

a quarter of a mile south by southwest from the present Toohey ranch house. By the present roadside, just below the Toohey ranch house, is a signboard that tells people, "Custer camped here June 23, 1876." The place where Sitting Bull's people had their Great Medicine dance is only half a mile southwest from this roadside signboard.

A few miles up the valley from this camp site are the deer medicine rocks. They are three or four miles below the present reservation northern gate. They may be seen about a mile west of the present road and off from the base of the hills. They are about half a mile or farther southwest from the big ranch house of a white man named Bailey. In the old times, both Cheyennes and Sioux had reverence for these separated cliff towers. As hunters were about to go for deer or antelope, they assembled on horseback and grouped around the deer medicine rocks. There they looked up to the tops and made prayers for success in the oncoming hunt. It is probable that the Indians at that camping time paid the usual respect to this old-time place of worship. But I do not know. I was not there. I then was traveling up the Tongue river valley, with ten other Cheyenne buffalo hunters.

VII

Soldiers from the Southward.

Our party of eleven buffalo hunters went over the same low pass that is traversed by the road now going from the Rosebud to Tongue river and Ashland. We did not find any big herd of buffalo. We had killed only four by the time we arrived at Hanging Woman creek. We decided then to go on over to Powder river. We followed Powder river almost up to the mouth of Lodgepole creek. On the way we came across a dead Indian on a burial scaffold. The body had been stripped of all wrappings and of clothing. We wondered if this had been a Sioux, a Crow or a Shoshone. We wondered also who had robbed the body.

One of our men named Lame Sioux went out to a hill for a look over the country. Pretty soon he began to signal. He had seen a camp of soldiers. All of us got out to look. Yes, this was a soldier camp. We dropped back into hiding. Ourselves and our horses all were put into concealment until darkness came. Then we dressed ourselves, painted ourselves and went on a night scout for a closer view. We saw the camp fires burning. We worked our way carefully toward them. It was after the middle of the night when we arrived at a point where we could see well the entire scene. But all of the soldiers then were gone.

We slept then until morning came. When we went to the abandoned camp-site the first thing to arouse our special interest was a beef carcass having yet on the bones many fragments of meat. The next interesting object was a box of hard crackers. It had been raining, and they were wet, but this made them all the better. We ate what we wanted of them. We cooked pieces of the beef on the fire coals. We enjoyed a fine breakfast. Then we set out on the trail of the soldiers.

The trail led us northwestward over the divide and down Crow creek. Near where Crow creek empties into Tongue river we saw the soldier camp.* The time was late in the afternoon. We retreated and skirted around up the river. At dusk we crossed it to the west side. The water was running high. We stripped and tied our clothing in bundles about our necks. We sat upon our riding horses and led our pack horses as they swam through the lively current. We hid ourselves among the trees on that side of the valley and slept until morning.

* Prairie Dog creek? Finerty writes that the soldiers were camped there June 8th.—T. B. M.

From a cliff the next morning we saw first a band of about twenty Indians riding away from the soldier camp. Were they Crows? Were they Shoshones? We exchanged guesses, but we did not know. We talked among ourselves about making an attack upon them. There was some talk of trying to steal soldier horses. We were anxious to do something warlike, to get horses or to count coups. But the general agreement was that it was too risky. We considered it most important that we return and notify our people on the Rosebud. We did not want to tire out our horses in an effort to get others or to get fighting honors. But we lingered to do some more looking. We saw soldiers walking about their camp. It had been flooded by the high waters. They were splashing about here and there and appeared to be getting ready to travel. We decided it was time for us also to travel.

Six of us, including myself, started out toward the hills between us and the uppermost Rosebud. The five other Cheyennes remained behind to see where the soldiers might go. During the day two of these came on and joined us. Before night the final three were with us. "They are coming in this direction," the three reported. We then were on the upper small branches of Rosebud creek.

We killed a buffalo there. We hurried in cutting

195

from it some of the choice pieces. We quickly divided up the liver and ate the raw segments. Over a hastily built fire we scantily toasted little chunks of buffalo meat. As we devoured them we spoke but few words. Whatever speech was uttered was in jerky sputterings. Everybody was excited. Every minute or two somebody was jumping up to go somewhere and look for pursuing soldiers. After the food had been bolted we hastened to move on. When darkness had well advanced we stopped for the night. Our horses needed rest and food. We picketed them. We felt safe during the night, so we slept soundly.

Before the sun was up we were several miles on down the Rosebud valley. We did not know just where our people were, but we knew they were somewhere on this stream. We found them strung along from the location of our present Indian dance hall there up almost to the present home of Porcupine. We wolf-howled and aroused the people. Cheyennes flocked to learn why we had given the alarm. We went on into camp and reported to an old man. Some Sioux were there, and they carried the news to their people. Soon all of the camp circles were in a fever of excitement. Heralds in all of them were riding about and shouting:

"Soldiers have been seen. They are coming in this direction. Indians are with them."

196

Councils were called. Lots of young men wanted to go out and fight the soldiers, but the chiefs would not allow this. Our chiefs appointed Little Hawk, Crooked Nose and two or three others to go scouting and find out about the further movements of the white men. Maybe some Sioux scouts also were sent out. I do not know, but I think they depended upon the Cheyennes to do the work.

The Indians all moved camp, going on up the valley about ten miles. Here the Cheyennes chose for their location a spot on the east side of the Rosebud, just across from the present Davis creek and on the land now occupied by Rising Sun. The Sioux following them set their circles on down the creek, the Uncpapas being below the present Busby school. My recollection is we stayed here more than one sleep, but I am not sure. When we left this place we went westward up Davis creek and across the hills beside it, going toward the dividing hills separating us from the Little Bighorn river. It was understood we were on our way to that valley.

We camped that afternoon just east of the divide. The place is about a mile north of the present road there, the camps extending northward up a broad coulee full of plum thickets. Dry camp, no water, at this place. One sleep here. The next morning we went on over the divide and down the slopes to what

197

we called Great Medicine Dance creek, but known now to the white people as Reno creek. We stopped where the main forks of the creek come together. Our circles were formed along the valley and on the bench. The Cheyennes were at the advance or west end, the Uncpapas at the rear or east end. From our camp to theirs the distance was about two miles. The grouped camps centered about where the present road crosses a bridge at the fork of the creek.*

Little Hawk and the other scouts returned to us here. They reported the soldiers as being on the upper branches of the Rosebud. The Sioux were told of this report, or they may have had information from scouts of their own. Heralds in all six of the camps rode about and told the people. The news created an unusual stir. Women packed up all articles except such as were needed for immediate use. Some of them took down their tepees and got them ready for hurrying away if necessary. Additional watchers were put among the horse herds. Young men wanted to go out and meet the soldiers, to fight them. The chiefs of all camps met in one big council. After a while they sent heralds to call out:

"Young men, leave the soldiers alone unless they attack us."

* Wooden Leg, Big Beaver and Limpy, each on a separate occasion, went with me and pointed out the exact locations of the 1876 Indian campings on the Rosebud and the Little Bighorn.—T. B. M.

198

But as darkness came on we slipped away. Many bands of Cheyenne and Sioux young men, with some older ones, rode out up the south fork toward the head of Rosebud creek. Warriors came from every camp circle. We had our weapons, war clothing, paints and medicines. I had my six-shooter. We traveled all night.

We found the soldiers * about seven or eight o'clock in the morning, I believe. We had slept only a little, our horses were very tired, so we did not hurry our attack. But always in such cases there are eager or foolish ones who begin too soon. Not long after we arrived there was fighting on the hillsides and on the little valley where was the soldier camp. In this early fighting, one young Cheyenne foolishly charged too far, and some Indians belonging to the soldiers got after him. They shot and crippled his horse. I and some other Cheyennes drove back the pursuers. I took the young man behind me on my horse, and we hurried away to our main body of warriors.

Jack Red Cloud, son of the old Ogallala Chief Red Cloud, was wearing a warbonnet. His horse was killed. According to the Indian way, in such case the

* General Crook's soldiers, June 17th, 1876. Historians have copied each other in repetitions that the hostiles here were "Crazy Horse and his Ogallalas," and that they were from the "Crazy Horse village" supposed to have been only a short distance down the Rosebud.—T. B. M.

warrior was supposed to stop and take off the bridle from the killed horse, to show how cool he could conduct himself. But young Red Cloud forgot to do this. He went running as soon as his horse fell. Three Crows on horseback followed him, lashed him with their pony whips and jerked off and kept his warbonnet. They did not try to kill him. They only teased him, telling him he was a boy and ought not to be wearing a warbonnet. Some of his Sioux friends interfered, and the Crows went away. The Sioux told us that young Red Cloud was crying and asking mercy from the Crows. He was my same age, eighteen years old.*

White Wolf, a Cheyenne almost thirty years old, had a repeating rifle. In drawing this weapon from its scabbard at his left side it was accidentally discharged. The bullet broke his left thigh bone. He finally recovered and is yet living (1930). He still limps on account of that accidental wound.

Until the sun went far toward the west there were charges back and forth. Our Indians fought and ran away, fought and ran away. The soldiers and their Indian scouts did the same. Sometimes we chased them, sometimes they chased us. One time, as I was

---

* The Crow aspect of this same story was told to me by Along the Hillside, an old Crow man who was a scout with Crook. He was one of the pursuers who jerked the warbonnet from the amateur Sioux.— T. B. M.

getting away from a charge, I caught up with a Cheyenne afoot and driving his tired horse ahead of him. My horse also was very tired, so I dismounted and we two drove our mounts into a brush thicket. There we rested a while. It appeared that all of the Cheyennes were in hiding just then.

Chief Lame White Man, the old Southern Cheyenne, rode out into the open on horseback. He called to us for brave actions. Our young men had high regard for him. The Cheyennes came out from hiding and went flocking to him. I and my companion joined them. It then became the turn of the soldiers and their Indians to get out of our way.

The soldiers finally left the field and went back southward, on the trail where they had come to this place. Some Sioux and Cheyennes followed them a short distance, but not far. The soldiers lost or left behind some of the packs from their mules.* We got crackers and bacon and other food material. I found a good white hat and a good pair of gloves. I picked up a little package of something and stuffed it under my belt. As I went riding away, the package rubbed between the belt and my body. The day was hot, and I was sweating freely. My nostrils perceived a pleasant odor. I traced it to the package. I took it

---

* Finerty writes that Crook had 1,000 pack mules, and that the Crows and Shoshones joined him on June 14th, at the Goose Creek camp.—T. B. M.

from my belt, sniffed at it, then fumbled at the heavy paper and tore off a corner.

"Oh, coffee!" My heart was glad. I had something good to take as a gift for my mother.

The only naked Cheyenne in that battle was Black Sun. All of the rest of us had on whatever war clothing he owned. I do not recollect having seen there any Sioux who was not dressed in his best. But Black Sun had a special medicine painting for himself. He spent a long time at getting ready. All of his body was colored yellow. On his head he wore the stuffed skin of a weasel. He wrapped a blanket about his loins. The soldiers and enemy Indians fired many shots at him without harming him. Finally some one of them got behind him and shot him through the body. He fell, not dead, but unable to stand up. Some of his friends rescued him. I caught his horse. When we were ready to go back to our camps we put him upon a travois and had his horse drag this bed for him. He died that night, at his home lodge. He was the only Cheyenne killed that day. Limpy was shot in his left side and had his horse killed. Other Cheyennes had slight wounds.

One Burned Thigh Sioux was killed during the battle, and one Minneconjoux died after arrival at the camps. I do not know how many other Sioux were killed, but some Cheyennes said there were twenty or more. I think the Uncpapas lost the most warriors. I remember that one of the dead Sioux was a boy about fourteen years old. Black Sun was buried in a hillside cave. I believe that all of the Sioux dead were left in burial tepees on the camp-site when we left there.

All camps were moved again early the next morning after the Rosebud battle. We followed a short distance down Medicine Dance creek and then turned southward across the benches to the Little Bighorn. In present times, where the Busby road joins the graveled highway there is a bridge over the river. About half a mile south of this bridge, on the west side of the highway and on the east side of the river, stood the camp circle of the Uncpapas. The Cheyennes were a mile or more farther up the river. The other four tribal camps were scattered here and there between the Uncpapas and the Cheyennes. There was not here nor at any other camping location a placing of the camp circles in line with one another. The groupings between Uncpapas and Cheyennes were according to the form of the land or the curves of the stream. The only strict rule of camp circle location was that none should be set up ahead of the Cheyennes nor behind the Uncpapas.

Six sleeps we remained at this first camping place on the Little Bighorn. We had beaten the white men

203

soldiers. Our scouts had followed them far enough
to learn that they were going farther and farther
away from us. We did not know of any other soldiers
hunting for us. If there were any, they now would
be afraid to come. There were feasts and dances in
all of the camps. On the benchlands just east of
us our horses found plenty of rich grass. Among the
hills west of the river were great herds of buffalo.
Every day, big hunting parties went among them.
Men and women were at work providing for their
families. That was why we killed these animals.
Indians never did destroy any animal life as a mere
pleasurable adventure.

Six Arapaho men came to the Cheyenne camp
while we were at this place. They said they were
afraid of soldiers, as they had killed a white man on
Powder river. Many Sioux and some Cheyennes suspected them as spies, but finally all of us were satisfied
they wanted to stay with us as friends. They were
invited into lodges of different ones of the Cheyennes.
Some more of our own people from the reservation
joined us here. It is likely some Sioux also arrived,
but I am not sure about that.

Our plans had been to go up the Little Bighorn
valley. But our game scouts reported great herds of
antelope west of the Bighorn river. Because of this,
the chiefs decided we should turn and go down the

Little Bighorn, to its mouth. From there our hunting parties would cross the Bighorn and get antelope skins and meat that we now wanted.

These councils of chiefs of all of the tribal circles were held sometimes at one camp circle and sometimes at another. In each case, heralds announced the meeting and told where it would be held. Each tribe operated its own internal government, the same as if it were entirely separated from the others. The chiefs of the different tribes met together as equals. There was only one who was considered as being above all of the others. This was Sitting Bull. He was recognized as the one old man chief of all the camps combined.

Almost all of our Northern Cheyenne tribe were with us on the Little Bighorn. Only a few of our forty big chiefs were absent. Two of our four old men chiefs, Old Bear and Dirty Moccasins, were here. Old Bear had been off the reservation throughout all of the past year, while Dirty Moccasins had come to us on the Rosebud. The absent two old men chiefs were Little Wolf and Rabbit, this last one known sometimes as Dull Knife, or Morning Star. Our tribal medicine tepee was at its place in our camp circle, and Charcoal Bear, its keeper, was with it. I believe all of the thirty chiefs of the three warrior societies were present, except Little Wolf, leading chief of the Elk warriors. I do not know how many Cheyennes in all were in the camp.* In fact, I do not know how many of us there were in our tribe at that time. I never knew of any count having been made during those times.

We crossed the Little Bighorn river to its west side and set off down the valley. Cheyennes ahead, Uncpapas behind, in the usual order of march. The journey that day was not a long one. After eight or nine miles of travel the Cheyennes stopped and began to form their camp circle. The tribes following us chose their ground, and their women began to set up the villages taken down that forenoon. The last tribe, the biggest one, the Uncpapas, placed themselves behind the others.

The Cheyenne location was about two miles north from the present railroad station at Garryowen, Montana. We were near the mouth of a small creek flowing from the southwestward into the river. Across the river east of us and a little upstream from us was a broad coulee, or little valley, having now the name Medicine Tail coulee.

The Uncpapas, at the southern end of the group

* At the Northern Cheyenne fair at Lame Deer in 1927 I estimated the encampment at about 1,100. Wooden Leg and some other old men were asked to compare this camp with the one on the Little Bighorn. After a consultation, it was generally agreed that there must have been 1,600 or more Cheyennes in their camp when the Custer soldiers came.—T. B. M.

206

and most distant from us, put their circle just north-east of the present Garryowen station. The other four circles were placed here and there between us and the Uncpapas.

Our trail during all of our movements throughout that summer could have been followed by a blind person. It was from a quarter to half a mile wide at all places where the form of the land allowed that width. Indians regularly made a broad trail when traveling in bands using travois. People behind often kept in the tracks of people in front, but when the party of travelers was a large one there were many of such tracks side by side.

VIII

On the Little Bighorn.

Every one of the six separate camp circles had its open and unoccupied side toward the east. Every lodge in each of these camps was set up so that the entrance opening was at its east side. This was the arrangement at all of our campings in this entire summer of combined movement. This was the regular Indian way of putting up a lodge or arranging a camp.

Some old Cheyennes talk of seven camp circles, and a few of them mention eight. But there were only six important ones. The extra one or two were not of tribal bands governing themselves as such. These additional Indians in considerable number were the Burned Thighs, Assiniboines and Waist and Skirt people. These kept themselves mainly in their own separated groups, but the groups would be placed close to some main camp circle and considered as belonging to it. At this particular camping place the Waist and Skirt Sioux were right beside the great Uncpapa circle, the Burned Thighs were partly with the Blackfeet Sioux and partly with the Ogallalas. Beginning with the Cheyennes at the north side and following up the river, four camp circles succeeded each other: Cheyennes, Arrows All Gone, Minneconjoux, Uncpapas. Away from the river and southwest of the Cheyennes and Arrows All Gone was the Ogallala camp. Between the Ogallalas and the Uncpapas, but nearer to the Uncpapas, was the Blackfeet Sioux camp, this also back a short distance from the river. A small and irregular camp of Burned Thigh Sioux was located by the river between the Cheyennes and the Arrows All Gone, or just east of the Ogallalas. All of the camps were east of the present railroad and highway.

One big lodge of Southern Cheyennes was in our circle. In it were eight men, six women and some children. Lame White Man, the Southern Cheyenne chief, had his own family lodge. He and his family had been with our northern branch of the tribe so long that they were looked upon as belonging to us. The six Arapaho men were attached to the lodge of Two Moons, one of the little chiefs of the Fox warrior society. One of his two wives was an Arapaho woman. There was not any white person nor any mixed-breed person with us. I never heard of there being any such person there with any of the Sioux tribes.

Our tribal medicine tepee, containing our sacred Buffalo Head and other revered objects, was in its

209

place at the western part of the open space enclosed by our camp circle. The medicine arrows, which belong to the Southern Cheyennes, were not here. Ours was the only tribal medicine lodge in the whole camp. The Sioux tribes did not maintain this kind of institution. They had tribal medicine pipes, but no special lodges for them.

Our family dwelling had in it seven people. These were my father and mother, my older brother Yellow Hair, my older sister Crooked Nose, myself Wooden Leg, a younger sister and a small boy brother. All of us together owned nine horses. I personally owned two of these. Other tepees had more people in them, some not as many. A few unmarried young men had little willow dome and robe shelters. Old couples likewise had this sort of temporary housing. These would be abandoned and built anew at each time of moving camp.

Three hundred lodges seems to me now as being about the size of our Cheyenne camp. The Blackfeet Sioux had about the same number, or a few less. The Arrows All Gone had more. The Minneconjoux and the Ogallalas each had more than the Arrows All Gone. The Uncpapas had, I believe, twice as many as had the Cheyennes.*

* Estimating the Cheyennes at 1,600, it appears the entire camp numbered about 12,000.—T. B. M.

The principal chiefs of the various camp circles were:

Uncpapas: Sitting Bull. He also was recognized as the one old man chief of the combined tribes. The Uncpapa medicine man chief was named Buffalo Calf Pipe.

Ogallalas: Crazy Horse, old man chief.

Minneconjoux: Lame Deer, old man chief.

Arrows All Gone: Hump Nose, or Hump, important chief of some kind.

Blackfeet: I do not know name of any chief there. Also, I do not know what chiefs may have been with the small irregular bands of other Indians.

Cheyennes: Old Bear and Dirty Moccasins, old men chiefs. Next to them, Crazy Head was considered the most important tribal big chief. Lame White Man was regarded as the most capable warrior chief among us, although Last Bull and Old Man Coyote also were held in special high esteem.

Our Cheyenne warrior society chiefs were these:*

Elk warriors: Leading chief—Lame White Man. Nine little chiefs—Left-Handed Shooter, Pig, Goes After Other Buffalo, Plenty Bears, Wolf Medicine, Broken Jaw, A Crow Cut His Nose, White Hawk and Tall White Man.

* List made up in various conferences wherein Wooden Leg was assisted by Sun Bear, White Wolf, Big Crow, Two Feathers and Big Beaver, all warriors at the battle.—T. B. M.

211

Crazy Dog warriors: Leading chief—Old Man Coyote. Nine little chiefs—Black Knife, Beaver Claws, Iron Shirt, Little Creek, Snow Bird, Crazy Mule, Strong Left Arm, Red Owl and Crow Necklace.

Fox warriors: Leading chief—Last Bull. Nine little chiefs—Wrapped Braids, Plenty of Buffalo Bull Meat, Little Horse, Sits Beside His Medicine, Two Moons, Bears Walks on a Ridge, Mosquito, Rattlesnake Nose and Weasel Bear.

The Fox warriors were on duty as camp policemen at this time. It was their business, while remaining on duty, to watch for the approach of enemies as well as to enforce the tribal laws. A few of the little chiefs of the warrior societies, and various members of the different ones, were not in the camp.

Our three leading warrior chiefs were allowed to talk in the tribal councils, where the tribal big chiefs and old men adviser chiefs assembled for the consideration of tribal affairs. The little warrior chiefs were expected to attend these councils, but they were not permitted to talk there. They were required to keep still and listen. The place for them to talk was in the warrior society meetings, where they were the instructors while the young warriors had to remain quiet and listening. The Sioux and other tribes had this same kind of system.

Guns were not plentiful among us. Most of our hunting had been with bows and arrows. Of the Cheyennes, Two Moons and White Wolf each had a repeating rifle. Some others had single-shot breech-loading rifles. But there was not much ammunition for the good guns. The muzzle-loaders usually were preferred, because for these we could mold the bullets and put in whatever powder was desired, or according to the quantity on hand. I believe the Sioux had, in proportion to their numbers, about the same supply of firearm material that we had. The Waist and Skirt people had few or no guns, were in every way very poor. My muzzle-loading rifle had been lost with my other personal effects when we had been driven out and had our lodges burned on Powder river.

Six or eight guns, I suppose, had been taken from soldiers at the Rosebud fight. I recall seeing only two, a rifle and a revolver, among the Cheyennes. Both of them used cartridges. The ammunition belt I saw taken there had a special piece of belting swung in a curve from the main girdle. Around the main circle were loops for forty rifle cartridges. The revolver cartridges were carried in twelve or fifteen loops on the suspended curve. On the surface of a revolver scabbard I saw were six other loops for its

213

cartridges. I never heard of the Indians getting from the Rosebud soldiers any ammunition except what was in the belts captured.

My cap-and-ball six shooter was my warring weapon. I had plenty of caps, powder and lead for it. I had a bullet mold to make its bullets from the lead. I kept the bullets and the caps in two small tin boxes. The powder I carried in a horn swung by a thong from my shoulder. For the gun I had a good scabbard. This was fastened to my leather belt.

The Cheyenne horses were put out to graze on the valley below our camp. Horses belonging to other tribes were placed at other feeding areas on the valley and on the bench hills just west of the combined Indian camps. The tribal herds were kept separate from each other. Boys from each tribe guarded their horse bands. An occasional riding horse was picketed near to or within each camp circle. It could get better feed with the herd, and probably it felt better satisfied there, but always there was somebody here or there, particularly among the policemen, who picketed a horse for ready use.

I had no thought then of any fighting to be done in the near future. We had driven away the soldiers, on the upper Rosebud, seven days ago. It seemed likely it would be a long time before they would trouble us again. My mind was occupied mostly by such thoughts as regularly are uppermost in the minds of young men. I was eighteen years old, and I liked girls.

That night we had a dance. It was entirely a social affair for young people, not a ceremonial or war dance. In the midst of the open area within our camp circle the women and girls cleared off and leveled a broad surface of ground. The young men brought a tall pole and set it up at the center of the dancing ground. Charcoal Bear, the medicine chief, brought the buffalo skin that regularly hung from the top of the sacred tepee. He tied it to the top end of our long pole before we raised it. We built a big bonfire. The drums and the Cheyenne dance songs enlivened the assemblage. It seemed that peace and happiness was prevailing all over the world, that nowhere was any man planning to lift his hand against his fellow man.

The same kind of amusement was going on in the Sioux camps. An occasional group from them came to our party. An occasional group of Cheyennes went visiting among them. I was enjoying myself in our own gathering. Finally, though, a young man friend of mine proposed:

"Let's go and dance a while with the Sioux girls."

Four of us went to the neighboring camp, that of the Arrows All Gone Sioux. Pretty soon the girls

215

were asking us to dance.* The Sioux women gave us plenty of food. We were treated well, so we did not go elsewhere nor back to our own people. We stayed there and danced throughout the remainder of that night.

At the first sign of dawn the dance ended. I walked wearily across to the Cheyenne camp. I did not go into our family lodge. Instead, I dropped down upon the ground behind it. I do not remember anything that might have happened during the two or three hours that followed. When I awoke I went into the family lodge. My mother prepared me a breakfast. Then she said: "You must go for a bath in the river."

My brother Yellow Hair and I went together. Other Indians, of all ages and both sexes, were splashing in the waters of the river. The sun was high, the weather was hot. The cool water felt good to my skin. When my brother and I had dabbled there a few minutes we came out and sought the shelter of some shade trees. We sat there a little while, talking of the good times each of us had enjoyed during the previous night. We sprawled out to lie down and talk. Before we knew it, both of us were sound asleep.

* The customary Indian way is for the women to choose partners at the social dances.—T. B. M.

The Coming of Custer.

In my sleep I dreamed that a great crowd of people were making lots of noise. Something in the noise startled me. I found myself wide awake, sitting up and listening. My brother too awakened, and we both jumped to our feet. A great commotion was going on among the camps. We heard shooting. We hurried out from the trees so we might see as well as hear. The shooting was somewhere at the upper part of the camp circles. It looked as if all of the Indians there were running away toward the hills to the westward or down toward our end of the village. Women were screaming and men were letting out war cries. Through it all we could hear old men calling:

"Soldiers are here! Young men, go out and fight them."

We ran to our camp and to our home lodge. Everybody there was excited. Women were hurriedly making up little packs for flight. Some were going off northward or across the river without any packs. Children were hunting for their mothers. Mothers were anxiously trying to find their children. I got my lariat and my six shooter. I hastened on down toward where had been our horse herd. I came across three of our herder boys. One of them was catching grasshoppers. The other two were cooking fish in the blaze of a little fire. I told them what was going on and asked them where were the horses. They jumped on their picketed ponies and dashed for the camp, without answering me. Just then I heard Bald Eagle calling out to hurry with the horses. Two other boys were driving them toward the camp circle. I was utterly winded from the running. I never was much for running. I could walk all day, but I could not run fast nor far. I walked on back to the home lodge.

My father had caught my favorite horse from the herd brought in by the boys and Bald Eagle. I quickly emptied out my war bag and set myself at getting ready to go into battle. I jerked off my ordinary clothing. I jerked on a pair of new breeches that had been given to me by an Uncpapa Sioux. I had a good cloth shirt, and I put it on. My old moccasins were kicked off and a pair of beaded moccasins substituted for them. My father strapped a blanket upon my horse and arranged the rawhide lariat into a bridle. He stood holding my mount.

"Hurry," he urged me.

I was hurrying, but I was not yet ready. I got my paints and my little mirror. The blue-black circle soon appeared around my face. The red and yellow colorings were applied on all of the skin inside the circle. I combed my hair. It properly should have been oiled and braided neatly, but my father again was saying, "Hurry," so I just looped a buckskin thong about it and tied it close up against the back of my head, to float loose from there. My bullets, caps and powder horn put me into full readiness. In a moment afterward I was on my horse and was going as fast as it could run toward where all of the rest of the young men were going. My brother already had gone. He got his horse before I got mine, and his dressing was only a long buckskin shirt fringed with Crow Indian hair. The hair had been taken from a Crow at a past battle with them.

The air was so full of dust I could not see where to go. But it was not needful that I see that far. I kept my horse headed in the direction of movement by the crowd of Indians on horseback. I was led out around and far beyond the Uncpapa camp circle. Many hundreds of Indians on horseback were dashing to and fro in front of a body of soldiers. The soldiers were on the level valley ground and were shooting with rifles. Not many bullets were being sent back at them, but thousands of arrows were falling among them. I went on with a throng of Sioux until we got beyond and behind the white men. By this time, though, they had mounted their horses and were hiding themselves in the timber. A band of Indians were with the soldiers. It appeared they were Crows or Shoshones. Most of these Indians had fled back up the valley. Some were across east of the river and were riding away over the hills beyond.

Our Indians crowded down toward the timber where were the soldiers. More and more of our people kept coming. Almost all of them were Sioux. There were only a few Cheyennes. Arrows were showered into the timber. Bullets whistled out toward the Sioux and Cheyennes. But we stayed far back while we extended our curved line farther and farther around the big grove of trees. Some dead soldiers had been left among the grass and sagebrush where first they had fought us. It seemed to me the remainder of them would not live many hours longer. Sioux were creeping forward to set fire to the timber.

Suddenly the hidden soldiers came tearing out on horseback, from the woods. I was around on that side where they came out. I whirled my horse and lashed it into a dash to escape from them. All others of my companions did the same. But soon we discovered they were not following us. They were running away from us. They were going as fast their tired horses could carry them across an open valley space and toward the river. We stopped, looked a moment, and then we whipped our ponies into swift pursuit. A great throng of Sioux also were coming after them. My distant position put me among the leaders in the chase. The soldier horses moved slowly, as if they were very tired. Ours were lively. We gained rapidly on them.

I fired four shots with my six shooter. I do not know whether or not any of my bullets did harm. I saw a Sioux put an arrow into the back of a soldier's head. Another arrow went into his shoulder. He tumbled from his horse to the ground. Others fell dead either from arrows or from stabbings or jabbings or from blows by the stone war clubs of the Sioux. Horses limped or staggered or sprawled out dead or dying. Our war cries and war songs were mingled with many jeering calls, such as:

"You are only boys. You ought not to be fighting. We whipped you on the Rosebud. You should have brought more Crows or Shoshones with you to do your fighting."

Little Bird and I were after one certain soldier. Little Bird was wearing a trailing warbonnet. He was at the right and I was at the left of the fleeing man. We were lashing him and his horse with our pony whips. It seemed not brave to shoot him. Be-

sides, I did not want to waste my bullets. He pointed
back his revolver, though, and sent a bullet into
Little Bird's thigh. Immediately I whacked the white
man fighter on his head with the heavy elk-horn
handle of my pony whip. The blow dazed him. I
seized the rifle strapped on his back. I wrenched it
and dragged the looping strap over his head. As I
was getting possession of this weapon he fell to the
ground. I did not harm him further. I do not know
what became of him. The jam of oncoming Indians
swept me on. But I had now a good soldier rifle.
Yet, I had not any cartridges for it.

Three soldiers on horses got separated from the
others and started away up the valley, in the direction
from where they had come. Three Cheyennes, Sun
Bear, Eagle Tail Feather and Little Sun,* joined
some Sioux in pursuit of the three white men. The
Cheyennes told afterward about the outcome of this
pursuit. One of the soldiers turned his horse eastward toward the river and escaped in the timber.
The other two kept on southward. Of these two, one
went off to the right, up a small gulch to the top of
the bench. There he was caught and killed. The remaining one rode on toward the mouth of Reno
creek. As he neared that point he swerved to the

---

* Little Sun, in the presence of Wooden Leg and other veteran
Cheyennes, told me of this incident.—T. B. M.

right. He made a circle out upon the valley and returned to the timber just across west from the mouth
of Reno creek. Here he dismounted from his exhausted horse and got himself into the brush. The
Sioux and Cheyennes surrounded him and killed him.
They told that he fought bravely to the last, making
use of his six shooter.

A warbonnet Indian belonging with the soldiers
was chased by Crooked Nose, a Cheyenne, and some
Sioux. The chase was afoot, across a wet slough and
into some timber northward from where the soldiers
had been hidden for a few minutes. After many exchanges of shots, after much dodging and shifting of
position, the enemy Indian was killed there.* I
was told afterward about this killing. I did not see
it. I was following the fleeing soldiers to and across
the river.

Indians mobbed the soldiers floundering afoot and
on horseback in crossing the river. I do not know
how many of our enemies might have been killed
there. With my captured rifle as a club I knocked
two of them from their horses into the flood waters.
Most of the pursuing warriors stopped at the river,
but many kept on after the men with the blue clothing. I remained in the pursuit and crossed the river.

* This apparently was Bloody Knife, Custer's favorite Arikara
scout.—T. B. M.

Whirlwind, a Cheyenne, charged after a warbonnet Indian belonging with the whites. The enemy Indian bravely charged also toward Whirlwind. The two men fired rifles at the same moment. Both of them fell dead. This was on the flat land just east of the river where the soldiers crossed.

Another enemy Indian was behind a little sagebrush knoll and shooting at us. His shots were returned. I and some others went around and got behind him. We dismounted and crept toward him. As we came close up to him he fell. A bullet had hit him. He raised himself up, though, and swung his rifle around toward us. We rushed upon him. I crashed a blow of my rifle barrel upon his head. Others beat and stabbed him to death. I got also his gun. It was the same as the one I had taken from the soldier, but the Indian's gun had a longer barrel. A Sioux said: "You have two guns. Let me have one of them." I gave him the one I had taken from the Indian just killed. I liked better the shorter barreled one, so I kept it. The Sioux already had the Indian's ammunition belt. He did not give me any of the cartridges. There were only a few of them. One of the Sioux scalped the dead man. Different ones took his clothing. I took nothing except the gun I had given away.

I returned to the west side of the river. Lots of

Indians were hunting around there for dead soldiers or for wounded ones to kill. I joined in this search. I got some tobacco from the pockets of one dead man. I got also a belt having in it a few cartridges. All of the weapons and clothing and all other possessions were being taken from the bodies. The warriors were doing this. No old people nor women were there. They all had run away to the hill benches to the westward. I went to a dead horse, to see what might be found there. Leather bags were on them, behind the saddles. I rummaged into one of these bags. I found there two pasteboard boxes. I broke open one of them.

"Oh, cartridges!"

There were twenty of them in each box, forty in all. Thirty of them were used to fill up the vacant places in my belt. The remaining ten I wrapped into a piece of cloth and dropped them down into my own little kit bag. Now I need not be so careful in expending ammunition. Now I felt very brave. I jumped upon my horse and went again to fight whatever soldiers I might find on the east side of the river.

The soldiers had gone up gulches and a backbone ridge to the top of a steep and high hill. Indians were all about them. Shots were going toward them and coming from them. A friend here told me that Hump Nose, a Cheyenne two years younger than I

225

was, had been killed on the west side of the river. My heart was made sad by this news, but I went on up the hill. I joined with others in going around to the left or north side of the place where were the soldiers. From our hilltop position I fired a few shots from my newly-obtained rifle. I aimed not at any particular ones, but only in the direction of all of them. I think I was too far away to do much harm to them. I had been there only a short time when somebody said to me:

"Look! Yonder are other soldiers!"

I saw them on distant hills down the river and on our same side of it. The news of them spread quickly among us. Indians began to ride in that direction. Some went along the hills, others went down to cross the river and follow the valley. I took this course. I guided my horse down the steep hillside and forded the river. Back again among the camps I rode on through them to our Cheyenne circle at the lower end of them. As I rode I could see lots of Indians out on the hills across on the east side of the river and fighting the other soldiers there. I do not know whether all of our warriors left the first soldiers or some of them stayed up there. I suppose, though, that all of them came away from there, as they would be afraid to stay if only a few remained.

Not many people were in the lodges of our camp.

Most of the women and children and old Cheyennes were gone to the west side of the valley or to the hills at that side. A few were hurrying back and forth to take away packs. My father was the only person at our lodge. I told him of the fight up the valley. I told him of my having helped in the killing of the enemy Indian and some soldiers in the river. I gave to him the tobacco I had taken. I showed him my gun and all of the cartridges.

"You have been brave," he cheered me. "You have done enough for one day. Now you should rest."

"No, I want to go and fight the other soldiers," I said. "I can fight better now, with this gun."

"Your horse is too tired," he argued.

"Yes, but I want to ride the other one."

He turned loose my tired horse and roped my other one from the little herd being held inside the camp circle. He blanketed the new mount and arranged the lariat bridle. He applied the medicine treatment for protecting my mount. As he was doing this I was making some improvements in my appearance, making the medicine for myself. I added my sheathknife to my stock of weapons. Then I looked a few moments at the battling Indians and soldiers across the river on the hills to the northeastward. More and more Indians were flocking from the camps to that direction. Some were yet coming along the hills from where the first soldiers had stopped. The soldiers now in view were spreading themselves into lines along a ridge. The Indians were on lower ridges in front of them, between them and the river, and were moving on around up a long coulee to get behind the white men.

"Remember, your older brother already is out there in the fight," my father said to me. "I think there will be plenty of warriors to beat the soldiers, so it is not needful that I send both of my sons. You have not your shield nor your eagle wing bone flute. Stay back as far as you can and shoot from a long distance. Let your brother go ahead of you."

Two other young men were near us. They had their horses and were otherwise ready, but they told me they had decided not to go. I showed them my captured gun and the cartridges. I told them of the tobacco and the clothing and other things we had taken from the soldiers up the valley. This changed their minds. They mounted their horses and accompanied me.

We forded the river where all of the Indians were crossing it, at the broad shallows immediately in front of the little valley or wide coulee on the east side. We fell in with others, many Sioux and a few Cheyennes, going in our same direction. We urged our horses on up the small valley. As we approached the place of battle each one chose his own personal course. All of the Indians had come out on horseback. Almost all of them dismounted and crept along the gullies afoot after the arrival near the soldiers. Still, there were hundreds of them riding here and there all the time, most of them merely changing position, but a few of them racing along back and forth in front of the soldiers, in daring movements to exhibit bravery.

I swerved up a gulch to my left, where I saw some Cheyennes going ahead of me. Other Cheyennes were coming here from the east side of the soldiers. Although it was natural that tribal members should keep together, there was everywhere a mingling of the fighters from all of the tribes. The soldiers had come along a high ridge about two miles east from the Cheyenne camp. They had gone on past us and then swerved off the high ridge to the lower ridge where most of them afterward were killed. While they were yet on the far-out ridge a few Sioux and Cheyennes had exchanged shots with them at long distance, without anybody being hurt. Bobtail Horse, Roan Bear and Buffalo Calf, three Cheyennes, and four Sioux warriors with them, were said to have been the first of our Indians to cross the river and go to meet the soldiers. Bobtail Horse was an Elk

229

warrior, Roan Bear a Fox warrior, and Buffalo Calf a Crazy Dog warrior. They had been joined soon afterward by other Indians from the valley camps and from the southward hills where the first soldiers had taken refuge.

Most of the Indians were working around the ridge now occupied by the soldiers. We were lying down in gullies and behind sagebrush hillocks. The shooting at first was at a distance, but we kept creeping in closer all around the ridge. Bows and arrows were in use much more than guns. From the hiding-places of the Indians, the arrows could be shot in a high and long curve, to fall upon the soldiers or their horses. An Indian using a gun had to jump up and expose himself long enough to shoot. The arrows falling upon the horses stuck in their backs and caused them to go plunging here and there, knocking down the soldiers. The ponies of our warriors who were creeping along the gulches had been left in gulches farther back. Some of them were let loose, dragging their ropes, but most of them were tied to sagebrush. Only the old men and the boys stayed all the time on their ponies, and they stayed back on the surrounding ridges, out of reach of the bullets.

The slow long-distance fighting was kept up for about an hour and a half, I believe. The Indians all the time could see where were the soldiers, because the white men were mostly on a ridge and their horses were with them. But the soldiers could not see our warriors, as they had left their ponies and were crawling in the gullies through the sagebrush. A warrior would jump up, shoot, jerk himself down quickly, and then crawl forward a little further. All around the soldier ridge our men were doing this. So not many of them got hit by the soldier bullets during this time of fighting.

After the long time of the slow fighting, about forty of the soldiers * came galloping from the east part of the ridge down toward the river, toward where most of the Cheyennes and many Ogallalas were hidden. The Indians ran back to a deep gulch. The soldiers stopped and got off their horses when they arrived at a low ridge where the Indians had been. Lame White Man, the Southern Cheyenne chief, came on his horse and called us to come back and fight. In a few minutes the warriors were all around these soldiers. Then Lame White Man called out:

"Come. We can kill all of them."

All around, the Indians began jumping up, running forward, dodging down, jumping up again, down again, all the time going toward the soldiers. Right away, all of the white men went crazy. Instead of

* The Indians differ as to the color of the horses ridden by these soldiers, but military students of the case believe this to have been Lieutenant Smith's troop.—T. B. M.

231

shooting us, they turned their guns upon themselves. Almost before we could get to them, every one of them was dead. They killed themselves.

The Indians took the guns of these soldiers and used them for shooting at the soldiers on the high ridge. I went back and got my horse and rode around beyond the east end of the ridge. By the time I got there, all of the soldiers there were dead. The Indians told me that they had killed only a few of those men, that the men had shot each other and shot themselves. A Cheyenne told me that four soldiers from that part of the ridge had turned their horses and tried to escape by going back over the trail where they had come. Three of these men were killed quickly. The fourth one got across a gulch and over a ridge eastward before the pursuing group of Sioux got close to him. His horse was very tired, and the Sioux were gaining on him. He was moving his right arm as though whipping his horse to make it go faster. Suddenly his right hand went up to his head. With his revolver he shot himself and fell dead from his horse.

I raced my horse to hurry around to the hillside north of the soldier ridge. The Indians there were all around a band of soldiers on the north slope.* I got off my horse and fired two shots, at long dis-

* Captain Keogh or Captain Tom Custer, or both troops.—T. B. M.

tance, with my soldier gun. I did not shoot any more, because the sagebrush was full of Indians jumping up and down and crawling close to the soldiers, and I was afraid I might hit one of our own men. About that time, all of this band of soldiers went crazy and fired their guns at each other's heads and breasts or at their own heads and breasts. All of them were dead before the Indians got to them.

Many hundreds of boys on horseback were watching the battle. They were on the hills all around, far enough away to be out of reach of the soldier bullets. The ridge north of the soldier ridge was crowded with these boys and some old men. When the warriors were crowding in close to the soldiers on the north slope, one soldier there broke away and ran afoot across a gulch toward the northward hill. I suppose he thought there were no warriors in that direction, as all of them were hidden and creeping through the sagebrush and gullies. But several of them jumped up and ran after him. Just after he got across the gulch he stopped, stood still, and killed himself with his own revolver. A Cheyenne boy named Big Beaver lashed his pony into a dash down to the dead white man. The boy got the soldier's revolver and his belt of cartridges, jumped back upon his pony, and hurried away again to the hilltop. A Cheyenne warrior scalped the soldier and hung the scalp on a bunch of sagebrush, leaving it there. While I was at this part of the field, a Waist and Skirt Indian said to me:

"I think I see the big chief of the soldiers. I have been watching one certain man who appears to be telling all of the others what to do."

He tried to point out this man. But just then another bunch of soldier horses went running wildly among them, kicking up a great dust and knocking down or jostling the men. So I did not get to see the special man the Indian was trying to show me.

I saw one Sioux walking slowly toward the gulch, going away from where were the soldiers. He wabbled dizzily as he moved along. He fell down, got up, fell down again, got up again. As he passed near to where I was I saw that his whole lower jaw was shot away. The sight of him made me sick. I had to vomit. I did not know him, and I did not learn whether he died or not.

I had remained on my horse during most of the long time of the fighting at a distance. I rode from place to place around the soldiers, keeping myself back, as my father had urged me to do, while my older brother crept close with the other warriors. I got off and crept with them, though, for a little while at the place where the band of soldiers rode down toward the. river. After they were dead I got

234

my horse and mounted again. I stayed mounted until I got around into the gulch north from the west end of the soldier ridge. By this time all of the soldiers were gone except a band of them at the west end of the ridge. They were hidden behind dead horses. Hundreds or thousands of warriors were all around them, creeping closer all the time. From the gulch where I was I could see the north slope of the ridge covered by the hidden Indians. But the soldiers, from where they were, could not see the warriors, except as some Indian might jump up to shoot quickly and then duck down again. We could get only glimpses of the soldiers, but we knew all the time right where they were, because we could see their dead horses.

I got down afoot in the gulch. I let out my long lariat rope for leading my horse while I joined the warriors creeping up the slope toward the soldiers. During all of the earlier fighting, when I had been most of the time going from place to place on horseback, I had fired several shots with my rifle captured from the soldier when we chased them across the river. I also had used my six-shooter. I had replaced the four bullets expended during the chase of the first soldiers in the valley. In this second battle I used up the six, reloaded the six-shooter, and fired all of these additional six shots at the soldiers. But

235

it is hard to shoot straight when on horseback, especially when there is much noise and much shooting and excitement, as the horse will not stand still. When I went crawling up the slope I could lie down and shoot. I could not see any particular soldier to shoot at, but I could see their dead horses, where the men were hiding. So I just sent my bullets in that direction.

A Sioux wearing a warbonnet was lying down behind a clump of sagebrush on the hillside only a short distance north of where now is the big stone having the iron fence around it. He was about half the length of my lariat rope up ahead of me. Many other Indians were near him. Some boys were mingled among them, to get in quickly for making coup blows on any dead soldiers they might find. A Cheyenne boy was lying down right behind the warbonnet Sioux. The Sioux was peeping up and firing a rifle from time to time. At one of these times a soldier bullet hit him exactly in the middle of the forehead. His arms and legs jumped in spasms for a few moments, then he died. The boy quickly slid back down into a gully, jumped to his feet and ran away.

A soldier on a horse suddenly appeared in view back behind the warriors who were coming from the eastward along the ridge. He was riding away to the eastward, as fast as he could make his horse go.

It seemed he must have been hidden somewhere back there until the Indians had passed him. A band of the Indians, all of them Sioux, I believe, got after him. I lost sight of them when they went beyond a curve of the hilltop. I suppose, though, they caught him and killed him.

The shots quit coming from the soldiers. Warriors who had crept close to them began to call out that all of the white men were dead. All of the Indians then jumped up and rushed forward. All of the boys and old men on their horses came tearing into the crowd. The air was full of dust and smoke. Everybody was greatly excited. It looked like thousands of dogs might look if all of them were mixed together in a fight. All of the Indians were saying these soldiers also went crazy and killed themselves. I do not know. I could not see them. But I believe they did so.

Seven of these last soldiers broke away and went running down the coulee sloping toward the river from the west end of the ridge. I was on the side opposite from them, and there was much smoke and dust, and many Indians were in front of me, so I did not see these men running, but I learned of them from the talk afterward. They did not get far, because many Indians were all around them. It was said that these seven men, or some of them, killed themselves. I do not know, as I did not see them.*

After the great throng of Indians had crowded upon the little space where had been the last band of fighting soldiers, a strange incident happened: It appeared that all of the white men were dead. But there was one of them who raised himself to a support on his left elbow. He turned and looked over his left shoulder, and then I got a good view of him. His expression was wild, as if his mind was all tangled up and he was wondering what was going on here. In his right hand he held his six-shooter. Many of the Indians near him were scared by what seemed to have been a return from death to life. But a Sioux warrior jumped forward, grabbed the six-shooter and wrenched it from the soldier's grasp. The gun was turned upon the white man, and he was shot through the head. Other Indians struck him or stabbed him. I think he must have been the last man killed in this great battle where not one of the enemy got away.

* The story of wholesale suiciding is such a reversal of our accepted conceptions that some reader may exclaim: "That is a villifying falsehood!" *But it is the truth.* Most of the Seventh cavalry enlisted men on that occasion were recent recruits. Only a few of them ever had been in an Indian battle, or in any kind of battle. It is evident, though, that they fought well through an hour and a half or two hours. Then, finding themselves vastly outnumbered, they "went crazy," as the Indians tell. They put into panicky practice the old frontiersman rule, "When fighting Indians keep the last bullet for yourself." A great mass of circumstantial evidence supports this explanation of the military disaster. The author hopes to attain publication, at some future time, of his own full analysis of the entire case.—T. B. M.

238

This last man had a big and strong body. His cheeks were plump. All over his face was a stubby black beard. His mustache was much longer than his other beard, and it was curled up at the ends. The spot where he was killed is just above the middle of the big group of white stone slabs now standing on the slope southwest from the big stone. I do not know whether he was a soldier chief or an ordinary soldier. I did not notice any metal piece nor any special marks on the shoulders of his clothing, but it may be they were there. Some of the Cheyennes say now that he wore two white metal bars. But at that time we knew nothing about such things.

One of the dead soldier bodies attracted special attention. This was one who was said to have been wearing a buckskin suit. I had not seen any such soldier during the fighting. When I saw the body it had been stripped and the head was cut off and gone. Across the breast was some writing made by blue and red coloring into the skin. On each arm was a picture drawn with the same kind of blue and red paint. One of the pictures was of an eagle having its wings spread out. Indians told me that on the left arm had been strapped a leather packet having in it some white paper and a lot of the same kind of green picture-paper found on all of the soldier bodies. Some of the Indians guessed that he must have been the

239

big chief of the soldiers, because of the buckskin clothing and because of the paint markings on his breast and arms.* But none of the Indians knew then who had been the big chief. They were only guessing at it.

The sun was just past the middle of the sky.** The first soldiers, up the valley, had come about the middle of the forenoon. The earlier part of the fighting against these second soldiers had been slow, all of the Indians staying back and approaching gradually. At each time of charging, though, the mixup lasted only a few minutes.

I took one scalp. As I went walking and leading my horse among the dead I observed one face that interested me. The dead man had a long beard growing from both sides of his face and extending several inches below the chin. He had also a full mustache. All of the beard hair was of a light yellow color, as I now recall it. Most of the soldiers had beard growing, in different lengths, but this was the longest one I saw among them. I think the dead man may have been thirty or more years old. "Here is a new kind of scalp," I said to a companion. I skinned one side of the face and half of the chin, so as to keep the long beard yet on the part removed.*** I

* Evidently this was Captain Tom Custer.—T. B. M.
** All old Cheyennes insist the battle ended about noon.—T. B. M.
*** This unfortunate soldier probably was Lieutenant Cook.—T. B. M.

got an arrow shaft and tied the strange scalp to the end of it. This I carried in a hand as I went looking further.

Somebody told me Noisy Walking was badly wounded. I went to where he was said to be, down in the gulch where the band of soldiers nearest the river had been killed in the earlier part of the battle. He was my same age, and we often had been companions since our small boyhood. White Bull, an important medicine man, was his father. I asked the young man: "How are you?" He replied: "Good." But he did not look well. He had been hit by three different bullets, one of them having passed through his body. He had also some stab wounds in his side. Word had been sent to his relatives in the camp west of the river, and it was said his women relatives were coming after him with a travois. I moved on eastward up the gulch coulee.

I discovered almost hidden the dead body of an Indian. I did not go up close to it, but I could see the scalp was gone. That puzzled me. Could this be a Crow or a Shoshone? I had not known of there being any Indians belonging to these soldiers killed here. As I stood there looking, it seemed there was something familiar about the appearance of that body. I backed away and went to find my brother Yellow Hair. We two returned to the place. We

241

got off our horses and walked to the dead Indian. We rolled the body over and looked closely.

"Yes, it is Lame White Man," my brother agreed.

We called other Cheyennes. Several of them came. All of them promptly confirmed our identification. All of us were satisfied some Sioux had scalped him, or maybe had killed him, finding him in among the soldiers and supposing him to be a Crow or a Shoshone belonging to them. We knew he had gone with the young men in their charge upon the soldiers there. Perhaps he had gone farther than the others and was killed on his way back to us, the killer mistaking him for an attacking enemy Indian. A bullet had gone in at his right breast and out at his back. He also had many stab wounds. He was still dressed in his best clothing, none of it having been taken. The Cheyennes never made any inquiries among the Sioux concerning the case. We just kept quiet about it.

My brother took the blanket from his horse and covered the body of the favorite Cheyenne warrior chief. A young man hurried away to go across the river and tell his people. When I came back to the place an hour or so afterward the dead man's wife and three or four women helpers had come with a horse dragging a travois. Four of us young men rolled the body into the blanket and put it upon the buffalo hide stretched across the lodgepoles. The women set off with it toward the river.

I helped likewise in putting my friend Noisy Walking upon the swinging bed when his father and mother and other women came after him. Judging by his appearance then, this was the last good act I ever should do for him. Various groups of women, many more of the Sioux than of the Cheyennes, were on the field searching for and taking away their dead and wounded men. Two Sioux had been killed in this same first charge upon the soldiers. I did not like to hear the weeping of the women. My heart that had been glad because of the victory was made sad by thoughts of our own dead and dying men and their mourning relatives left behind.

I noticed decorations on the shoulders and stripes on the arms of some of the soldier coats. I did not think of their meanings. I did not hear any of the Indians there talk about any meanings for these special marks. If I thought about it at all, I may have thought these were particular medicine ways the soldiers had for preparing themselves. It was a long time after that day before I learned that the wearers of these were the soldier chiefs.

Each Indian horse used for going into the battle had only a blanket strapped upon its back and a lariat rope about the neck. In riding, the lariat was looped into the horse's mouth, or was looped over the head and then into the mouth, for a bridle. The surplus of the long rope was coiled and tucked into the rider's belt. If a man fell from his horse the coil would be jerked from his belt, so he would not be dragged. Also, the uncoiling as the horse might move away would leave a long rope trailing after it, so it was easy to recapture the animal. That was the regular Indian way of riding.

Warbonnets were worn by twelve Cheyennes among the three hundred or more of our warriors in the battle. It may be I have forgotten a few of them, but as I recollect it our warbonnet men on that day were these: * Crazy Head, Crow Necklace, Little Horse, Wolf Medicine, White Elk, Howling Wolf, Braided Locks, Chief Coming Up, Mad Wolf, Little Shield, Sun Bear and White Body. Three of these were little warrior chiefs. Ten of the warbonnets had trails. Sun Bear had a single buffalo horn projecting out from the front of his forehead band. Crazy Head was a big chief of the tribe, had been a great fighter in past times, but was not now a warrior chief. While he had on his warbonnet here, I suppose he stayed in the background and let the young men do the fighting. Chief Lame White Man

* Various old Cheyennes helped Wooden Leg in making this list.— T. B. M.

was not wearing a warbonnet on this occasion. It was not usual for a man of his high standing to go into the battle as he did. I suppose he did so because he had not there any son to serve as a warrior.

Not any Cheyenne fought naked in this battle. All of them who were in the fight were dressed in their best, according to the custom of both the Cheyennes and the Sioux. Of our warriors, Sun Bear was nearest to nakedness. He had on a special buffalo-horn head-dress. I saw several naked Sioux, perhaps a dozen or more. Of course, these had special medicine painting on the body. Two different Sioux I saw wearing buffalo head skins and horns, and one of them had a bear's skin over his head and body. These three were not dressed in the usual war clothing. It is likely there were others I did not see. Perhaps some of the naked ones were No Clothing Indians.

A dead Uncpapa Sioux received something of the same kind of mistaken attention given to our Lame White Man. The dead Sioux was mixed in with dead bodies of the soldiers. An Arapaho and a No Clothing Indian supposed him to be a Crow or a Shoshone belonging to the white men fighters. They jabbed spears many times into the body. They were much embarrassed when they learned of their mistake.

245

I found a metal bottle, as I was walking among
the dead men. It was about half full of some kind
of liquid. I opened it and found that the liquid was
not water. Soon afterward I got hold of another
bottle of the same kind that had in it the same kind
of liquid. I showed these to some other Indians.
Different ones of them smelled and sniffed. Finally
a Sioux said:

"Whisky."

Bottles of this kind were found by several other
Indians. Some of them drank the contents. Others
tried to drink, but had to spit out their mouthfuls.
Bobtail Horse got sick and vomited soon after he
had taken a big swallow of it. It became the talk
that this whisky explained why the soldiers became
crazy and shot each other and themselves instead of
shooting us. One old Indian said, though, that there
was not enough whisky gone from any of the bottles
to make a white man soldier go crazy. We all agreed
then that the foolish actions of the soldiers must
have been caused by the prayers of our medicine men.
I believed this was the true explanation. My belief
became changed, though, in later years. I think now
it was the whisky.*

I took a folded leather package from a soldier hav-

* The whisky explanation is regularly advanced by the warrior
veterans nowadays. It appears none of them have any conception of
suicide to avoid capture.—T. B. M.

ing three stripes on the left arm of his coat. It had in it lots of flat pieces of paper having pictures or writing I did not then understand. The paper was of green color. I tore it all up and gave the leather holder to a Cheyenne friend. Others got packages of the same kind from other dead white men. Some of it was kept by the finders. But most of it was thrown away or was given to boys, for them to look at the pictures.*

I rode away from the battle hill in the middle of the afternoon. Many warriors had gone back across the hills to the southward, there to fight again the first soldiers. But I went to the camps across on the west side of the river. I had on a soldier coat and breeches I had taken. I took with me the two metal bottles of whisky. At the end of the arrow shaft I carried the beard scalp.

I waved my scalp as I rode among our people. The first person I met who took special interest in me was my mother's mother. She was living in a little willow dome lodge of her own. "What is that?" she asked me when I flourished the scalp stick toward her. I told her. "I give it to you," I said, and I held it out to her. She screamed and shrank away. "Take it," I urged. "It will be good medicine for

* Paper money. The soldiers received two months' pay after they had left Fort Lincoln. There had been no opportunity for them to spend a cent, except among themselves, since that time.—T. B. M.

247

you." Then I went on to tell her about my having killed the Crow or Shoshone at the first fight up the river, about my getting the two guns, about my knocking in the head two soldiers in the river, about what I had done in the next fight on the hill where all of the soldiers had been killed. We talked about my soldier clothing. She said I looked good dressed that way. I had thought so too, but neither the coat nor the breeches fit me well. The arms and legs were too short for me. Finally she decided she would take the scalp. She went then into her own little lodge.

I passed one bottle of the whisky among friends. Each took a small drink of it until all of it was gone. The other bottle I gave to Little Hawk. He himself drank all of the whisky in it. Pretty soon, though, he became sick and he vomited up everything in his stomach.

Some special excitement was going on over beyond the Arrows All Gone camp. A big crowd of Sioux were gathered there. I went to see what they were doing. They had surrounded some Indians just then arrived in the camp. "Kill them, every one of them," some Sioux were shouting. Others were saying: "Wait. Let us be sure." Above the confusion of threats and general noise of the excited throng I heard an angry thundering:

248

"No. I had nothing to do with the soldiers. I am all Indian, all Cheyenne."

It was the voice of Little Wolf, most respected of the four old men chiefs of the Cheyennes. He was speaking in our language. He could not talk Sioux. He never had mingled much with them, so not many of them knew him.

Yellow Horse, an old Southern Cheyenne man, was with me. He said to me: "Let us go to Little Wolf. You are his relative, you know the Sioux language, and you should talk for him." We crowded our way through to the old chief. Both of us shook hands with him. The Sioux began talking to us about him. Some Cheyennes also were accusing him. One of these was White Bull. He knew Little Wolf, but he said the chief ought to have been with the Cheyennes long ago, that he ought not to have waited until after the fighting before joining us, that he stayed too long on the reservation. I knew that White Bull's heart was troubled, though, about his own son, Noisy Walking. Finally, Yellow Horse called out: "Wait until this young man talks to Little Wolf. He will find out and tell everybody."

"Have you been with the soldiers?" I asked the chief.

"No, you foolish boy," he flared back at me. "Do these people think I am a crazy man? I have with

249

me seven lodges of our people. There are families of women and children. They have their tepees, their packhorses, all of their property. Does anybody suppose that is the way to join the soldiers and help them? Not any part of me ever was white man. I am all Indian. I am willing to fight any man who says I am not."

He went on to tell all about the experiences of his little band of Cheyennes. On their way out from the reservation they saw soldiers camped on the upper Rosebud, just the afternoon before. They kept hidden back in the hills and watched the soldiers go on toward the divide leading to the Little Bighorn. His people did not set up their lodges that night. Instead, they traveled a while and rested a while, their scouts all the time watching the soldiers. Early in the morning, some of Little Wolf's young men out in front found a box of something the soldiers had lost. Just then, some soldiers came back, shot at these young men, and they returned to Little Wolf.* The band continued to follow the soldiers, but kept themselves hidden. From the hilltops they heard the guns and saw some of the fighting. It appeared that

---

* Here appears to have been the key incident that misled Custer into supposing his presence revealed to the camps and that caused him to attack at once, lest they escape. Big Crow, Black Horse and Medicine Bull, all of them with the Little Wolf band, told me the details of this experience.—T. B. M.

all of the Indians in the camps were running away. Finally, the shooting mostly died down. The frightened little band peeped over the hilltops and saw that the camps and the Indians still were on the valley. Then they cautiously came on to join us.

I repeated all of this story to a Sioux chief. He told the assembled Sioux warriors and I told the Cheyennes. Some grumbling continued, many saying that Little Wolf ought to have been with us long ago, but all of them became satisfied that neither he nor his companions deserved killing. The crowd scattered, and the newcomers moved on to join the Cheyenne camp. There were some additional scoldings of them on account of their having stayed so long at the reservation. But their women had plenty of sugar and coffee in their packs, and with gifts of these desirable extra foods they soon quieted all complaints. Little Wolf at that time was fifty-five years old.

Burial parties of Cheyennes were going to the hill gulches west of our camps, to put our dead into rock crevices. Each warrior lost was disposed of by his women relatives and his young men friends. A big band of people went out to help bury Lame White Man. I accompanied the relatives of Limber Bones, one of our young men who had been killed. We took him far back up a long coulee. We found there

251

a small hillside cliff. Four of us young men helped the women to clear out a sheltered cove. In there we placed the dead body, wrapped in blankets and a buffalo robe. We piled a wall of flat stones across the front of the grave. His mother and another woman sat down on the ground beside it to mourn for him. The rest of us returned to the valley.

The Sioux likewise were disposing of their dead. Their customary way was to set up burial tepees. It appeared that in all of the Sioux camps these were being set up. They were placed where had been the dwelling lodges, or near them. In some cases the original dwelling lodges of the dead ones were left standing, in each case the body being all dressed for burial and left on a scaffold in the lodge or on the dirt floor, the dwelling being then abandoned by the inhabitants. This was a common mode of Sioux burial, and sometimes the Cheyennes did it in this way.

All of the camps were being moved. This was in accordance with a regular custom among the Indian tribes. When any death occurred in a camp, either from battle or from other cause, right at once the people began to get ready to move camp to some other place. The Cheyennes selected a camping spot down the river about a mile northwestward. The Sioux all began moving northwestward and back from the Little Bighorn toward the base of the bench hills west from the river. In the new locations, all of the camps except the Cheyennes were west of the present railroad and highway.

Most of the women and children and older people in the camps had fled toward the hills to the northward and westward when the first band of soldiers made the attack upon the Uncpapas at the upper part of the group of camps. I suppose there were very few people left in the camps at that end until after those soldiers had been chased away and across the river. When I rode up there and around the west and south sides of the Uncpapa and Blackfeet circles it was hard to keep from running over the Indians who were hurrying afoot toward the bench lands to the westward.

Our Cheyenne people who were not active warriors started to go toward the north, down the valley, and some of them crossed the river. But when the second band of soldiers were seen on the high ridge far out eastward these Cheyennes who had crossed the river returned to the camping side. Of course, nobody knew how many soldiers were coming. Nobody knew what would be the outcome of their attack. They had surprised us by their sudden appearance. We were not prepared for battle.

At the first time of the flight from the camps, many

women and some of the men seized small packs of food or other precious possessions and carried them away. The fleeing ones stopped on the benchlands west of where had been their camp circles. They stayed there and watched the fighting. After a little while, since no more of the soldiers had come to that side of the river, people began hurrying to the camps, quickly gathering up other things, then hurrying back to the hilltops. Later, as none of our warriors were returning, it became evident that we were winning the contest. Our people then became more confident. The old men who were making medicine prayers for our success added words of encouragement to the waiting families.

Throngs of women now were busy going back and forth between the old and the new camp positions. They were carrying water from the river and wood from the timber. All of the lodges not abandoned were taken down. Most of them were packed, not set up in the new spots of location. The poles were wrapped, the buffalo skin coverings were put into bundles, packs were made up, all put into readiness for quick movement elsewhere if need be. Only the cooking pots and other essential articles were left in use. The women went by hundreds to cut willows for making little skeleton dome shelters, in substitution for the regular tepee lodges kept packed. It had not rained here during all of that day, but rain might come at any time. Not all of the Indians, though, prepared shelters. Many depended only upon robes for shielding them if shielding should become needful. The lodges of mourning Cheyennes were torn or cut to pieces or burned, and their furnishings were cast away. These bereft people, according to our customs, now had to live during their time of mourning without any lodge or any property of their own. They dwelt outside or with hospitable friends. The poles and skins of any travois used to carry dead bodies were also thrown away. Sometimes the horses used to drag the travois of a dead person were killed or were turned loose to be captured by whoever might want them.

After sundown I visited Noisy Walking. He was lying on a ground bed of buffalo robes under a willow dome shelter. His father White Bull was with him. His mother sat just outside the entrance. I asked my friend: "How are you?" He replied: "Good, only I want water." I did not know what else to say, but I wanted him to know that I was his friend and willing to do whatever I could for him. I sat down upon the ground beside him. After a little while I said: "You were very brave." Noth-

255

ing else was said for several minutes. He was weak. His hands trembled at every move he made. Finally he said to his father:

"I wish I could have some water—just a little of it."

"No. Water will kill you."

White Bull almost choked as he said this to his son. But he was a good medicine man, and he knew what was best. As I sat there looking at Noisy Walking I knew he was going to die. My heart was heavy. But I could not do him any good, so I excused myself and went away.

There was no dancing nor celebrating of any kind in any of the camps that night. Too many people were in mourning, among all of the Sioux as well as among the Cheyennes. Too many Cheyenne and Sioux women had gashed their arms and legs, in token of their grief. The people generally were praying, not cheering. There was much noise and confusion, but this was from other causes. Young men were going out to fight the first soldiers now hiding themselves on the hill across the river from where had been the first fighting during the morning. Other young men were coming back to camp after having been over there shooting at these soldiers. Movements of this kind had been going on all the time since the final blows fell upon all of the soldiers

256

in the second and greatest battle. Old men heralds were riding about all of the camps, singing the brave-heart songs and calling out: "Young men, be brave." The only fires anywhere among us were little camp fires for cooking. Or, there may have been at times a larger blaze coming from some mourning family's lodge being burned.

I did not go back that afternoon nor that night to help in fighting the first soldiers. Late in the night, though, I went as a scout. Five young men of the Cheyennes were appointed to guard our camp while other people slept. These were Big Nose, Yellow Horse, Little Shield, Horse Road and Wooden Leg. One or other of us was out somewhere looking over the country all the time. Two of us went once over to the place where the soldiers were hidden. We got upon hill points higher than they were. We could look down among them. We could have shot among them, but we did not do this. We just saw that they yet were there.

Five other young men took our duties in the last part of the night. I was glad to be relieved. I did not go to my family group for rest. I let loose my horse and dropped myself down upon a thick pad of grassy sod.

X

The Spoils of Battle.

I slept late that next morning after the great battle. The sun had been up an hour before I awoke. I went to the willow lodge of my father and mother. When I had eaten the breakfast given to me by my mother I got myself ready again to risk death in an effort to kill other white men who had come to kill us. I combed and braided my hair. My braids in those days were full and long, reaching down my breast beyond the waist belt. I painted anew the black circle around my face and the red and yellow space enclosed within the circle. I was in doubt about which clothing to wear, but my father said the soldier clothing looked the best, even though the coat sleeves ended far above my wrists and the legs of the breeches left long bare spots between them and the tops of my moccasins. I put on my big white hat captured at the Rosebud fight. My sister Crooked Nose got my horse for me. Soon afterward I was on my way up and across the valley and on through the river to the hill where the first soldiers were staying.

I had both my rifle and my six shooter. I still

was without my medicine shield and my other medicine protectors that had been lost on Powder river. Most of the other Cheyennes and Sioux had theirs. The shields all were of specially shrunken and toughened buffalo skin covered with buckskin fringed and painted, each with his own choice of designs, for the medicine influence. I went with other young men to the higher hills around the soldiers. I stayed at a distance from them and shot bullets from my new rifle. I did not shoot many times, as it appeared I was too far away, and I did not want to waste any of my cartridges. So I went down and hid in a gulch near the river.

Some soldiers came to get water from the river, just as our old men had said they likely would do. The white men crept down a deep gulch and then ran across an open space to the water. Each one had a bucket, and each would dip his bucket for water and run back into the gulch. I put myself, with others, where we could watch for these men. I shot at one of them just as he straightened up after having dipped his bucket into the water. He pitched forward into the edge of the river. He went wallowing along the stream, trying to swim, but having a hard time at it. I jumped out from my hiding place and ran toward him. Two Sioux warriors got ahead of me. One of them waded after the man and struck him with a rifle barrel. Finally he grabbed the man, hit him again, and then dragged him dead to the shore, quite a distance down the river. I kept after them, following down the east bank. Some other Sioux warriors came. I was the only Cheyenne there. The Sioux agreed that my bullet had been the first blow upon the white soldier, so they allowed me to choose whatever I might want of his belongings.*

I searched into the man's pockets. In one I found a folding knife and a plug of chewing tobacco that was soaked and spoiled. In another pocket was a wad of the same kind of green paper taken from the soldiers the day before. It too was wet through. I threw it aside. In this same pocket were four white metal pieces of money. I knew they were of value in trading, but I did not know how much was their value. In later times I have learned they were four silver dollars. A young Cheyenne there said: "Give the money to me." I did not care for it, so I gave it to him. He thanked me and said: "I shall use it to buy for myself a gun." I do not remember now his name, but he was a son of One Horn. A Sioux picked up the wad of green paper I had thrown upon the ground. It was almost falling to pieces, but he

*In a letter published in Brady's book, Private Wm. E. Morris tells of the death of Tanner, of Troop M, while he was after water for the Reno wounded men.—T. B. M.

began to spread out some of the wet sheets that still held together. Pretty soon he said:

"This is money. This is what white men use to buy things from the traders."

I had seen much other paper like it during the afternoon before. Wolf Medicine had offered to give me a handful of it. But I did not take it. I already had thrown away some of it I had found. But even after I was told it could be used for buying things from the traders, I did not want it. I was thinking then it would be a long time before I should see or care to see any white man trader.

I went riding over the ground where we had fought the first soldiers during the morning of the day before. I saw by the river, on the west side, a dead black man. He was a big man. All of his clothing was gone when I saw him, but he had not been scalped nor cut up like the white men had been. Some Sioux told me he belonged to their people but was with the soldiers.*

As some of us were looking at the body of an Indian who had been with the soldiers, an old Sioux said:

"This is a Corn ** Indian, not a Crow nor Shoshone."

* Isaiah, a negro, Sioux interpreter for the Seventh cavalry.— T. B. M.
** The Arikaras were known as Corn people.—T. B. M.

261

He showed us the differences in appearance, especially the earrings and the hair dressing. The Crow men wore their hair cut off above the forehead and roached up. The Shoshones had almost the same way of placing this foretop. The Corn Indians kept their hair in braids, parted like that of the Sioux and Cheyennes, but the Corn Indian parting was not in the middle of the top, as ours was. I examined again the one I had helped in beating to death. I learned he also was a Corn Indian. I found yet a third one. We who had killed them were young men, and there was great excitement at the time, so we had not observed their tribal connection. We had supposed them to be the same Crows and Shoshones we had fought on the upper Rosebud creek a few days before. Now there began to be talk that maybe these soldiers were not the same ones we had fought there. Or, perhaps they had added the Corn Indians to their forces since that time. There were different opinions on the matter.

Some Sioux caught a mule that wandered out from the place where the soldiers were together on the hilltop. The animal was going down toward the river when the Indians got it. They tried to lead it toward their sheltered place behind a knoll, but it would not go. It appeared to be wanting a drink of water. One Sioux got behind it and whipped it, while a companion pulled at the leading strap. But the mule just stood there, would not move. On its back were packs of cartridges. The Sioux took these and let the mule go.

I went with other Cheyennes along the hills northward to the ground where we had killed all of the soldiers. Lots of women and boys were there. The boys were going about making coups by stabbing or shooting arrows into the dead men. Some of the bodies had many arrows sticking in them. Many hands and feet had been cut off, and the limbs and bodies and heads had many stabs and slashes. Some of this had been done by the warriors, during and immediately after the battle. More was added, though, by enraged and weeping women relatives of the Sioux and Cheyennes who had been killed. The women used sheathknives and hatchets.

A dog was following one of the Sioux women among the dead soldiers. I did not see any other dog there, neither on that day nor on the day before, when the fight was on. There were some Indian dogs tangling among the feet of the horses at the time of the fighting of the first soldiers, on the valley above the camps. But even here most of them were called away by the women and old people going to the western hilltops.

Three different soldiers, among all of the dead in

both places of battle, attracted special notice from the Indians. The first was the man wearing the buckskin suit and who had the colored writing and pictures on his breast and arms. Another was the black man killed among the first soldiers on the valley. The third was one having gold among his teeth. We did not understand how this metal got there, nor why it was there.

Paper boxes of ammunition were in the leather bags carried on the saddles of the soldiers. Besides, in all of the belts taken from the dead men there were cartridges. Some belts had only a few left in them. In others the loops still contained many, an occasional one almost full. I did not see nor hear of any belt entirely emptied of its cartridges.

All during that forenoon, as well as during the afternoon and night before, both in the camps and on the battle grounds, Indians were saying to each other: "I got some tobacco." "I got coffee." "I got two horses." "I got a soldier saddle." "I got a good gun." Some got things they did not understand.

One young Cheyenne took something from a dead soldier just after all of them had been killed. He was puzzled by it. Some others looked at it. I was with them. It was made of white metal and had glass on one side. On this side were marks of some kind.

While the Cheyenne was looking at it he got it up toward his ear. Then he put it up close.

"It is alive!" he said.

Others put it to their ears and listened. I put it up to mine.

"Tick-tick-tick-tick-tick-tick," it was saying.

We talked about its use. We agreed generally it was that soldier's special medicine. Many Indians came and wondered about it. The young man decided to keep it for his own medicine.

When I was getting ready the next morning to go and fight again the soldiers staying on the hilltop, the Cheyenne young man had a crowd around him again examining his strange white man medicine. They were listening, but it made no sound. After different ones had studied it, he finally threw it away as far as he could throw it.

"It is not good medicine for me," he said. "It is dead."

I saw another soldier medicine thing something like this one, but the other one was larger and it did not make the ticking noise. It acted, though, like it was alive. When it was held with the glass side up a little arrow fluttered around. When it was held quiet for a while the arrow gradually stopped fluttering. Every time it stopped the point of the arrow was toward the north, down the valley. There was talk then of other soldiers coming from that direction, so it was decided this medicine object was useful for finding out at any time where might be soldiers. Little Shield had it when I saw it. He gave it to High Walking. Another Cheyenne got a pair of field glasses. We understood them. This was a big pair.

Cleaners for the rifles puzzled us a while. They were in joints and were carried in a long hole in the end of the wooden stock. Pretty soon we learned what was their use. I saw one rifle that had a shell of cartridge in its barrel. A Sioux had it. He could not put into the gun any other cartridge, so he threw it into the river.

Yellow Weasel, a Cheyenne, got a bugle. He tried to make a noise with it, but he could not. Others tried. Different ones puffed and blowed at it. But nobody could make it sound out. After a while we heard a bugle making a big noise somewhere among the Sioux. The Cheyennes said: "The Sioux got a good one. This one Yellow Weasel has is no good. He might as well throw it away." But he kept it, and it was not long until he was making it sound.

One Cheyenne got a flag. There were several others among the Sioux. I do not know just how many they got, but I believe I saw nine of them.

Bridle bits were thrown away, but the leather parts were kept. I got two sets of bridle reins, but no other parts of the bridles. A Cheyenne gave them to me. All of the soldier boots were taken from them. But they were not worn by the Indians. The bottoms were cut off and discarded. Only the tops used. These made good leather pouches, or the leather was cut up to make something else. Old men were allowed to have all of the saddles. But only a few of the Cheyenne old men got them. I saw lots of Sioux old men riding around on soldier saddles, either on the soldier horses or the Indian horses.

All of the soldier horses taken by the Indians were good. They were fat and sleek and strong and lively. They were better than any of the Indian horses. Some were killed or were so badly wounded we did not want them. But when we could scare them away from the soldiers as the fighting was going on, we did this. Any time that horses got among us we turned them toward the river, for the old men or the boys to capture. It was easy to do this, as they were very thirsty. One big band of them went down from the west end of the ridge.

Noisy Walking died during the night after the great battle. Six Cheyennes now had been killed. Another man, Open Belly, was badly wounded and was expected to die. He was about thirty years old, but he had neither wife nor children. The six dead were:

Lame White Man, age about thirty-eight, wife and two children.

Limber Bones, age twenty, not married.

Black Bear, age twenty, not married.

Noisy Walking, age eighteen, not married.

Hump Nose, age sixteen, not married.

Whirlwind, age sixteen, not married.

Others had wounds that crippled them but did not threaten to kill them. Little Bird got a bullet through a thigh. Many had scratch wounds. Sun Bear almost got killed. He went into the first great Cheyenne charge. A bullet glanced off his forehead. He was dazed and he fell down. But he got up right away and went on fighting.

Hump Nose and Whirlwind were killed during the first battle, above the camps. Hump Nose fell on the west side of the river, in the valley fighting. Whirlwind's death took place on the east side, when he had the fight with the Corn Indian, who also was killed. Lame White Man and Noisy Walking received their bullets at the time of the first charge among the Custer soldiers who rode down toward the river. Open Belly, our man who died after we arrived east of Powder river, was hit by a soldier bullet when he was riding across the bench where the stone house of the Custer Battlefield National Cemetery now is standing. Limber Bones and Black Bear were killed on the steep slope just north of the present Custer stone monument. Both Limber Bones and Black Bear were a little taller than I was. After they were gone I was the tallest young man in the tribe, I believe. I heard of a few women riding out to watch the fighting, but I did not see any women there during that time. None of them was doing any fighting. All of them kept far back.

The Indians supposed all the time that these were the same soldiers we had fought on the upper Rosebud valley. Little Wolf and his people, arriving just after the fight ended, explained to us that these men just killed came from another direction. Then, when we learned that the Indians with these soldiers at the Little Bighorn were Corn Indians, not Crows or Shoshones, it began to appear that the Little Wolf band had it right, that these really were not the Rosebud battle soldiers.

During the afternoon it was learned that yet another band of white men were coming up the Little Bighorn valley.* All of the young men wanted to fight them. A council of chiefs was held. They decided we should continue in our same course—not fight any soldiers if we could get away without doing so. All of the Indians then got ready to move.

* The Terry-Gibbon forces. They camped that night on the site of the present Crow Agency.—T. B. M.

Mourning families abandoned and left behind their meat, robes, cooking pots and everything else they owned, as well as their vacated or destroyed lodges. That was a custom among all of the Sioux tribes the same as with the Cheyennes. I saw several Sioux tepees left standing. I supposed there were dead warriors in some of them, or perhaps in all of them. Some Cheyenne tepees were left standing. These had belonged to families wherein a member had been killed. But, except the lodges and property abandoned by mourning people, all of the possessions of the Indians were taken with us.

Late in the afternoon the procession of tribes was in movement. Again, as at all other times, the Cheyennes went ahead and the Uncpapas came last. Several parties of young men went aside to go across the river and shoot again among the soldiers camped on the high hill. A few stayed there until darkness came. Uncpapa scouts watched behind, observing particularly the new band of soldiers coming up the Little Bighorn valley.

We set out southwestward up the small valley of a creek just south of the present Garryowen railroad station. Soon we mounted to the benchland and traveled southward. Late in the night, the whole caravan stopped and rested a few hours, all sleeping in the open, with no lodges. At daylight we traveled on, now following up the Little Bighorn valley. During the afternoon we stopped for camping. The Cheyenne circle, at the leading or southern end, was about two miles below the mouth of Greasy Grass creek, below the place where now is located the town of Lodge Grass, Montana.

XI

Rovings after the Victory.

All of the lodges were set up here below the mouth
of Greasy Grass creek. All of the six tribal camp
circles were arranged as they had been before the
soldiers came and troubled us. The Cheyennes again
were on one of their favorite old camping spots.
They still were at the advance side of the group of
circles. The Uncpapas still were at the opposite
side.

I was stationed as a wolf to keep lookout from a
hill near our camp. As I sat there, an Indian young
man rode up to me. He asked me, in Sioux language,
"Who are you?" I said, "I am a Cheyenne." He
got down from his horse. He had tobacco and a pipe,
and we had a smoke together. He told me he belonged to the Waist and Skirt people, but I already
could see that, by his earrings. All of the Waist and
Skirt men wore elk teeth hanging from their ears.
After we had smoked and visited a while, he said:·

"I think the big chief of the soldiers we killed
was named Long Hair. One of my people killed him.
He has known Long Hair many years, and he is sure
this was him. He could tell him by the long and
wavy yellow hair."

This was the first time I ever had heard of any such person as Long Hair. The news was interesting to me at first, but after I had thought a few moments about it the story seemed not very important. I recalled myself having seen at least three soldiers having long and light-colored hair. One of these I had shot after he was dead. Just after the end of the fighting I saw this long-haired soldier lying there without any appearance of wounds on him. So I put the muzzle of my rifle against the side of his head and sent a bullet through it. This man's clothing was gone when I first saw him. I had not any thought about whether or not he was a chief.

A great council was held at the Greasy Grass camp that night. Chiefs of all of the tribes were there. It was out of doors, in the midst of the camp circles. I believe it was at the Ogallala camp, but I am not sure. At this council I heard an Uncpapa Sioux war chief say:

"Long Hair was big chief of the soldiers. I saw him there, and I killed him. I know it was him. I could not mistake the long and wavy yellow hair." *

I did not hear anyone else during that time make claims of knowing who was the soldier big chief.

---

* In fact, his wife and others to whom he was well known assert that General Custer was not wearing his hair long at the time he was killed. For some time before that occasion he had kept his hair cut short.— T. B. M.

273

There was some talk, though, that all of those soldiers had been chosen specially for their bravery and had been sent out direct from Washington. It was generally agreed that whoever was the big chief of them, he must have been the big chief of all of the white man soldiers in the world.

At this council I heard chiefs of the different tribes announce the number of their killed. The Cheyennes had lost 6. Uncpapas, 7. Arrows All Gone, 4. Minneconjoux, 3. Ogallalas, 2. I have forgotten the numbers from the Waist and Skirt, Burned Thigh and Blackfeet Sioux. I think, though, that all of these three tribes together might have lost 7 or 8. Total deaths, about 30.*

The Cheyenne warriors had a dance at this Greasy Grass camp. Charcoal Bear, our medicine chief, brought the buffalo skin from the sacred tepee and put it upon the top of a pole in the center of our camp circle. We danced around this pole. No women took part in the dancing. Many of them had sore legs from the mourning cuts. Our dance was not carried very far into the night. It was mostly a short telling of experiences, a counting of coups. My father told, in a few words, what his two sons had done. When he had ended the telling of my

* The small loss is explainable by the extensive suiciding among the soldiers.—T. B. M.

warrior acts, he said: "The name of this son of mine is Wooden Leg." Up to this time some people still used my boyhood name, Eats From His Hand. But now this old name was entirely gone.

Some of the Sioux people had little dances here, the same as the Cheyennes were having. But not all of them did this. The Uncpapas did not dance. They said it was not time, that we ought to mourn yet a while. Some of them came to look on quietly at our gathering.

Only one sleep we stayed at the Greasy Grass location. The great band of Indians trailed from there on up the Little Bighorn valley. Our next stop was near where is the present town of Wyola.

An accidental killing took place during the time we were at this next camp. That afternoon, as we were traveling, a Cheyenne named Coffee was among the men who hunted buffalo along the way. He got a load of meat on his pack horse and joined us just after the camp had been set up. He belonged to our tribal medicine lodge, as a helper for the chief medicine man. He rode to the medicine lodge and made a movement to dismount from his horse. He had a rifle strapped in front of his body. As he swung himself from the horse, his rifle accidentally was discharged. Coffee originally had been a Southern Cheyenne, but for many years he had been a mem-

275

ber of our tribe. He was an old man, but he never was married. He said that one having his position as helper to the medicine chief ought not to have a wife. But Charcoal Bear, the medicine chief, had a wife and two children.

After one sleep at this place we turned eastward and went over the hills to the extreme upper Rosebud. One sleep at this place. We moved on down, going past the ground where we had fought the soldiers on this creek. We camped a few miles below where this fight had taken place. One sleep here. The movement was kept up down this valley. The next camp was pitched near the present Busby. After one sleep here we traveled on northward. This time we stopped at our favorite old camping place on the Rosebud above the mouth of Muddy creek.

I was not with the camps at all of these stopping places. Like many others, I was out a part of the time looking for meat. I took it to my people when I could get any. Buffalo were scarce along the line of travel, so most of the game killed was elk, deer or antelope. Many people among the Indians were hungry for more food. Partly because of the fast traveling and partly because the hunters were not going far on account of soldiers in the country, the food demands of the people could not be supplied to their full satisfaction.

I went out with one party, though, as far as the present town of Sheridan, Wyoming. We found there plenty of buffalo. We loaded our pack horses and started to return to the moving Indians. But somebody saw soldiers, or it was said they had been seen. I did not see them. But I quickly threw off the meat from my pack horse, the same as the others did, and we rode away southward as fast as our horses could go. Not far off we got into a wooded canyon and hid there until darkness came. At night we went back and picked up all of our meat. We then traveled on, and the next day we got to our people.

We Cheyennes had a dance at our camp near the mouth of Muddy creek, on the Rosebud. I do not recollect any dance in any other tribal circle at this place. Our warriors again talked in public of acts at the great battle. One would dance, flourish a gun, and say, "I killed a white man soldier." Another would do the same. Each one who did this had to have witnesses to verify his claims. A few women took part in the dance. My grandmother was one of them. She had the bearded face scalp I gave to her, and she told of my doings in the fight with the first soldiers. After this dance, she threw away the scalp.

One sleep we stayed here. Then we continued down the Rosebud. The next stop was below the

277

mouth of Lame Deer creek, as it now is known. We moved from there on down to the mouth of the stream now called Greenleaf creek. All along the Rosebud we had seen the trail of the soldiers we had killed at the Little Bighorn. We now had full proof that they had come up this valley from the Yellowstone. After one sleep at the Greenleaf camping place we left the Rosebud valley.

The direction of movement was turned eastward. We followed the little branch stream to its head and went on over the divide to Tongue river. Stopped there, one sleep. Next day, traveled up this valley to Otter creek and on up this little valley several miles. One sleep in the camp on Otter creek. The next camp was set up at the head of Otter creek. The day after that our great band of tribes went over another divide and camped on what the white people call Pumpkin creek. One sleep, then eastward to a branch of Powder river. Next, to Powder river. Following, one day of travel down Powder river and one more camping beside this stream. Crossed the river and went up a creek flowing into its east side. This creek is the next one south of that one where the combined Indians had traveled in starting from east of Powder river toward the valleys westward from there.

We now were in the same region where all of the

tribes had come together three months before this time. In coming back to the gathering place all of the Indians traveled together, as we had done in going westward from it. The Cheyennes still were moving in the advance and camping in the advance. The Uncpapas still were following last and camping last. On the return we hurried from place to place. There was no stopping for special hunting. I believe we remained only one sleep at each of the camps. I may have forgotten one or two places of our camping. I think, though, that it was sixteen or more sleeps from the battle camp on the Little Bighorn back to this place on the creek east of Powder river.

Open Belly, our badly wounded man, died here east of Powder river. One wounded Sioux had died along the way. This brought the Cheyenne loss from the battle up to seven. Some Sioux count also was increased by one. All of the Indians then had lost about thirty-two warriors as a result of the great battle. The wounded men had been carried during all of the journey on travois beds. That makes easier riding than any other way I know. But it may have been they could have become well if during all the time they had been quiet in a lodge.

The Indians were hungry. Our meat was all gone. The horses had been traveling hard every day and were tired. The fat and sleek soldier horses we had

279

were more tired than the Indian ponies. It was said this was because they were not used to living on grass alone, as the Indian ponies were.

We stayed four or five sleeps at this camping place. Every day the chiefs met in council. Finally, they decided on a separation of the tribes. It seemed there was no danger just now from soldiers. By traveling separately, or in small bands, more meat and skins could be taken by each tribe or band. The horses all could get more grass when scattered. Everybody agreed it was best to separate. I think this was the intention of the chiefs all the time, but we were staying together for yet a few days of final visiting in a quiet camp before the separation.

The Cheyennes went first down the Powder river. We followed it to where it flows into Elk river. We found a big pile of corn in sacks by Elk river. We fed some of it to our soldier horses. Some people cooked a little and ate it. We emptied out most of the remainder and took the sacks.

By Powder river we saw lying dead an old man and an old woman. They were Sioux. Both of the bodies were humped down close together among some brush as if they had been in hiding there when they had been shot. Many bullet wounds were in both of them, all of the holes in the back of the head and back of the body. There were lots of tracks of soldier horses there. The old man was scalped, but the woman was not.

We saw a steamboat on Elk river. Soldiers were on the boat. As they passed along, some of the Cheyennes shot at them. I do not know whether or not any soldier was hit by the shots. They did not shoot back at us. The boat did not stop.

We moved back up Powder river. We camped and hunted all along far above the forks of the Powder and the Little Powder. We went over to Tongue river, to the upper Rosebud, to the upper Little Bighorn branches. We moved back and forth among the valleys of these higher regions. We got plenty of game and our horses had plenty of grass.

Four Cheyennes, Bear Man, Bullets Not Harm Him, Big Nose and myself Wooden Leg, went out from a camp on the upper Rosebud to get buffalo meat. We went far out southward. We got our pack horses loaded and started back. We heard many shots following close after each other.

"Soldiers are after somebody," we agreed.

We hurried away from that neighborhood. None of us went to look. The next day at camp we learned what had happened. Some soldiers had been after a mixed hunting party of Sioux and Cheyennes. Tall Bear, a Cheyenne, had been killed.

All during the remainder of the summer the Chey-

281

ennes traveled and hunted. We kept mostly in the upper parts of the valleys. Not many of our people went to the reservation. But some more came out and joined us. Dull Knife, the old man chief, was with us soon after the separation of the tribes. All of the four old men chiefs now were here. Charcoal Bear kept our tribal medicine lodge set up at every place of camping. When the leaves began to fall we were on Powder river. We camped and hunted along up its valley. As the snows of winter began to fall we moved farther up.

Ten of us young men decided to go on a war party against the Crows. Black Hawk and Yellow Weasel were the big men or leaders of this party. We left the tribal camp on a small creek flowing into the west side of Powder river. It was located then almost in the Big Horn mountains, far up beyond where now is Buffalo, Wyoming.

Six sleeps we ten Cheyenne warriors traveled westward and northward, looking all the time for Crows. We would kill any Crow found, if we could, or whatever horses of theirs we might find would be made ours if we could get them. Our sixth sleep was on the west side of the Bighorn river, just below the place where in past times had been the soldier fort.*

* Fort C. F. Smith.

We now were in Crow land.   But we had not yet seen any Crow Indian.

We followed on down the west side of the Bighorn to its mouth.   We crossed there to its east side and went a little distance down the Elk river.   There we saw a Crow man, woman and some children traveling up the valley with only their one lodge.   We hid back.   They did not see us.   We decided not to harm them.   We turned back and set off up the east side of the Bighorn.   When we got to the mouth of the Little Bighorn we followed up this valley.   Our tenth sleep of the war journey found us camping where now is Crow Agency, only a short distance down the river from where had been the great combined camp when we had fought the soldiers during the early summer.

We rode next morning all about the camping places of the Indians when the soldiers had come. We looked where had been the little shelter camps after the battle with them.   We went then across the river and over to the ridge where we had killed all of the soldiers.   The weather was clear and chilly, but not cold.   There was no snow on the ground.   We led our horses as we walked all over the battle field. Each man told the others of his own experiences during the fight.   I showed them where Noisy Walking had been found and where my brother and I came upon the body of Lame White Man.   The places where all of the killed Cheyennes and many of the Sioux had fallen were known by some one or other of us. We visited all of these places and talked of the dead Indian friends.

Dirt and sagebrush mounds now were at the places where had been the dead soldiers. In a few places we could see some parts of their bodies exposed. But mostly the graves were good, except they had no stones piled over them. At one end of many different ones of the graves was a straight board stuck into the ground, to stand up there. They were straight boards, not crosses. Dead horses were lying in decay here and there among the graves. Wolves had been eating at the horses. I did not notice any place where it appeared wolves had been at the graves.

I found a folding knife that had belonged to some soldier. Another of our party found a Sioux sheath-knife. Soldier boot bottoms and other pieces of soldier belongings were scattered here and there. I saw some broken Cheyenne spears. There were many hundreds of arrows lying all along the ridge and on its sides. Some were Cheyenne arrows, but mostly they were from the bows of the Sioux.

I hunted specially for cartridges. The others also picked them up, but they were getting them to give to friends. I was the only one of this party having a soldier rifle. There were lots of empty shells, and from place to place we picked up loaded ones. Near a dead horse I found a whole pasteboard boxful of good cartridges. There were forty of them in the box. The box had been rotted by rain and had fallen apart, but the cartridges were good. They only needed to be wiped dry. I filled my belt and put the remainder into my pockets. Others found other boxfuls.

We went on southward over the hills to the place where the first soldiers had hidden themselves on the hilltop. We found other cartridges here. After having looked a while at this place we forded the river to the west side and walked about over the valley where the first fight had taken place. One other man and myself were the only two in this party who had been in this battle. We told our companions about how we chased the soldiers and killed them. I showed them right where I had taken my rifle from the soldier and where I had helped in killing the Corn Indian. I pointed out to them the place where I was hidden and where was the soldier when I shot him as he was dipping up water. I told of my getting the wet tobacco from a hip pocket and the metal money from another pocket. They laughed when I told of having thrown aside the wet paper money the soldier had folded and laid into a little paper box.

We slept this night only a little distance up the

285

valley from this first battle ground. Here we made
for ourselves the same kind of little brush shelters
we had been making each night. We slept by twos
or in groups, to keep warm.

The next morning we set out over the divide eastward toward the Rosebud. We followed the same
trail regularly used by the Indians traveling this region, the same that had been used by the soldiers in
coming to us. Four more sleep camps we made in
going on eastward to Tongue river and up this valley.
Somewhere below the mouth of Hanging Woman
creek our scouts caught sight of Indians coming down
the valley. All of us got to where we might see.
Most of the Indians were afoot. Only a few had
horses. We watched and wondered. Who were
these people?

The band of walking Indians were our Cheyennes,
the whole tribe. They had but little food. Many of
them had no blankets nor robes. They had no
lodges. Only here and there was one wearing moccasins. The others had their feet wrapped in loose
pieces of skin or of cloth. Women, children and old
people were straggling along over the snow-covered
trail down the valley. The Cheyennes were very
poor.

Our people told us of soldiers and Pawnee Indians
having come to the camp far up Powder river where

we had left them. The Cheyennes had to run away with only a few small packs, as our small band had done on lower Powder river during the late winter before this time. The same as we had done, they had to see all of their lodges burned and most of their horses taken. Many of our men, women and children had been killed. Others had died of wounds or had starved and frozen to death on the journey through the mountain snow to Tongue river. Three Cheyenne women and a boy had been captured by the Pawnees.*

The tribe were hunting now for the Ogallala Sioux, where Crazy Horse was the principal chief. These Sioux were somewhere in this region. We crossed to the east side of Tongue river just above the present white man town of Ashland, Montana, and went over the benches to Otter creek. After a night of sleep here we moved on eastward over the little mountains. Travel and sleep, travel and sleep, we kept going. Eleven sleeps the tribe had journeyed when we arrived at the place on Beaver creek where now is a white man trading store and a postoffice called Stacey. Here we found the Ogallalas.

The Ogallala Sioux received us hospitably. They had not been disturbed by soldiers, so they had good lodges and plenty of meat and robes. They first as-

* This Powder river fight was on November 26th, 1876.—T. B. M.

sembled us in a great body and fed us all we wanted to eat. To all of the women who needed other food they gave a supply. They gave us robes and blankets. They shared with us their tobacco. Gift horses came to us. Every married woman got skins enough to make some kind of lodge for her household. Oh, how generous were the Ogallalas! Not any Cheyenne was allowed to go to sleep hungry or cold that night.

We had traveled and hunted much during past times with these Sioux people. At all times there was some one or more families of them with us or some of our Cheyennes with them. Of our friendly intermarrying, there was more connection with the Ogallalas than with any other tribe. Their people during the summer and fall had been going to and from the agency more than ours had been. Our few incoming Cheyennes had brought us some news about the soldiers we had fought on the Little Bighorn. But the Ogallalas informed us more fully. From them we learned that the big chief of the soldiers was Long Hair, the same man who several years before this time had fought the Southern Cheyennes.

After we had rested with the Ogallalas a few days the chiefs counciled together and decided that the tribes should join in movement up the Tongue river. All of us then followed our back trail over to Otter creek and on to Tongue river. We moved slowly and hunted along the way. The Cheyennes got a new supply of buffalo meat and many more skins for enlarging their lodges. We crossed Tongue river on the ice, to the east side. Not far up the valley we went back over the ice, to the west side. We traveled then on up the benchland trails, to Hanging Woman creek. The Ogallalas had some cattle they had taken from white people or from soldiers. These were butchered along the way. They had yet also a few of the horses taken at the battle on the Little Bighorn. But these horses that had been so fat and strong were now poor and weak. Most of them already had died. They did not know how to find winter food like the Indian ponies could find it.

At Hanging Woman creek it was decided the two tribes would separate. The Ogallalas would go eastward up this stream. The Cheyennes would continue on up the Tongue river valley. As usual, a few Cheyennes joined the Sioux and a few of their people decided to come with us. My sister Crooked Nose started with the other people. Chiefs Crazy Horse and Water All Gone and a few other Ogallalas came to us. Just as the tribes were about to separate, some scouts brought in the report:

"Soldiers are coming!"

The two bands of Indians began to come again to-

289

gether. The warriors mingled themselves as being of one tribe. The women and children and older men of both sets of people moved together up the Tongue river. The young men put themselves behind their fleeing people. Somebody said to me:

"They have captured some women. Your sister is one of them."

My heart jumped when this news came to me. I lashed my horse into a run toward where it was said they had been captured. There I saw tracks of soldier horses. The trail led to the river ice. On the opposite side of the river, the west side, were soldiers. They began shooting at me. I had to get away. I did not see any of the women, so I supposed they had been killed. My heart then became bitter toward these white men.

I hid my horse in the brush at the foot of a ridge where some warriors were on its top. I walked up there. Many Indians were hidden behind rocks and were shooting toward the soldiers. I chose for myself a hiding place and did the same. I had my soldier rifle and plenty of cartridges. Many soldiers were coming across on the ice, to fight us. But we had the advantage of them because of our position on the high and rocky ridge.

Big Crow, a Cheyenne, kept walking back and

forth along the ridge on the side toward the soldiers. He was wearing a warbonnet. He had a gun taken from the soldiers at the Little Bighorn battle. He used up his cartridges and came back to us hidden behind the rocks, to ask for more. Cheyennes and Sioux here and there each gave him one or two or three. He soon got enough to fill his belt. He went out again to walk along the ridge, to shoot at the soldiers and to defy them in their efforts to hit him with a bullet. All of us others kept behind the rocks, only peeping around at times to shoot. Crazy Horse, the Ogallala chief, was near me. Bullets glanced off the shielding rocks, but none hit us. One came close to me. It whizzed through the folds of my blanket at my side.

Big Crow finally dropped down. He lay there alive, but apparently in great distress. A Sioux went with me to crawl down to where he was and bring him into shelter. Another Sioux came after us. When we got to the wounded man I took hold of his feet and the two Sioux grasped his hands. The three of us crawled and dragged him along on the snow. Bullets began to shower around us. We let loose our holds and dodged behind rocks. When the firing quieted, we crept out and again got him. My brother just then called out to me: "Wooden Leg,

291

come, we are going away from here." I let loose
again and went to my brother. The two Sioux continued to drag Big Crow.

The Indians moved back and forth, down and up,
fighting the soldiers at different times all day. After
darkness came, the fighting stopped. The group
where I was built a little fire, so we might warm ourselves. As soon as the light of it showed, the bullets
began to sing over our heads. We quickly threw
snow upon the fire. Then we moved to another place.
I got down where I had left my horse. It was still
there. I mounted and joined my friends. All of the
Indians left there during the night. Some of the
Ogallalas already had gone on up Hanging Woman
creek. Chiefs Crazy Horse and Water All Gone, with
many lodges of their people, attached themselves to
the Cheyennes. We went up Tongue river. We
traveled all night and all the next day before we
stopped to camp.

We did not know where these soldiers had come
from.* We did not know either how far they might
follow us. But our scouts remaining behind saw
them go back down Tongue river. At the camp, Big
Crow's relatives went about inquiring for him. I

* These soldiers were commanded by Colonel Nelson A. Miles. They
had come from Fort Keogh, which he had established on the Yellowstone just above the mouth of Tongue river. This fight was on
January 1, 1877.—T. B. M.

told where I last had seen him. Finally, they found the two Sioux who had been with him when I left him. These men said he was dead. That was our one man lost in the battle. Two Sioux were killed.

The missing Cheyennes were: Sweet Woman, an old woman, age fifty or older. Lame White Man's widow and her two girls. Little Chief's wife, their girl and their boy. My sister Crooked Nose, past twenty-one years old. A boy belonging to some other family. There were four women and five children. These were said to be in one group together, and all were captured by the soldiers. We were not sure, though, but some of them or all of them might have been wounded or killed.

The Cheyennes and the few Ogallalas now with us traveled far up Tongue river. We found plenty of buffalo there. We went on west to the upper Little Bighorn. After camping and hunting there, we went farther west to the Bighorn at the mouth of Rotten Grass creek. We did not stay here long. We returned to the Little Bighorn. Most of the last part of the winter was spent in camp on this valley. All of the time during the next few months we had good hunting. Soldiers did not trouble us nor we did not trouble them.

Almost the entire Northern Cheyenne tribe was in this winter camp on the upper Little Bighorn. Little

Wolf, Dull Knife, Dirty Moccasins and Old Bear, our four old men chiefs, were here. Charcoal Bear, the medicine chief, had kept possession of the sacred buffalo head through all of our distress. We had now as good a medicine lodge for it as we ordinarily had. This lodge was at its usual place at the back part of the space within our horseshoe camp circle. All of the people had good lodges. In every way we were living yet according to our customary habits. We were not bothering any white people. We did not want to see any of them. We felt we were on our own land. We had killed only such people as had come for driving us away from it. So, our hearts were clean from any feeling of guilt.

XII

Surrender of the Cheyennes.

Just before the grass began to show itself in the early part of the spring, two visitors arrived at our camp on the Little Bighorn. One of these was our captured old woman, Sweet Woman. The other was a half-breed Sioux we called White.* Each had a horse to ride and each was leading a pack horse. In their packs were tobacco and other things, for gifts to the principal chiefs. The visitors said they had been sent out from the soldier fort at the mouth of Tongue river, to invite us to come there and surrender peaceably. They brought a promise from Bear Coat,** the soldier chief there, that we should not be harmed and should be given plenty of food.

Sweet Woman told us all of the captives were well. She said they had been treated well, that they had a lodge for themselves and that Bear Coat had a soldier guard near their lodge at all times to keep other soldiers from bothering them. This Sweet Woman was a sister of White Bull's wife. She was a widow. Her husband had been dead many years. He had been

---

* Bruyere, a Frenchman-Sioux scout for Miles.
** The Cheyenne name for General Miles.

a black man, and the name for him was Black Man. As a boy he had been captured by the Cheyennes. She was a tall and thin woman, but she was healthy.

Our chiefs counciled about this proposal. It was decided quickly that we might as well go in that direction. The final decision could be made at some other place. We moved then eastward by camps and sleeps of one night each. We stopped one night at the mouth of Hanging Woman creek, where we had fought the soldiers in the middle of the winter before. Some other young men and I climbed up among the rocks where we had fought. We searched for Big Crow's body. We found it. It was lying with the back partly propped up against a bush in a thin group of small pines. The right hand was up and behind the head. The left hand was over the breast. We could not decide whether he had been dead when left there or had put himself into this position and had frozen to death. We stretched out the dead man and covered him with stones. His people felt better when we told them what we had done.

The half-breed Sioux traveled with us to Tongue river. Some of the chiefs decided to go with him to the soldier fort and find out what might happen to the Cheyennes if all should go there. They left us and went down the valley. The Cheyennes going on this journey of peacemaking were: Old Wolf and

Crazy Head, tribal big chiefs. Little Creek and Two Moons, little chiefs of the Crazy Dog and Fox warrior societies. White Bull, a medicine man but not a chief. The Elk warriors did not send any chief.

The tribe and the Ogallalas with us kept on moving eastward. At Powder river it was decided to wait for the return of the chiefs who had gone to the fort. The Ogallalas with us separated from us and traveled on. Most of them said they were going to the agency. A little band of them went down Powder river. All of the Cheyennes remained in tribal circle camp on the west side of Powder river, above the mouth of Little Powder river, only a short distance above the place where we had been burned out a year before this time.

The four chiefs came back to us at this Powder river camp. White Bull was not with them. They told us he had stayed with the soldiers, to scout for them in hunting for Indians. This news did not please us. As we looked at it, the surrendering to the soldiers was good if one felt like doing this. But an offer to help them to kill friends showed a bad heart.

I was affected more, though, by other news the chiefs brought. It was concerning my sister Crooked Nose, one of the captives. When the chiefs were only a part of the first day out in coming back from the fort, somebody followed them to tell them about her. She had been very sad in heart because of a belief she never again would see her people. She had felt better when the chiefs came, but when they went away again she fell into deep grief. Her sorrow was so great that she got out her hidden six-shooter I had given to her and shot herself dead. My heart almost stopped beating when I heard about her death in this way. She had been a good sister, kind to everybody.

Seven Cheyennes from the agency came to the camp on Powder river. They had one tepee lodge but no women were with them. They came only to tell us we ought to surrender at the agency. They said all of the Indians there were being fed well, were being treated well in every way. Nobody was being punished in any manner for past conduct in warfare against the soldiers. To my father and to most of the Cheyennes this sounded more attractive than the invitation to go to the Elk river fort.* Our people were better acquainted with conditions at the agency. Besides, the Ogallalas had the same agency with us, so these people also would be there. Our old men counciled about whether the tribe should surrender. And, if so, where they should go. It was decided to let every Cheyenne choose for himself.

* Fort Keogh, at the mouth of Tongue river.

Little Wolf and the other principal chiefs chose to go to the agency. Charcoal Bear, the medicine chief, said the sacred buffalo head and the medicine lodge should follow them. Their choice influenced the course of most of the tribe. My father said we ought to go with them. For two or three days, I believe, the chiefs and the people talked about the matter. Finally, the main body of the tribe set off toward the agency. A smaller part of it determined to go to the Elk river soldier fort. These were convinced by Two Moons and White Bull's relatives that they would receive better treatment there.

But not all of the Cheyennes were ready yet to surrender at any place. Fourteen or fifteen men, six or seven of them having wives and children, separated off to go westward. White Hawk, a little chief of the Elk warriors, was with them. They said they were going to join the Minneconjoux Sioux, who then were in camp on Rosebud creek or on a branch of it that afterward was called Lame Deer creek. The principal chief of these Minneconjoux Sioux was Lame Deer.

I joined another band still desiring most the freedom we considered to be ours by right. Thirty-four Cheyennes made up this band. Last Bull, leading chief of the Fox warrior society, was the big man of our party. His warrior followers at this time were from all three of the societies. The people making up this group of further hunters were these:

Last Bull, his wife and two daughters.

Many-Colored Braids, his wife, two daughters and a son.

Little Horse, his wife, two daughters and a son.

Black Coyote, his wife and small daughter.

Dog Growing Up, his wife and one small boy.

Fire Wolf, Yellow Eagle, Spotted Wolf, Chief Going Up a Hill, White Bird, Buffalo Paunch, Big Nose, Meat, Medicine Wolf, Horse Road, Little Shield, Yellow Horse, my brother Yellow Hair and myself Wooden Leg. All of these were unmarried young men.

Five tepee lodges were taken along and set up at each camping place, by the wives of the five married men. The unmarried young men slept mostly unsheltered, or at each camping they made for themselves little willow or tree branch lodges. They did their own cooking, most of the time, but often some young man would give a part of his meat to some woman as payment to her for cooking his meat for him. I dwelt all the time in the lodge of Last Bull, as a member of his family. He felt very friendly to me because of my having helped his wife and children at the time the soldiers came to the Cheyenne camp the year before, on Powder river.

Every man in this band had a good gun of some kind. I had my rifle taken from the soldier. I had not used up much of the ammunition I had found on the battle grounds at that time and afterward. I did not do any more shooting than was necessary in getting plenty of meat. I was saving my cartridges for fighting whatever soldiers might come.

We traveled and hunted all about the country on the upper Powder river and the upper Tongue river. We had to be moving often, because game was not plentiful. Every day scouts were out trying to locate buffalo. All of the time they were on the lookout too for soldiers or for Crows or Shoshones. We were not loafing idly. We were working and earning our living.

A baby boy was born to the wife of Black Coyote at one of the camps. The wife of Many-Colored Braids took care of her, as medicine woman. As we moved from place to place, the young woman and her baby were put into a travois bed. The other women helped in taking down and setting up her lodge. Her personal name was Calf Road. She was specially famous because she had fought as a warrior with her husband Black Coyote at the battle with the soldiers on the upper Rosebud. Now there were thirty-five people in our band.

I was sent alone from this band one time to scout

301

for buffalo. I took with me a pack horse to bring back whatever meat I might get. I had on the led horse a soldier pack saddle belonging to Last Bull. I stayed out three sleeps. I saw a few deer and antelope but no buffalo.

We were having a good many days of hunger. Our horses had plenty of grass, but our own ribs were becoming thin. Our clothing was wearing out, and we could not get enough of skins to renew them and to keep our beds and our lodges in good order. My soldier coat and breeches were gone, and my last shirt and cloth breeches were almost in tatters. The only good article of wear I had now was my big white hat I had captured at the Rosebud battle.

A Cheyenne named Yellow Eagle added himself to us. He had been at the agency not long before. We decided to have him and White Bird go there together and spy out the conditions. They went. In a week or so they were back among us.

"Good treatment, plenty of food, blankets, everything, nobody punished," they reported.

We started right away for the agency. But not all of us yet were ready to go there. Medicine Wolf, Growing Dog, Meat and my brother Yellow Hair said they were going to stay out hunting. They said it would not be long before lots of Indians would be back out here, the same as had been here during the

302

year before. I was almost persuaded to remain with them, but Last Bull said he now was convinced the Indians would not come back to this country. So I kept with the main part of our band. We traveled southeastward toward the White River agency of the Cheyennes and the Ogallalas.

At a white man house far along our way we stopped to see if the people there might give us some food. The only people there were two white men. They acted as if they were badly frightened, but we made peace signs to them, and only two of us went to their door. We made signs that our Indians all were very hungry, and we asked them for something to eat. They gave us a little beef meat and some sugar and coffee. We were glad to get this, and we told them our hearts were good toward them.

Three strange Indians on horseback approached us from our front as we arrived about a day's journey from the agency. We could see they were Indians, but they had on soldier clothing. This alarmed us. All of our men cocked their guns and went out in front of the women and children. We watched and waited. The three Indians stopped. At a distance they made signs to us. They told us they were soldier scouts come out to help us find our way to the agency. We allowed them to join us and remain with us the remainder of the way. One of them was a

Cheyenne, another was a Sioux, the third was a Cheyenne-Sioux named Fire Crow.

It made all of us feel good to see the hundreds of Indian lodges as we came near to the agency.* We galloped our horses forward. We cheered and fired gunshots into the air. Some soldiers came running out from their tents, but they soon saw we were friendly and were only celebrating and notifying our people we had come. We saw great camps of Arapahoes and Ogallalas as well as the tribal camp circle of our own Cheyennes. Many soldiers also were there, in their own separate camp. Several of the soldier chiefs came and shook hands with our men and said, "How." One of these soldier chiefs we specially liked. We learned from a Cheyenne his name among the Indians was White Hat.** He could make good signtalk. It appeared he understood Indians better than any white man soldier I ever had seen. I suppose that was why we liked him.

A white man married to a Cheyenne woman was acting as interpreter for the soldiers. His name was Rowland. But White Hat did not need any interpreter in talking to us, he could make the signtalk so well. After the general handshaking, White Hat said:

* White River agency, Fort Robinson, Nebraska.
** Lieutenant W. P. Clark, who wrote a book on sign language.

"Now, you men must give to me your guns and your horses."

We were not expecting this, but we trusted him, so we began to do as he had asked. But Black Coyote jumped back and said he would not give up his gun. He cocked it and stood there. He was much excited. Just then three Sioux dressed in soldier clothing came riding toward us. Black Coyote aimed his gun at them. Last Bull pushed the gun aside and said:

"Don't shoot. You are crazy."

He talked to Black Coyote, telling him that a shot just now might cause all of us to get killed. White Hat motioned the three Sioux to go away, and they did so. Black Coyote then quieted down. He gave his gun to Last Bull, and this leader gave it to a soldier with White Hat. I was the only one among us having a gun captured from the soldiers at the battle on the Little Bighorn. When I handed it to a soldier he gave it to White Hat. White Hat examined it with apparent great interest. He then called other soldier chiefs to look. Finally he asked me:

"Where did you get this gun?"

I did not answer him at once. He asked me again, making signs so clear that I could not help but make some kind of answer. I told him the truth. I showed him just how I had seized it and wrenched it away from a soldier riding toward the river during the first

part of the great battle a year before this time. The
way they talked about it, it appeared the Indians had
not been giving them these guns taken from the soldiers. After a little while, White Hat shook hands
again with me and made signs to me: "You are a
brave man. Do not be afraid any soldier will want to
kill you."

The next morning all of us went to the agency
buildings for gifts we had been told would be there
for us. Wagons came with the presents. They were
unloaded in piles. Blankets, clothing and different
kinds of food were in the piles. Two of our people
were appointed to divide up and distribute the articles
among all of us. Our hearts now were glad. It
seemed good to be here with plenty and not be in
fear of soldiers.

I received other gifts. An Ogallala Sioux presented me with a medicine pipe, the first one I had
owned since the loss of mine when the soldiers burned
out our forty lodges on lower Powder river. A Cheyenne young man gave me a wad of paper money like
I had seen at the time of the great battle. He said:
"You can buy things at the trader's store with this
paper." I put it into my pocket. After a while I
got a Sioux young man friend to go with me to the
agency trader's store. I took out my money and

gave it all to the trader. He counted it over and over.
Then he asked me, in Sioux speech:
"Where did you get all of this money?"
My Sioux friend quickly answered:
"He got it from Custer."
The trader said to me:
"The soldiers are going to hang you." This
startled me at first, but both he and my Sioux friend
laughed, so I knew he was only joking.
"Now, what all do you want?" the trader asked,
after they had joked me a little while.
I got first a red and yellow shirt. Then I got some
breeches that fitted me much better than the pair
that had been given to me by the agency people. I
picked out a fine red blanket, a hat and a big silk
scarf. I got plenty of tobacco. I bought coffee,
sugar, meat and other things. I did not want all of
the goods I bought, but the trader kept telling me of
what I ought to have. After each time he brought me
what I asked for, he took from the money some part
of it. Then he would ask:
"And what else?"
I did not know how much the different articles were
worth. I kept on choosing some other until finally
the trader said:
"Your money is all gone."
My friend helped me to carry all of my property to

my home lodge. I wore the new hat just bought. But I took along the old white hat I had captured from the soldiers. I gave this old one to my father. He was much pleased to get it. It was the first white man hat he ever owned. He threw away then the old Indian buffalo hat he had been wearing.

Some of the Cheyennes who had gone to the Elk river soldier fort were here now. They had been sent here by the soldiers. Other Cheyennes had stayed at that fort, the men joining the soldiers as scouts for them. All of these Cheyennes brought here were dwelling in soldier tents. Many other Indians, Cheyennes, Ogallalas and Arapahoes, also had the soldier tents. These were larger than most of the Indian tepees then in use. The tepees were smaller than usual because only a few buffalo skins had been taken during this summer.

There was some dissatisfaction among the Cheyennes on account of talk of them being taken to the South. The agent and the soldier chiefs had said we ought to go there and be joined as one tribe with the Southern Cheyennes. Our people did not like this talk. All of us wanted to stay in this country near the Black Hills. But we had one big chief, Standing Elk, who kept saying it would be better if we should go there. I think there were not as many as ten Cheyennes in our whole tribe who agreed with him.

There was a feeling that he was talking this way only to make himself a big Indian among the white people. The white men chiefs would not talk much to any Cheyenne chief but him. They gave him extra presents and treated him as if he were the only chief in the tribe, when he was but one of our forty tribal big chiefs. One day he went about telling everybody:

"All get ready to move. The soldiers are going to take us from here tomorrow."

Lots of Cheyennes were angry. We had understood that when we surrendered we were to live on our same White River reservation. We had given up our guns and our horses and had quit fighting because of this promise. Now, after we had put ourselves at this great disadvantage, the promise was to be broken. But we could not do anything except obey him. So, three sleeps after my small band had come to what we thought was to be our home, the whole tribe was on its way to what we now call Oklahoma.

XIII

Taken to the South.

The soldier leader of our movement to the South was known to us as Tall White Man. He was a good man, always kind to the Indians. We had to do whatever he said we must do, but he talked good to our chiefs, so all of us were pleased to have him guiding us. He had with him a band of soldiers. I do not know how many, but I think there may have been almost a hundred of them.

Our horses that had been taken away from us at the agency were now returned to us. Still, many Cheyennes did not own any. Old people who had no animal to ride were provided with them from the soldier herd. Or, very old or sick people were allowed to ride in the soldier wagons. Young men who owned no horses had to walk or borrow from friends. I owned four. I had three of them loaned out most of the time.

Soldier tents were used by the Indians as well as by the soldiers. I think the Indians had a few canvas cone tepees, but I do not remember seeing among us any buffalo skin lodges. We had not killed for a long time enough buffaloes to renew the old dwelling

310

shelters we liked so well. Wagons were used to haul the tents. Other wagons were loaded with bread, crackers, coffee, sugar and other food. Every day, rations were issued to all of the soldiers and all of the Indians.*

A drove of cattle was kept moving along behind us. Some of them were butchered every day for meat. This was good, but the Indians liked better the wild meat when it could be found. Our chiefs talked to Tall White Man about this. He listened to their talk. He said it was good. He told them how it would be arranged for some of the Indians to hunt along the way.

Thirty men, ten from each of the three warrior societies, were chosen by our warrior chiefs to do the hunting. Each of these thirty was given a rifle. At every time of hunting, each of them was allowed to have five cartridges for his gun. Other Indians were allowed also to hunt, but they had to use the bows and arrows or whatever else they might have for use. A few took out guns they had kept hidden when we had surrendered at the agency, but they had to be sly about this so the soldiers would not find out about them.

We traveled slowly and camped often, so there

---

* The movement to the South began in early May, 1877. Seventy days were spent in the journey.—T. B. M.

was plenty of time for hunting at distances from the moving people. The soldiers went always ahead. The Indians followed them. The wagons came behind the Indians. The drove of cattle were last. We kept mostly along the old trails of the Cheyennes as they had gone back and forth between the Black Hills and the South. These were across the high lands at the headwaters of the rivers. Not yet were many white people living here.

Buffalo and antelope were plentiful. There were a few deer, but no elk. I rode out at times with the hunters, but I had neither gun nor bow and arrows. I could do nothing but look on and wish I could do some killing. I knew of one certain Cheyenne who had a rifle hidden. One night in camp I said to him:

"I see every day lots of antelope. Let me take your gun tomorrow."

I killed a buffalo the next day with his gun. I killed also two antelope. I gave him half of the meat. Both of us had plenty to distribute among our friends. The soldiers never knew anything about it. Or, none of them said anything to me.

Soldiers hunted with the Indians. All of the soldiers were friendly and good to us. They were good shooters and they killed lots of game. They gave us most of the meat. I became specially friendly with two or three of them. I liked to be with them, and they appeared to like me. I went at times to their camp in the evening and visited with them. When we were about half along our journey I asked one of them:

"Let me take your gun tomorrow."

"Yes, you may take it," he told me.

He let me have five cartridges when I got the gun the next morning. Oh, how good I felt—on horseback, having a good rifle, and after buffalo! I killed one and brought in the best parts of its meat. I gave the soldier his choice of it and all he wanted, when I returned his gun that night in camp.

Either a rifle or a six shooter was loaned to me for a day at other later times. Each time, with the rifle came five cartridges. Each time, with the six shooter came six loads for it. Each time, I returned the borrowed gun at the night camp and gave the friendly soldier whatever meat he might want. Most of them did not want much of it, so I had at all times plenty of the food we liked most, for our family group and for our friends who might need it.

We camped near one certain big town far along on our journey. None of us were allowed to go into the town, but I went walking all about the outside of it to look at it. As I walked I found a big piece of wood that I wanted. I had seen at past times this same kind of wood, and I knew its usefulness to us.

313

It was the heavy piece that lays across the necks of cattle when they draw a wagon. The Indians liked to get these, because they made the best kind of bows and arrows. I picked it up and lifted it over a shoulder   I went right away to my home tent lodge.

I made a good bow. My mother had in her packs some dried sinew from buffalo back tendons. This I used to string my bow. I made then ten arrows. I got here and there some pieces of metal for the points. My mother made a pouch for the bow and arrows. She made it of a calfskin she had tanned as we were moving. I was glad now, with the full pouch slung from my shoulder and dangling at my left side. Two days I spent most of our camping time at this work.

On the first day out with my new bow and arrows I killed a buffalo. I could have killed more, but I did not want any more. There were not so many of them here as we had found farther north, but we still were finding a few. There were yet plenty of antelope feeding out on the rolling hills and level lands. An antelope, though, is hard to hit with arrows. It can run fast and can dodge quickly. Still, if one be chased a long time it becomes tired. Any ordinary horse then can catch up with it. It is easy enough then to shoot arrows into its body. One arrow often is enough to kill it. I killed several of them, as many

314

as I wanted to kill, while we were going on our way. I killed also a few more buffalo.

One sleep before we got to the Southern Cheyenne agency we had some special doings. The agent there came out to see us. He had with him a half-breed Cheyenne as interpreter. They went to every tent of the Indians. At each place the interpreter asked the names and he wrote them on paper. We were in camp beside a soldier fort. That evening I saw some of the soldiers there trying to rope loose horses. I went to them and asked them to let me try it. They did. I could loop the lariat noose over a running horse almost every time I tried. The soldiers cheered. They were very friendly to me.

The thirty Cheyennes who had been allowed to have soldier guns for hunting were told now they must give back these guns. But Little Wolf and Standing Elk talked to Tall White Man about this. They said: "Let us keep these guns for hunting, or we might need them for protecting ourselves." But the good soldier chief replied: "No, I cannot do that. They must be returned to us." Others of our chiefs joined Little Wolf and Standing Elk. Tall White Man sat in a long council with them. Finally, he agreed:

"Yes, the Cheyennes may keep the few guns they have."

I learned in the South the white man name of Long Hair, the soldier big chief we had killed on the Little Bighorn. I was told he was called General Custer. I had heard this name spoken at the White River agency, but I did not understand clearly who was meant by it. The Southern Cheyennes knew of him because of his having fought against them before he had come into our northern country. They had surrendered to him.

A few of our Northern Cheyennes had not yet joined us before we left the White River agency, at the North. Or, some of these fled from us as soon as it was decided we must go to the South. My brother Yellow Hair had not yet come in to surrender. He stayed hunting or he went to the Ogallalas. Not long after we became settled in the new home the news came to us that he had been killed. He was hunting on Crow creek, a stream flowing into the east side of upper Tongue river, when some white men not soldiers shot him. Our family now was made up of my father and mother, myself, my younger sister and the small boy brother.

My first shoes were given to me at the southern agency. They were too big, but I wore them a part of the time. All of my life before this, I had worn only the moccasins made by Indians. I yet liked best the moccasins, but we did not have skins enough to make all of them we needed.

I did some hunting in the southern country. But the hunting was not for the large food game animals. Very few of these got on the reservation, and we were not allowed to go off the reservation for hunting. So, my searching for something to shoot at with bow and arrows or with gun was for whatever small game could be found there.

On one certain bow and arrow hunt I was afoot and alone. The weather was hot. I was tired and sweating. I went to the shade of two big trees. As I rested there, a fluttering noise attracted my attention to the tops of two trees. I looked. There sat an eagle perched high up. I aimed an arrow and shot. No harm done. I drew out another arrow and fitted it to my bowstring. I aimed more carefully this time. In a moment after the second shot, the eagle fluttered and tumbled to the ground out a little distance from the trees. I ran out there. The big bird flopped and hobbled along away from me. Before I could get hold of it the eagle had lifted itself into the air. It flew on and up, farther and higher. I watched it until it was gone entirely from my view.

I learned how to hunt specially for eagles. Their

317

regular sleeping places were at the tops of big trees. I would go out on horseback and locate myself under a big tree just as darkness was about to come. One night I sat under a tree waiting. I had both a rifle and a six shooter. Two eagles came. I shot and killed one with the rifle. I jerked out the six shooter and fired at the other one. It too tumbled down dead. That was good shooting, considering that the light was dim. But always in shooting eagles at night the dark body against the sky made a good enough target.

On another eagle hunt at night, when I shot up into the tree the eagle fell to the ground wounded but not dead. It lay there moving about a little but not much. I ran to it and seized it, to hold it while I might beat it with the handle of my pony whip. It grasped in its two taloned feet my left forearm and my right thigh just above the knee. I struck it with the whip handle, but this only made it sink the talons in more deeply. I had to pry them loose. Then I beat it to death. I still own and make regular use of a fan made from a wing of that eagle.

I shot one certain eagle in a tree above my head one night. Right after I fired the shot it tumbled. But it did not fall to the ground. I looked up among the branches, but I could not see it. I began to look about me on the ground. Just then a heavy thump

318

on top of my head almost knocked me down. The eagle had lodged somewhere and then had fallen. It seized my hat in its talons and bounced off my head to the ground. There I killed it with my six shooter.

One night, as I stood watching under a tree I saw something moving along on a branch high up. It did not appear to be an eagle, but when it stopped on the branch I aimed my rifle and fired. It dropped straight down and plumped hard upon the ground. It was dead. It was to me a strange animal. It looked somewhat like the badgers of the northern country, except this animal I had killed was smaller. I remembered, too, that badgers do not live in trees. When I took it to the home lodge I found out what it was. The white people call this kind of animal a coon. I afterward saw others. I saw also what the white people call possums. We ate these little animals when we could get them.

The tallest Indian I ever saw was a Southern Cheyenne young woman. I first saw her at one of our Omaha dances. I stood beside her, for measurement. The top of my head came just above the level of her shoulders. She was extremely slender and she stood up straight, not stooping. Her name was Slit Eyes. I did not see her father, but I saw her mother. The mother was a short woman. This very tall young

319

woman died when she was about twenty years old.

After we had been a year on this reservation, many of our people began to ask to be taken back to the North. There was no game here, we were not allowed to go off the reservation for hunting, and we were not given food as it had been promised we should be given. At times, some of our young men would violate the orders and would slip away from the reservation to get a buffalo or some other animal good to eat. Some white people said the Indians were killing their cattle. I do not know. I did not do this. I stayed all the time on the reservation. But if any Indians did kill the white men cattle they did so because they were very hungry and could not find any wild game. We ate the beef because it was the best we could get. We always liked better the wild game.

There was much sickness among the Northern Cheyennes. To us it was a new kind of sickness. Chills and fever and aching of the bones dragged down most of us to thin and weak bodies. Our people died, died, died, kept following one another out of this world. Finally, Chief Little Wolf declared that he for one was going to move back North, whether the white people consented or not. Others said they would follow him. The agent told them that soldiers would go on their trail and would kill them. They were promised more food. They waited for it, but it did not come. More people flocked to Little Wolf's side. Dull Knife said he too would go. Late in the summer, more than half of the tribe started out. Little Wolf's last message to the agent was:

"The soldiers may kill all of us, but they cannot make us stay in this country."

Soldiers went after them. Other soldiers from other places were sent out to head them off. The Cheyennes were hunted from all directions. They were found many times, but each time the Cheyennes fought off their pursuers and kept on going northward. Many of our people were killed, but the most of them got back to their old home country and were allowed to stay there.

My father and I considered joining Little Wolf. But we had managed in one way and another to keep our family from starving, and we believed that after a while the food would be more plentiful. Some of us had been sick at times, but none of us yet had come near to death. We sympathized fully with our deceived and suffering people, and both of us had a high admiration for Little Wolf. But we settled our minds to stay here and keep out of trouble.

From the Southern Cheyennes I learned a great deal about General Custer's dealing with them in that country. All of them said he had smoked the peace pipe with them at the time they had surrendered to him, seven years before he was killed. According to the custom among us, this was understood as a promise by him that never again would he fight against the Cheyennes. When they learned that he had been killed by our people and the Sioux, they considered him as having deserved that kind of death, on account of his failure to keep his peace pipe oath.

They told us also about the band of Southern Cheyennes who started out for the North, to join us, during the summer when we fought the great battle. Their medicine man chief was with the band, and he had the tribal medicine arrows and its tepee with him. Soldiers got after them. The medicine man chief and his wife separated themselves in the scattering flight from the soldiers, each of the two taking two of the four sacred àrrows. After a few days the band all got together again, on upper Powder river. But there were so many soldiers in the country that they decided to go back to the South.

An assemblage of army officers asked me to tell them about the Custer battle. When they sent for me my heart said thump—thump—thump. I was afraid they might hang me. I went, but I told only a little. They asked for more talk. They assured me their hearts were good toward me. They gave me lots of money, about five dollars, I believe. Good! My heart quit thumping. I told them all they asked, answering many questions. Some things I kept to myself, but all that I told them was true.

I got a wife from the Southern Cheyennes. She was my same age, twenty years old. All of my people and all of her people appeared to be pleased at our marriage. They gave us presents and we set up our own lodge. She had been a girl in the Cheyenne camp at the Washita river when Custer and his soldiers came there and killed many Cheyennes and burned their lodges (November, 1868). Chief Black Pot was one of the killed.

The women and children fled, the same as ours had done at the Powder river. It was winter, and there was at that time a deep snow for that country. Soldiers chased the women and children and killed many of them as well as the men. My wife, at that time a girl, was barefooted, as others also were. They had been surprised early in the morning. She stopped and cut off pieces of buffalo robe to tie about her feet, to keep them warm as she ran. They went to a camp of Snake Indians (Comanches), farther down the river.

My wife told me she also was with the Cheyennes when they surrendered to General Custer (1869) after he had smoked the pipe with their chiefs. When

323

they surrendered, some of the chiefs were put into prison and had chains put upon their ankles. When I heard all of this from my wife, as well from many others of the Southern Cheyennes, it seemed the Great Medicine may have directed Custer to his death, as a punishment for having broken his promise to the Cheyennes.

When I had been six years in the South, the Northern Cheyennes were told they might go back now to their old country. The Little Wolf people had been given lands on the Rosebud and Tongue rivers. We could go to them or back to the White river, where the agency had become known as Pine Ridge.

My father had died while we were in the land of the southern Indians. My wife and myself, my mother and her two remaining children all agreed we would move. A few of our tribal people decided to remain as members of the Southern Cheyenne tribe. We who left them went first to Pine Ridge. After not a very long stay there we were located in a region I always liked, the Tongue river country in Montana.

XIV

Home Again on Tongue River.

Many changes had taken place in the affairs of
our tribe when I got back among the principal body
of them in Montana. Most of the men who had
surrendered at Fort Keogh went into service there
as scouts for the soldiers of General Miles, whose
Indian name was Bear Coat. They had many stories
to tell of these experiences. They helped in finding
and in fighting some bands of our old friends the
Sioux, who remained hunting through the country
after we had gone from it. I did not like to hear
these stories. I could not help but think these tribesmen of mine had done wrong in this kind of warfare. That was the way the Pawnees, Crows and
Shoshones had done in past times, and we had been
enemies to them because of their having done so.
There came into my heart thoughts that possibly the
death of my own brother Yellow Hair had been
brought about by reason of some Cheyenne having
guided the white men who killed him.

The Nez Perces had come through the country
soon after the part of our tribe had surrendered at
the Elk river fort. The Cheyennes went with the

soldiers to fight these other Indians. They had a battle far to the northward. Most of the Cheyennes were not in special danger during this battle, but two of them were said to have been very brave. These two were White Wolf and All See Him. White Wolf received a bullet wound across his scalp. He was stunned and he fell, but he was not killed. A Sioux scout dragged him into safety. The white soldiers gave money to the Sioux for his action. This was the same White Wolf who shot himself through the left thigh at our battle with the soldiers on the Rosebud and had to lie in his bed while his companion warriors fought the soldiers of Custer. All See Him had been a brave man in the Custer battle. He has another name, John Bighead Man. White Wolf also got another name after the Nez Perces bullet had hit him. His new name was Shot in the Head.

Two Moons and White Moon were two Cheyenne scouts of that time who were not in the Nez Perces fight. They were out with some Cheyennes chasing buffalo as the soldier and Indian army traveled in their hunt for the Nez Perces. In the course of the chase Two Moons accidentally shot White Moon through the body. White Moon was entirely disabled, and Two Moons did not feel then like fighting anybody. He helped in taking care of White

Moon, and he paid the Indian doctor a horse for curing him.

People told me all about the journey of Little Wolf's band from the South, with the soldiers after them all along the way. They had come to Fort Keogh and had surrendered to General Miles. Many of their men also enlisted as scouts. The Cheyennes at this place stayed a part of the time about the fort and a part of the time were allowed to live on the Rosebud and the Tongue rivers, near the fort. These combined Fort Keogh Cheyennes had been the beginning of our Tongue River reservation.

The Little Wolf people had some trouble among themselves on their way from the southern country. One case was where a man who had become angered to craziness about something went at beating his whole family. He clubbed every one of them he could reach. All of them were put into an insane fright. An adult daughter, screaming and struggling to get away from him, stabbed him with her sheathknife. He let loose of her, walked away staggering, and soon fell dead. The young woman was in great grief because of her having killed her own father. The chiefs and all of the people sympathized with her. She was not punished. That was the only case I ever knew of a Cheyenne woman having killed anyone.

Black Coyote was the cause of one big trouble. He was the same man of our little band who was about to shoot when we were giving up our guns at the time of our surrender at the White River agency. At a camp east of Powder river, during the last part of this flight with the Little Wolf people, an old chief said to him:

"Black Coyote, you have been riding during all of the journey. Many women are walking. You should let some one of them have your horse."

"No, it is my horse, and I want to ride," Black Coyote answered.

"But some of the women are old, and they are very tired," the chief persisted.

"It is my horse, and I intend to ride it," the young man stubbornly responded.

"Black Coyote, you are crazy."

"No. You are the crazy one."

The chief flourished his pony whip and lashed Black Coyote. He laid on stroke after stroke, many of them. The humiliated man humped his body and stubbornly hugged his rifle. He was sitting in front of his lodge. Suddenly he jumped up and ran away. A short distance off he turned and fired at the chief. The old man fell dead.

Black Coyote ran on out of the camp. Some Cheyennes shot at him, but he was not injured. He kept on going, and he never returned. His wife at once gathered a few of their belongings and followed out to join him. Her two children and an old woman went with her. Whetstone, another Cheyenne man, also left the camp and stayed away with the outcast people.

The two men went, just after dark one night, to a camp on Powder river, where were a few soldiers having a Sergeant with them. The Indians said, "How," and approached the campfire in a friendly way. The soldiers were fearful and were on the lookout, but they replied, "How." After the Indians had warmed themselves a little, Black Coyote said:

"Give us some bread."

"How," the Sergeant answered, and he gave them bread.

As the two walked away, for some reason Black Coyote jerked up his rifle and killed the Sergeant. Then they rushed off into the darkness.

The soldiers took the body of their Sergeant and went to Fort Keogh. Soldiers and Cheyennes from there went out to search for the bad Indians. They captured them and brought them to the fort. The two men were put into jail with chains upon their ankles. A soldier chief known to the Cheyennes as Little Chief talked to them:

"Did you kill the Sergeant?" he asked them.

329

"No," they answered him.

The next day Little Chief again asked them: "Did you kill the Sergeant?" Still they said: "No." After a few days, Black Coyote said: "Yes, I killed him."

Both of the men were hanged. I was told their bodies were not taken by the Cheyennes, but were buried by the white people. The hanging was at Miles City, I believe.

Black Coyote's wife, the woman warrior at the Rosebud battle, died while he was in jail. Cheyennes made signs to him from a distance, through the jail windows, and told him she was sick. Every day he asked: "How is my wife today?" She was dying, but to cheer him they told him, "She is better now." When finally somebody told him she was dead, he went entirely crazy. He would take no food, and he fought every white man who came to him. He had to be beaten and tied first when they went to hang him. His relatives said it was her death that caused him to say he had killed the Sergeant. They say the Sergeant and the soldiers were trying to kill him at the time. But I know that Black Coyote was a very excitable man. Bad Indians like him made lots of trouble for the whole tribe.

The most sorrowful new condition we found in

coming back to our Cheyenne country was in the case of Little Wolf himself. Some white men about the fort were selling or giving whisky to the Indians. One night, Little Wolf got a bottle of whisky and right away he drank all of it. He went into the fort trader's store and leaned forward upon the counter. He was quiet, but he was dizzy and stumbling here and there. The trader said: "Little Wolf, you had better go to your lodge." But he said: "No, I want to stay here."

Some Cheyenne men and women were playing cards at a table in the store. Famished Elk, a young man Sergeant of the scouts, was with them. He talked to Little Wolf. But the old chief paid no attention to his talk. Famished Elk took hold of Little Wolf's arm and said: "Come, I will help you to get to your lodge." He spoke and acted respectfully, but Little Wolf was angered because of the taking hold of him. He pulled himself away. His eyes blazed like fire. He stood a moment looking at the young man. Then he said:

"I will kill you."

He staggered on alone out from the store. Famished Elk returned to sit in the card game. Nobody was expecting any further trouble. But not long afterward the door was opened and Little Wolf stum-

331

bled into the room. He straightened himself, leveled a rifle and fired. Famished Elk sank down dead upon the floor.

The old chief went back to his lodge and told his two wives what he had done. "We must go," he added. The three of them went out into the darkness of the night. Soldiers and Cheyennes searched for them. They searched during the next day and the next. The missing man and his two wives appeared in Miles City and sat themselves down at a place in plain view of the people there. A Captain and some soldiers went to him. This Captain we knew as Little Chief. He told Little Wolf what it was said he had done. He further told him:

"You are no more chief of the Cheyennes."

"That is true and just," Little Wolf agreed.

All of the Cheyennes said: "How. It is right. Little Wolf shall be not any more a chief among us." But their hearts were sad, not angry, when they said this. He was not punished in any other way. But he further punished himself. Before he and his wives had left their lodge he smashed into pieces his medicine pipe. Our old tribal laws required this. It was allowable for him afterward to smoke alone any small and short-stemmed pipe, such as might be made from a deer leg bone. But he did not do this. He denied himself all smoking. He never made any offer even to sit in the company of other Cheyennes smoking together. White men sometimes offered him cigarettes, but he always refused them. After a time he learned to chew tobacco, a habit never followed by the old-time Cheyennes. It seemed he did this deliberately, for self-humiliation. He never tried to intrude himself into any tribal public affairs. The people remembered his great services in past times. But nobody consulted him on tribal matters in present times. Truly, in every way he never more was chief among the Cheyennes.

Some Cheyennes who had run away or who could not be found, when we had been told we must go to the South, joined other tribes. Of these, some stayed away, others finally came back to us. Two of them came back to us on Tongue river. One was Joseph Tall White Man. He had dodged from the southern movement by escaping and joining the Blackfeet Sioux. The other was Little Crow. He had joined some tribe of the Sioux.

When I was thirty-one years old (1889) I enlisted with other Cheyennes to form a new band of scouts for the soldiers at Fort Keogh. For a long time we did not do much except to drill and work at getting out logs from the timber and building houses for ourselves. The soldier officers bought horses for us to ride. All of the new horses were wild. We had to break them. I got bucked off at times. But finally, all of us had horses that would not buck.

I learned to drink whisky at Fort Keogh. The trader at the fort sold whisky and beer to the soldiers, but he was not allowed to sell anything of this kind to the Indians. That made only a little difference. White men not soldiers would get whisky for us whenever we had money to give to them. They may have bought it at the fort trader's store or it may have come from Miles City. I spent most of my scout pay for whisky. I never got into any trouble for being drunk, but sometimes an Indian did get into trouble.

Tall Bull and some other scouts got drunk and went at night to where some soldiers were sleeping. The Cheyennes pointed their six-shooters at the soldiers and said: "Give us blankets." The soldiers were scared, so blankets were given the Indians. A Sergeant went to tell the officers. A Lieutenant officer came back with him. But the Lieutenant was as drunk as were the Indians. He went away without doing anything about the matter.

We had plenty to eat at the fort. A soldier named Jules Chaudel was the cook for our thirty Cheyennes. A part of my work was to haul water in barrels for him. I never got so drunk that I forgot to keep the barrels filled. He often gave me meat when it was not time for the Indians to eat.

All of the scouts went for making war the next year after I enlisted. We were taken to Pine Ridge reservation. We were told the Sioux were going to fight against the Cheyennes in that country, so we were willing to help our own people. Our scouts were led by an officer we knew as Big Red Nose.* Willis Rowland, the half-Cheyenne, was our Sergeant. Soldiers from some other fort came to Fort Keogh and went with us to Pine Ridge.

When we got to Pine Ridge we learned that it was mostly the other Sioux tribes, not the Ogallalas, who were wanting to fight against the white people. The Cheyennes living there did not want any trouble, so the bad Sioux were angered also at the Cheyennes. Some Ogallalas joined the bad Indians. Our Cheyenne relatives had their lodges torn down and burned. Big Foot was the principal chief of the Sioux making the trouble. We knew him, and we were sorry at having to fight against him, but we were willing to be on the side of the whites and our own Cheyennes.

We Cheyenne scouts did not get into any battle. At one time we were all dressed and ready, but the officers made us stop behind a hill while the soldiers

* Lieutenant Casey.

335

went on and killed many Sioux at a camp on a little valley just over the hill. A Sioux started that fight by killing an officer who was taking all guns from them. The soldiers then began to shoot, and many women and children as well as men were killed. This trouble was on Wounded Knee creek. At the time of our advance up the hill I was wearing a warbonnet for the first time at any battle.

Big Red Nose, our officer, was killed by a Sioux before this fight. White Moon and Rock Roads, two of our scouts, were out riding somewhere with him. They saw four or five Sioux coming on horseback. The Sioux were riding slowly, and it appeared they did not intend any harm. But while Big Red Nose had his head turned in another direction one of the Sioux fired his rifle. The bullet went through the head of the officer, from back to front, and he fell dead from his horse. The two Cheyennes whipped their horses and got away. The Sioux scalped Big Red Nose and took all of his clothing.

As the Wounded Knee fight was going on, the Sioux fled in all directions. The soldier officer now leading us was White Hat. He sent me out to a little hilltop to watch where the people running away might go. I saw one Sioux man ride to a big house. He limped when he got off and walked into the house. I told White Hat about him. After a while he got some soldiers, and all of us went to the place. From a distance, I called out in Sioux language for all people in the house to come out and surrender. Nobody came out. We went close to the door. I called to ask how many people were in there. A man's voice answered me that there were three of them. I told him they must come out, but he did not answer me. White Hat knocked on the door. He knocked a second time and a third time. Then he and the soldiers smashed the door and went into the house. I followed them.

A Sioux man was lying on a floor bed. A boy was lying on another floor bed. A woman was sitting beside the boy. The man had a sheet covering all of him but his head and neck. I did not know what else might be under the sheet, but I said:

"You must give up your gun. You will be treated kindly."

He at once drew a rifle out from under the sheet and handed it to me. We learned that he had bullet holes through both legs, but no bones were broken. The boy had been shot through the left arm. The woman was not injured. The soldiers got a wagon and took them to the agency. A soldier doctor there took care of them.

The troublesome Sioux were gathered out in what the Indians knew as the Bad Lands. It was a very rough country having no trees and not much grass. The Cheyennes went out with soldiers and camped between the agency and that country. We kept watching to try to find out how many were there and how many were going there or coming back to the reservation. It was winter, and the wind blows hard there much of the time. We had some cold rides.

One night our officer gave me a writing on paper and told me to take it to the agency. He had the interpreter explain to me which officer there was to receive it. The air was full of whirling snow. The gusts of wind appeared to come from everywhere except behind me. I wrapped my blanket tightly about me and kept my body humped up as my horse moved along the trail. At first I was not afraid, as it seemed the night was too stormy for any Sioux to be traveling. Then I began thinking that perhaps the Sioux might suppose the same thing about the Cheyennes and the soldiers, and so there might be many of them along the way. I was startled and my heart was jumping at every little doubtful sight or noise. But I could not do anything but keep on going. I tried to make myself feel better by thinking of what a good sleep I should have after so hard a ride.

At the agency I found the officer and gave to him the paper. Then I lay down on the floor behind his stove and went to sleep. Pretty soon the interpreter awakened me. The officer wanted me. He said: "You are a good scout. I want you now to take a message for me back to your officer." I was yet half asleep. But right away I became all awake again and got myself ready to go. I was as much afraid on the way back as I had been in coming. The snow and the wind whirling it were the same. I did not freeze, though, and I got to our camp and gave this paper to my officer. He said: "Good. Now you may go and sleep." It was almost morning. I slept far into the day. Nobody awakened me this time.

All of the scouts and Long Yellow Neck, the officer now with us, were out one night after some Sioux who had been seen. The Cheyennes were afraid. We thought there might be many more Sioux not seen. I went off a little distance aside from the others, to look and listen where there was more quietude. I saw the flash of a match. I went cautiously in that direction. I got down into a deep gulch. I could hear Sioux voices talking above me. My heart seemed to be jumping all around in my breast. I kept still until the sound of the voices went beyond my hearing. I could not see anybody, but the sounds told me the direction the Sioux were traveling. I went back to the band and told of what had occurred. All of us then followed a trail along the rim

339

of the gulch. It led us to two lodges. We surrounded them and then let them know we were there. They did not fight us. We captured ten Sioux. We made them give us their guns. I was one of ten scouts appointed to take them to the agency.

Some Ogallalas were with the Cheyennes as scouts. All together our band must have numbered sixty or more. I do not know exactly how many there were of either Cheyennes or Ogallalas, but I know there were more of the Cheyennes. Three Cheyennes and three Ogallalas were sent out one night to watch the trails. I was one of the three Cheyennes. Long Yellow Neck said: "I want you to find out how many bad Indians are going out from the reservation."

The six of us got upon our horses and rode away together into the night storm. One Ogallala and I separated off and dismounted, to look and listen. We watched particularly for match lighting, as any Indian who had tobacco was likely to stop long enough to light a match for smoking. After a little while, we saw what we were looking for. We moved quickly, but carefully, toward where we had seen the flash. We heard voices.

"Yes, they are Sioux," we whispered in agreement.

We rejoined our companions and told them. Everybody said we ought to go back and tell the officer. All of us went then to our camp. An Ogal-

340

lala knocked on the post at our officer's tent. "Come in," he said. All of us went into the warm shelter. Long Yellow Neck was writing. He put aside his paper and called the interpreter. We told what we had seen.

"How many of them were there?" the officer asked one of the Ogallalas.

"I don't know," the Indian replied.

"You are foolish," the officer told him.

He asked others. Each one said: "I don't know." I said the same. But we explained that it was too dark to see anybody, that only the flash of the match had been seen and the voices had been heard. The officer said:

"Good. Now, all of you go out again. If you see any Sioux, count them."

We found a fresh trail of horses going toward the Bad Lands. By a creek we saw that different campings had been made. Many carcasses of cattle were there. They were white men cattle that had been stolen and butchered by the Sioux.

We three Cheyennes separated off from the three Ogallalas. The two parties scouted at a little distance from each other. After our three had traveled only a short while, I left my horse to be held by one of the others while I crept to the top of a bluff for looking and listening. A commonly traveled trail

341

followed along past this bluff. Pretty soon I heard horses coming. I hugged close to the ground behind a rock. Four Sioux men rode past me toward the Bad Lands. They were almost close enough to reach out and strike me. I kept as still as the rock, except for my shivering from fright. When they were gone far enough I slid back a little distance and then jumped up and ran to my two companions. We found the three Ogallalas. They also had seen the four men. All six of us hurried back to our camp. The others appointed me to do the talking for our report. I told of how I had hidden behind the rock and counted them as they had passed by me. "There were four of them," I said. Long Yellow Neck wrote my name on a piece of paper. Then he said:

"Good. All of you may go now and sleep."

I believe I slept, but I am not sure whether I was sleeping and dreaming or was only lying there and thinking. I kept my cartridge belt buckled on me and I hugged my rifle to my body. It seemed that angry Sioux Indians were all about me. They were searching for me, to kill me. Some of them were striking at me with war clubs and slashing at me with knives. I heard calling of my name: "Wooden Leg." I jumped up and stood there wide awake.

Long Yellow Neck and a soldier with him were

in our tent. The soldier was reading off our names from a paper he had in his hands.

"The same six are to go and scout again," he said. Another Cheyenne was added to us. The seven of us got our horses. We were about to go when an Ogallala rode into camp. He had come from the agency. We wondered what was his errand. We waited to find out. He went to Long Yellow Neck's tent. Pretty soon everybody was saying:

"All of the scouts and soldiers go back to Pine Ridge."

I do not know how the others felt, but my own heart fluttered in pleasure. I did not want then to fight any Sioux. We were only a short time in getting all of the camp ready to move. When we were about to start on our way, Long Yellow Neck said: "Now, I want someone to stay behind and watch, to see if any of the Sioux are following us." He asked if I would stay. I said, "No, I do not want to stay behind." He asked Bad Horses, Foolish Man, White Bird, Sweet Grass and others. Some Ogallalas were asked. Everybody asked said, "No." While this was going on, three of the Ogallalas slipped away afoot, leaving their three horses. Long Yellow Neck told us he had thought all of us were brave men, but he had learned now that we were not brave. Finally

343

I said: "I will stay behind and watch." Little Thunder, an Ogallala, then said he would stay with me.

We two caught the three horses left by the Ogallalas who had run away afoot. Little Thunder said: "I am hungry." I too was hungry, but we had no food. We drove the three horses ahead of us and hurried forward. Soon we caught up with the scouts and soldiers. "Give us something to eat," we asked. A soldier took a big box of crackers from a pack mule and gave it to us. He gave us also plenty of bread. We ate until we were full up, and then we put what was left upon one of the three horses we had been driving. We led the three now and followed on far behind the other people.

The three Ogallalas afoot came to us. They asked us for bread and crackers. "If you will stay with us we will give you some," we told them. They agreed. We gave them all they wanted. We let them have their horses. They rode with us all of the remainder of the way to the agency, helping us in watching back to see if any Sioux were following. We kept ourselves far behind. None of us saw any of the bad Indians anywhere along the way. When we rode into the agency camp, all of the soldiers and scouts were already there. We told Long Yellow Neck that we had not seen any Sioux following us. He said:

"Good. Now you may sleep."

During the time we were scouting for the soldiers at Pine Ridge I got a Sioux head dress. It was a cap of some kind of skin having at its front a buffalo horn. I got it while the soldiers and scouts were camped on lower Wounded Knee creek. I was wearing it as I rode into camp. A soldier Sergeant said to me: "I wish you would give that to me." "What would you give to me?" I asked him. "Five dollars," he said. He gave me the five dollars and I gave him the buffalo horn head dress.

About four hundred Cheyennes came with us when we left Pine Ridge to return to Fort Keogh. These were people of ours who had fled from the South with Little Wolf and Dull Knife, and who had been staying since then among the Ogallalas on the Pine Ridge reservation. But now they were allowed to come and join the main body of Cheyennes in Montana. A few Cheyennes still remained with the Ogallalas, but this movement of the big band brought together what was considered to be the entire Northern Cheyenne tribe. An officer known to us as Small Chief * brought us back.

Cheyenne visitors from the Rosebud and Tongue river lands were camped at all times near Fort Keogh. We scouts who had families kept lodges for them

* Lieutenant McEniney.

345

among the visiting campers. Relatives and friends were shifting constantly to or from the fort, Miles City and our Cheyenne country seventy miles south of us. I had my food with the other scouts, from the soldier supplies and at our eating room at the fort. But I spent much of my time at the home lodge. One day I saw the old man Little Wolf at the camp. I said to my wife:

"I see Little Wolf. He is my relative. One of his wives is a sister of my father. I think I ought to invite him to eat at our lodge."

"I am glad to hear you say that," she answered me. "Tell him to come now." Right away she began to prepare bread and meat and coffee.

When I brought Little Wolf I found he was partly drunk. He fumbled the food as he sat and ate. He ate freely, as though he were very hungry. He kept quiet and kept looking downward during all of the time. When he was done eating, I told him of my sympathy with him in his great trouble. He then told me all about the affair. "I loved the young man and all of his people," he said. "I was crazy when I shot him." At this time of conversation, Little Wolf was about seventy years old.

This man gave away all of his horses after he had been put out of his position as our greatest chief. After that, all of his traveling was done afoot. Sometimes he went alone, sometimes one or both of his wives accompanied him. They took along whatever packs they could carry, and they slept in temporary shelters or with no shelter. He went at times to visit the Crows. He visited also the Arapahoes, in Wyoming, walking two hundred miles or more and back again. He died in 1904, at the age of eighty-three years. His wives and close friends stood his dead body upright on a high hill overlooking the Rosebud valley, where many Cheyennes had their reservation homes. A great heap of stones was built up to enclose him thus standing upright. Twenty-four years later, his bones were brought to the agency cemetery and put into a grave there. Bird,* the old-time Indian story white man who lives in New York, had a stone put at the head of this agency grave.

Even the nearest relatives of Famished Elk never kept bad hearts against Little Wolf. At different times I have heard talk of him from Bald Eagle, a brother of the young man killed. Bald Eagle said:

"Little Wolf did not kill my brother. It was the white man whisky that did it."

---

* Dr. George Bird Grinnell, the author.

347

XV

A Tamed Old Man.

Thirty years after the great battle against Custer, there was a gathering of Indians and white people at the Little Bighorn. Besides a few of our people, there were Crows, Sioux, Arapahoes, Shoshones, Nez Perces, Kiowas, Piegans, Gros Ventres and Paiutes, these last known to us as Fish-Eaters.

All Cheyennes who had fought in the battle were asked to come and join the other Indians and the white people in a peace feast. The place is only two short days of wagon traveling from our Lame Deer agency. But only a few Cheyennes would go there for the gathering. Among us there was much of such talk as: "Soldiers will be there. Seeing us might anger them so much as to make them want to kill us." * Seven of us decided to go. These were the younger Chief Little Wolf, White Elk, Bobtail Horse, Two Moons, Buffalo Calf, myself Wooden Leg, and Brave Bear, a Southern Cheyenne. Four of the seven men took along their wives and their lodges.

In a big council lodge of the Crows a white man

---

* A few old Cheyennes still talked this way in 1926. Fear kept them from attending the fiftieth anniversary of the battle.—T. B. M.

348

medicine doctor * asked different ones to tell something of the great battle. He said he had heard the white people say that Two Moons was a great warrior there, and he asked Two Moons to make a speech. This Cheyenne stood up and talked a long time. He said he had been the big chief of all the Cheyennes during the fight. He filled the ears of his hearers with lots of other lies, while the rest of us laughed among ourselves about what he was saying. Other Cheyennes and Sioux were asked to get up and talk, but none of them would do so.

The medicine doctor looked at my cousin, the younger Chief Little Wolf, and asked him:

"Were you at the Custer battle?"

"Yes."

"Were you in the first fight above the camps?"

"No."

"Who took the soldier horses?"

"The Sioux took most of them. The Cheyennes got a few. There were many Sioux and only a few Cheyennes in the fight."

"Who took the soldier guns?"

"The same—the Sioux got many, the Cheyennes got a few."

---

* The Cheyenne interpreter for them on that occasion informed me this man was Doctor Dixon.—T. B. M.

"Did you see Custer, either before or after he was killed?"

"I do not know. Nobody knew anything about Custer."

"Our soldiers afterward could not find the bodies of all the white men killed. What became of them?"

"I do not know."

"Were any of them taken away and hidden?"

"I think not, but I do not know."

"Were any of them, either dead or alive, taken to the camps?"

"I think not. I never heard of any taken there."

"Tell me all about what you saw and what you did at the battle."

But Little Wolf would not tell. I said to him: "Go on, tell the truth, but do not talk like Two Moons did." He was afraid, though. There were many white people and soldiers all around us, and he feared they might become angry.

White Elk, Bobtail Horse, Two Moons, Brave Bear, Buffalo Calf and the Sioux men all answered the same kind of questions in the same way. But none of them except Two Moons would say anything further about the fight. Bobtail Horse was either nervous or scared, so he got tangled a little. The doctor asked him the same kind of questions. Then he asked:

"How old are you?"

Bobtail Horse sat there as though he did not understand what was being asked. Pretty soon he began to count on his fingers. He counted them over and over. Finally he said: "I do not know." All of us knew exactly one another's age, but none of us interfered to help him in answering the question. The doctor did not ask him any further questions.

In my turn at the talking I was asked the same kind of questions:

"Wooden Leg, were you in the Custer battle?"

"Yes, I was there."

"Were you in the first fight up above the camps?"

"Yes."

"Good. How old were you at that time?"

"Eighteen winters."

"How old are you now?"

"Forty-eight."

"Good. Tell me where you were during all of the time. Tell me what you saw and what you did."

I told him. It happened I was the only Indian at this gathering who had been in the first fight with what the white people call the Reno soldiers. It began with my brother and I being awakened by the shooting and our running to get our horses. I followed my own doings up the valley and into the chase after the soldiers through the river and up the hill. I showed how I had taken a rifle from a soldier.

I described the killing of the Corn Indian and my taking his gun. The doctor wrote on a piece of paper as I talked. My cousin Little Wolf interrupted me: "You tell too much. Stop talking."

But I did not stop. It appeared none of the soldiers nor other white people listening to me were angry. This medicine doctor looked to me like a good man, one who understood that we had killed soldiers who had come to kill us. I described to him the way I had helped to kill the soldier getting water at the river. I told about the Indians surrounding the Custer soldiers on the long ridge and about many things that happened there. The doctor still was writing on the paper. He broke in with some questions and I answered each one as straight as I knew how to answer it. Little Wolf said to me: "Tell him Custer killed himself, and see if he becomes angry." But I did not say anything about that. Other Indians, at other times, had tried to tell of the soldiers killing themselves, but the white people listening always became angry and said the Indians were liars, so I thought it best to keep quiet. Other questions came:

"Did you see Custer?"

"I suppose I did, but I do not know. I think that no Indians there knew anything about him being with the soldiers."

"Did you see soldiers having special marks on the shoulders of their coats?"

"Yes, I noticed some of them."

"Did you know they were chiefs among the soldiers?"

"I did not know then, but I know now."

"How many soldiers did you see having the markings on the shoulders?"

"I do not know. When we were fighting them they all looked alike to us, the same as a herd of buffalo."

"How many Indians were killed?"

I told him the number of dead Cheyennes, Uncpapas and others.

"Good," he said, and he wrote the numbers on his paper.

The Cheyennes and some other Indians went with a few soldiers to Fort Custer, not far from the place where had been the great battle. The soldier officers at the fort shook hands with all of us. We gathered together, and some friendly speeches were made by officers and by Indians. All I said there was: "A long time ago we were enemies. Today we are friends." The medicine doctor rode beside me as we were going to and from the fort. We made sign-talk together along the way. I showed him the only place where the Cheyenne tribe ever camped west of the Bighorn river. From the top of the Fort Custer hill we could see the place, just across from the mouth of the Little Bighorn.

Many pictures were made of Cheyennes, Sioux, Nez Perces and Crows. Some were made on the valley and by the river where had been the first fight, others were made on the battle ridge and at its northern side. Pictures were made at night when the Indians were dancing. The bright flashes scared some of the Indians, but soon it was learned what was being done.

Wagons came loaded with rations. We were given plenty of beef, bacon, bread, crackers, coffee, sugar, meat in cans, and other food. We were on the valley by the river, where had been the fight with the Reno soldiers. A soldier officer rode about, saying:

"All Indians who were in the Custer battle get rations. No others are to be given any food."

But when the distribution began, lots of Crows came running. They crowded forward saying:

"Oh, meat! Give some to us."

Their actions made me angry. I let loose my tongue:

"You—Crows—you are like children. All Crows are babies. You are not brave. You never helped us to fight against the white people. You helped them in fighting against us. You were afraid, so you joined yourselves to the soldiers. You are not Indians."

Bobtail Horse said to me: "Ssh, keep your temper." My cousin Little Wolf said: "You are doing right. Tell them what we think of them." The Crows stopped asking for the rations. All of them went back and kept quiet.

Besides the rations given to us every day, each of us was paid three dollars at the end of each day, for four days. When the gathering ended and we were getting ready to go back to our reservation, we were given plenty of extra food to eat along the way. Some of it was eaten by ourselves and our friends after we arrived home.

Another great gathering of whites and Indians assembled there fifty years after the battle. All of the Cheyennes, particularly the men who had been in the battle, were invited to go. Many lodges of our people traveled over the divide to that place and camped there, but I stayed at my home. Two times I was called to our Ashland district telephone for a talk from the agency. "We want you to go to the great peace celebration," I was told. At each time of this talking I made reply: "I will think about it." The more I thought about it, the more I felt like staying away. The battlefield is on the present Crow Indian reservation. I do not want to go upon their lands. I have made up my mind never again to go to any place where I might be called upon to shake hands with a Crow.

The younger Chief Little Wolf, my cousin, had the boyhood name Thorny Tree. His mother was a sister of my father and of the older Little Wolf's first wife. The young nephew Thorny Tree showed special bravery at a battle with the Shoshones. The old chief was so pleased at this manly conduct of his wife's relative that he told the young warrior:

"I give you my name. From this day on you shall be Little Wolf."

This younger man stayed with the Cheyennes at the Pine Ridge reservation, after the peaceful times came. Among them he was made a tribal chief. When the band of them were moved to our Tongue River reservation he was made a chief of the entire tribe. A few years later he was accepted as the principal old man chief. He told me that during the years he was living at Pine Ridge he often was mistaken for the same Little Wolf who led the Cheyennes in their flight from the South. In fact, he was with that band of fleeing Cheyennes, but he joined that group of them who went to Pine Ridge. The older Little Wolf and his last followers .came to Powder river and on to Fort Keogh. The old

chief never was at Pine Ridge after that time.
My cousin told me that white people often embarrassed him also in supposing him to have been famed as Chief Little Wolf at the Custer battle. In this case, the older man was not in the fight, he and a small band of Cheyennes having followed on the trail of the soldiers and having arrived at the camps after the white men all had been killed. The younger Little Wolf was already there with the great tribal assemblage. The family lodge of his father, Big Left Hand, was near to my own father's family lodge. This last Chief Little Wolf, my cousin, died in 1927, at the age of 76 years.

I visited the Arapahoes and the Shoshones, in Wyoming, several years ago. Eight Cheyenne men, some of us with our wives and our tepees went on this trip. I had a Custer gun, borrowed from a Cheyenne who kept it in hiding. We saw a big band of elk in a valley of the Bighorn mountains. I was chosen to lead the hunters in getting ourselves close to them. I said: "Yes, I will lead, but you others must stay back until I tell you it is time for all to show themselves and begin to shoot." As we got well toward the elk band they suddenly ran away into a forest. I soon learned that one of our men had pushed on ahead and frightened them. "You are foolish," was all I could say to him. We saw trails of other elk, plenty of them, but we did not see any others of the elk themselves.

High up on the top of a rocky bluff we saw a bighorn, what the white people call a mountain sheep. Different ones of us shot at it and missed it. Another man and I then shot, at the same moment. The animal tumbled down the mountain. When we got to it we found that both of our bullets had struck the front part of its body. We enjoyed that meat. It was the first bighorn meat I had eaten for several years.

Nine sleeps we made on our way to the reservation where we were going. We stopped with the Arapahoes, good friends of the Cheyennes all during the old times. There had been friendly intermarriages between our people and theirs. There was much of inquiring about Arapahoes living among us on our reservation. These people made gifts to us. They could not give much, because they were as poor as the Cheyennes.

We moved camp for a visit with the Shoshones. In the old times they and the Cheyennes were constantly on terms of enmity. But now they received us cordially. From all sides came, "How," "How," "How." An old chief of theirs went riding among them and calling out: "Everybody come and shake hands with our guests, the Cheyennes. Let them know we are glad they came to visit us."

Men, women, old people, boys, girls, all moved along past our group and greeted us with handshakes. They brought food. There were big piles of all kinds of things the Indians like to eat. After a while, they began to bring horses. One after another they kept giving these to us. Every Cheyenne among us had more horses than he could lead, when we parted from the Shoshones. I had nine of them presented to me. When we got back among our own people at home we were the richest Indians in our tribe. We had horses to give away to our friends. All of the Cheyennes agreed that the Shoshones have good hearts, that they are a good people.

An Arickaree Indian visited me at my place on Tongue river a few years ago. We talked of the Custer battle. He told me one of their chiefs had been killed there. He described him. The special features of his war clothing were a fine buckskin shirt and a necklace made of bear claws. I described to him the Arickaree I had helped to kill. This one had on a buckskin shirt. An eagle feather stood up from his back hair. A red string tied his hair together behind. If he had a bear-claw necklace I did not see it. I did not see this kind of necklace on any of the three Arickarees I saw dead. It may be one of the other two had one and it had been taken from him before I saw the dead body.

I went to Washington when I was fifty-five years old. Little Wolf, Two Moons and Black Wolf were old men with me as delegates to speak for our tribe. Three younger men who could talk the white man language went with us. They were Willis Rowland, Ben Shoulderblade and Milton Little White Man. At a meeting with white men, there were some speeches made. Two Moons did most of the talking for us. The rest of us did not care to make any long talks. Two Moons told these people he was a big chief leading all of the Cheyennes at the Custer battle. None of us said anything in dispute of him at the meeting, but when we got away to ourselves Black Wolf said to him: "You are the biggest liar in the whole Cheyenne tribe." Two Moons laughed and replied: "I think it is not wrong to tell lies to white people."

The same white man medicine doctor who had been at the gathering by the Little Bighorn was in Washington. He was good to us, helping us to see the strange sights in the big city. He could make good signs, so he and I talked much together. We went up to the top of a very tall stone he said was Washington's monument. We rode up to the top and walked a long and winding stairway to the bottom.

A big ship took us Cheyennes out upon the great water. All of us became sick and vomited. "It is the same as whisky," we said to each other. The ship took us to New York. There we visited our friend Bird, the old-time Indian story white man. The white man medicine doctor was traveling with us. He went with us on to Philadelphia, where we visited the biggest trader store I ever saw. In a theater in this city we sat upon a platform before a great crowd of white people. I was asked to make a speech. I talked, but only for a short time. One of our interpreters repeated to them what I said. This visit to the great cities was at some time during the spring (1913), in March or April, I believe.

I lied to one man in New York. He asked me many questions. For a while I answered them as best I could. But it began to appear he was trying to show the old-time Indians as being low and mean people. I had told him a great deal about the fighting, about the taking of horses and saddles and guns, about other matters of this kind. I found I did not like him, so I decided to end our talk.

"What time of day was it when all of the Custer soldiers had been killed?" he asked me.

"I don't know," I answered him.

"Did the Indians keep the money they took from the soldiers?"

"I don't know."

"Did you get any of it?"

"I don't know."

After these answers he quit talking to me and went away.

The medicine doctor friend came several years afterward from Washington to our Lame Deer agency. I saw and talked with him here. I still keep a big flag he gave to me. I liked him. He was a good man, one having a heart good toward Indians.

The guns taken by Cheyennes from the Custer soldiers were given up or had been thrown away by those of our people who surrendered at the White River agency. I think that all of the Sioux also had to give their guns of all kinds to the soldiers chiefs at their reservations. But at Fort Keogh General Miles was good to the Cheyennes. He allowed them to keep their guns. I suppose that many Indians threw away their Custer guns, for fear of being found out and punished for having killed those soldiers. But the Fort Keogh Cheyennes kept theirs hidden. A few of these have been buried with the owners who died. But even to this day, I know of several of the Custer rifle guns hidden among the people on our reservation. White Elk and Spotted Wolf used to have Custer soldier six-shooters. These two men are dead. I do not know what became of their six-shooters. The Cheyennes also have yet some of the Custer soldier ammunition belts and saddle-bags. They do not like to tell of having these captured war things, because there are some white people who become angry when they talk of the old times of warfare between the whites and the Indians.*

I have yet four of the ten arrows I made from the cattle neckyoke picked up at the town when we were on our way to the South. For keeping my comb and paints I have a flat pouch made from a bootleg. The boots I got at the White River agency the next day after my hunting party went there to surrender. Another young man and I were walking in the neighborhood of the soldier tents there. I found a pair of soldier boots among some other articles also cast aside by the white men. The soles were worn, but the tops were good. I knew how to make use of them. I cut off the worn bottom parts and kept the tops. My mother sewed one of them into the pouch. I know of some Cheyennes who still have such carriers made from bootlegs of Custer soldiers.

* During 1926 and 1927 I came into possession of six carbines, three ammunition belts, one full pair of saddle-bags and one half-pair of same, that these Fort Keogh Cheyennes had kept hidden ever since their having been taken from the Custer soldiers in 1876.—T. B. M.

I lost the medicine pipe given to me by the Ogallala Sioux man at the White River agency. That was my second medicine pipe. The third one came to me when I was somewhere past forty years old. An Uncpapa Sioux visiting me at my place gave it to me. I still have it. It is made of the red stone found in their part of the country. After he had given to me this pipe I went on a journey into the Bighorn mountains. There I got some blue stone of the kind used for making Indian pipes. I made two of them. I now have three pipes, one red one and two blue ones. I have kept all three of them for several years, and I do not expect to sell any of them.

I was baptized by the priest at the Tongue river mission when I was almost fifty years old. My wife and our two daughters were baptized too. I think the white people pray to the same Great Medicine we do in our old Cheyenne way. I do not go often to the church, but I go sometimes. I think the white church people are good, but I do not believe all of the stories they tell about what happened a long time ago. The way they tell us, all of the good people in the old times were white people. I am glad to have the white man churches among us, but I feel more satisfied when I make my prayers in the way I was taught to make them. My heart is much more contented when I sit alone with my medicine pipe and talk with the Great Medicine about whatever may be troubling me.

Our old ways of worship were kept up through several years after we came to this reservation. Our Great Medicine dances and other old ceremonies were carried out as we had them in the days when we traveled over the whole hunting region. Then the government compelled us to quit them. I think this was not right. Lately, though, the conditions have changed. We were allowed to have our Great Medicine dance in 1927, again in 1928 and in 1929.

We had good medicine men in the old times. It may be they did not know as much about sickness as the white men doctors know, but our doctors knew more about Indians and how to talk to them. Our people then did not die young so much as they do now. In present times our Indian doctors are put into jail if they make medicine for our sick people. Whoever of us may become sick or injured must have the agency white man doctor or none at all. But he can not always come, and there are some who do not like him. I think it is best and right if each sick one be allowed to choose which doctor he wants. When Eddy was agent he let us keep our own old ways in all these matters. Our people liked him the best of all the agents we have had.

A policeman came to my place, one time, and told me that Eddy wanted to see me at the agency office. He did not say what was wanted. I thought: "What have I done?" I went right away. I never had been much about the agency, and I did not know Eddy very well. But the people all the time were saying he was a good man, so I was not afraid. When I got there, a strange white man was at the office. The interpreter told me this man was from Washington. Eddy and the other man talked to me a little while, about nothing of importance. Then Eddy said:

"We want you to be judge."

The Indian court was held at the agency. My home place was where it now is, over a divide from the agency and on the Tongue river side of the reservation. I accepted the appointment. I was paid ten dollars each month for going to the agency and attending to the court business one or two times each month. Not long after I had been serving as judge, Eddy called me into his office. He said:

"A letter from Washington tells me that Indians having two or more wives must send away all but one. You, as judge, must do your part toward seeing that the Cheyennes do this."

My heart jumped around in my breast when he told me this. He went on talking further about the matter, but I could not pay close attention to him.

My thoughts were racing and whirling. When I could get them steady enough for speech, I said to him:

"I have two wives. You must get some other man to serve as judge."

He sat there and looked straight at me, saying nothing for a little while. Then he began talking again:

"Somebody else as judge would make you send away one of your wives. It would be better if you yourself managed it. All of the Indians in the United States are going to be compelled to put aside their extra wives. Washington has sent the order."

I decided to keep the office of judge. It appeared there was no getting around the order, so I made up my mind to be the first one to send away my extra wife, then I should talk to the other Cheyennes about the matter. I took plenty of time to think about how I should let my wives know about what was coming. Then I allowed the released one some further time to make arrangements as to where she should go. The first wife, the older one, had two daughters. The younger wife had no children. It seemed this younger one ought to leave me. I was in very low spirits. When a wagon came to get her and her personal packs I went out and sat on a knoll about a hundred yards away. I could not speak to

367

her. It seemed I could not move. All I could do was just sit there and look down at the ground. She went back to her own people, on another reservation. A few years later I heard that she was married to a good husband. Oh, how glad it made my heart to hear that!

I sent a policeman to tell all Cheyennes having more than one wife to come and see me. One of them came that same afternoon. After we had smoked together, I said:

"The agent tells me that I as the judge must order all Cheyennes to have only one wife. You must send away one of yours."

"I shall not obey that order," he answered me.

"Yes, it will have to be that way," I insisted.

"But who will be the father to the children?" he asked.

"I do not know, but I suppose that will be arranged."

"Wooden Leg, you are crazy. Eddy is crazy."

"No. If anybody is crazy, it is somebody in Washington. All of the Indians in the United States have this order. If we resist it, our policemen will put us into jail. If much trouble is made about it, soldiers may come to fight us. Whatever man does not put aside his extra wife may be the cause of the whole tribe being killed.

Many of our men were angered by the order. My heart sympathized with them, so I never became offended at the strong words they sometimes used. Finally, though, all of them sent away their extra wives. Afterward, from time to time, somebody would tell me about some man living a part of the time at one place with one wife and a part of the time at another place with another wife. I just listened, said nothing, and did nothing. These were old men, and I considered it enough of change for them that they be prevented from having two wives at the same place. At this present time I know of only one old Cheyenne man who has two wives. They are extremely old, are sisters, and they have been his two wives for sixty or more years. He stays a part of the time with one of them and a part of the time with the other. The sister-wives visit each other, but they have different homes, several miles apart.

Throughout ten years I kept the position of judge. I rode my horse or went in my wagon to the agency once or twice each month. It became tiresome to me. Eddy went away, and we had another agent. I decided to resign, and I did so. After I had been out of the office a few years there was another change in agents. The man we now have, the one we have named Sioux Agent, was put in charge of our reservation. One day, Sioux Agent sent a message calling me to his office.

"I want you to be judge again," he said. "You will be paid twenty-five dollars each month."

That was better than the ten dollars each month I had been paid during the ten years of my first service. I took his offer. So now, in my old age, I am helping my people to learn the ways of the white man government. For the old people, it is a great change, so I try to apply my thoughts at teaching the young Cheyennes whatever I am expected to teach.

I was chosen two times as a little chief of the Elk warriors, in the old times. But in each instance I got somebody else to take my place. Also, at two different times of election of tribal chiefs, since we have been on the reservation, a band of warriors came to me and said: "We want you to be a big chief of the tribe." But I did not want to have that position, so in each instance I told my friends to choose some other man, some one who would like to have it. Some white people, at different times, have called me, "Chief Wooden Leg." But I never was a chief, neither of my warrior society nor of the tribe.

My younger brother's name was Twin. When he grew up to manhood he went from here to the Minneconjoux Sioux. There he was appointed a policeman. He continued in that duty until his death, a few years age. My mother died here at my home, on the Tongue river reservation. My younger sister and myself are the only members of my father's family yet living. This sister is the wife of Little Eagle. Their farm place is only a few miles down the valley from mine.

Both of my daughters went to school at the Tongue river mission. They lived there during the school months. Each Sunday we were allowed to take them to our home. At other times we might go to the mission and see them for a few minutes. Later, I built a house only a quarter of a mile from the Mission, and on a sloping hillside above it. We could look from our front door and see the children at any time when they might be outside of the school buildings. My wife and I were pleased at their situation in life. "They will have more of comfort and happiness than we have had," we said to each other.

But the younger daughter fell into an illness when she was about fourteen years old. We expected she soon would be herself again, but she grew worse instead of better. She became so weak she could not stay any longer at the school. She continued to go on downward after we brought her to our home. Finally, her spirit went back to the Great Medicine.

All of our love now was fixed upon the other daughter. She advanced to full young womanhood.

371

She could read the white man books, and she could write letters to our friends far away. But she too became ill, the same as her younger sister. During all of one winter she gradually wasted away. Every afternoon her body burned with fever. Every night her bed was soaked with the sweating. Every morning she coughed almost to strangling. Neither the medicines of the agency physician nor the prayers of our own medicine men could help her. Just when the spring grass was coming up, she was buried in our mission cemetery.

My heart fell down to the ground. I decided then that the white man school is not good for Indian children. I think they do not get enough of meat at the boarding schools. I think too that they are kept in school too much during each year. They ought to be out and free to go as they please during all of the good weather of the autumn and the spring. It may be that white children can stand it to be in school most of the year. I do not believe, though, that Indian children can stand it. It is not good sense to have the whites and the Indians living by the same rules.

My sister's daughter and her husband had pity for me and my wife. They gave to us their oldest son. He makes his home with us. On the agency roll his name is Joseph White Wolf. But according

372

to the Indian way he is our boy, our grandson. He is a good boy, comforting and helpful to us. I pray often that he may become a good man, may get a good wife, may have many children and may live far into old age.

My farming land is back from the valley, on a creek flowing into Tongue river. Each year I have some alfalfa hay and some oats or wheat, or both. I have a garden of vegetables, including an acre or more of corn for our own food. All together, twenty-one acres was the most land I had in cultivation in one season. That was a few years ago. I do not have that much now. I become tired more quickly than I did in past times. It appears my legs are not now made of wood, as they used to be.

I get pension money each month because of my service as a scout at Fort Keogh. For a while it was twenty dollars monthly. Then it was increased to thirty dollars. Now it is forty dollars. As I grow older it will be further increased. My pay as judge added to this pension money makes enough for me to buy food and clothing for my wife and boy, without need for farming. But I like to have more than I need, so I can help my friends. I can not do this many more years.

A few other old Cheyennes get the pension money. We few are the rich men of our tribe of very poor

373

people. Many of our old men and women have a hard time getting enough food. Some white people say to them: "You have good land, so you ought to be prosperous." They appear not to understand that Indians are not born farmers. Besides, many among us are older than I am. Even if these did know how to farm, they have not the strength to do it.

Another thing the white people appear not to understand: The old Indian teaching was that it is wrong to tear loose from its place on the earth anything that may be growing there. It may be cut off, but it should not be uprooted. The trees and the grass have spirits. Whatever one of such growths may be destroyed by some good Indian, his act is done in sadness and with a prayer for forgiveness because of his necessities, the same as we were taught to do in killing animals for food or skins. We revere especially the places where our old camp circles used to be set up and where we had our old places of worship. There are many of such spots on our reservation. White people look at them and say: "These Indians are foolish. There is good land not plowed." But we like to see these places as they were in the old times. They help to keep in our hearts a remembrance of the virtues of the good Cheyennes dead and gone from us.

XVI

Clearing the Docket.

Cheyennes still disagree among themselves about the number of sleeps the combined tribes stayed at different camps along the way from east of Powder river to the Little Bighorn and back again to the Powder river country. For a long time there was disagreement as to the length of time we had been at the battle camp before the Custer soldiers came. Some said we had been there only one sleep, others said two sleeps. This dispute was settled, though, several years ago, when a band of Ogallalas visited us on this reservation. In a great gathering with them at our Lame Deer agency there was a general rehearsing of the battle at the Little Bighorn. Little Hawk, a Cheyenne, spoke of us having slept there two nights before the soldiers came. Somebody corrected him:

"We had slept there only one night."

"I bet you we had been there two sleeps," Little Hawk replied. He spread out a blanket and laid upon it some money.

His money was matched. Other bets were made, by other Indians differing in their beliefs on the subject. Old men then were called upon, one after another, to tell what was in their memories concerning the question. White Elk, young Chief Little Wolf, Wooden Leg, various other old Cheyennes and several of the old Sioux, all were asked for expressions of their beliefs. Each one of them said:

"One sleep."

Little Hawk and his supporters finally had to admit themselves mistaken. In the general exchange of talk, many corroborating incidents were mentioned. There came then a full agreement that we had been in this camp only one night, that the soldiers attacked us the next morning, that after the fighting had ended we moved our camps a short distance northwestward and stayed there all of this night, and that in the late afternoon of the day after the great battle we left the place and traveled all night and all the next day up the Little Bighorn valley. Of the two nights at the battle place, one had been at the first camping spot where the soldiers attacked us and the other had been at the second camping spot, a short distance away, where we moved on account of our death losses.

For fifty years we old Cheyennes talked of Bear Coat, or General Miles, as having been big chief of the soldiers who came up the Little Bighorn valley the next day after the Custer battle.* We have been corrected by our present white man doctor friend. He informs us that General Miles did not come into this country until more than a month after that time. He says that a General Terry and a General Gibbon were the chiefs of these soldiers. I never before had heard of either of these two men.

I never had heard of any of General Custer's relatives having been killed with him, until our present white man doctor friend told us about the two brothers and the brother-in-law and the nephew. He tells us also that General Custer's body was not cut up. I do not know why he was spared, if such was the case. I never heard of any favorings of any dead man there. I do not know of any reason for intentional difference in treatment of them.

It was not then known to us who was the chief of these white men soldiers. It was not known to us where they had come from. We supposed them to be the same men we had fought on the Rosebud, eight days before. We had not known who was the chief of those soldiers on the Rosebud. I never heard any Indians at that time guessing as to who he may have been. It made no difference to us.

* This mistake of the old Cheyennes arose from their having found Miles in command of the soldiers at Fort Keogh when they surrendered there in 1877. They supposed, and kept right on supposing, that he had been the leader of the Yellowstone river soldiers who came up the Bighorn and the Little Bighorn in June, 1876.—T. B. M.

I have been told that certain different ones of Indians have claimed special honor for having killed Custer himself. All such men are only boasting to get attention. There was no talk of this kind during the hours and days right after the battle. If there had been, all of us would have known of it. I tell you again: None of us knew anything about Custer being there. The few Southern Cheyennes and the few Sioux warriors who had seen him in earlier times did not learn until many weeks later that he had been killed in this battle. It was weeks or months later when the most of us first learned that there ever was such a man. The white people, not the Indians, told us.

Even if some white man soldier in the battle had been well known to all of the Indians it would have been hard to recognize him there. During the first hour or two of the fighting we were too far away to single out and recognize any particular one. As we got close, the air became more and more full of smoke and dust. The Indians were greatly excited. All of the white men went crazy. It must have been that not any one of them looked like his natural self. I believe that not any warrior then was thinking of trying to find out which one was the chief of the soldiers nor which soldier might be a past acquaintance. Every fighter, on both sides, was sweating and dust-covered. The dead soldiers were dirty and bloody. Very soon, they were much worse than that. Their best friends would not have known them.

Of the thirty Indians killed in both fights, I believe about half fell from the bullets of the Custer men. Of these fifteen or so killed by the Custer men, there were more of them fell during the first close fighting, when Lame White Man led us and himself was killed, down toward the river, than fell at any other one section of the field. The soldiers in the entire battle with the Custer men could have killed a great many more of us, or we should have gone away and left them after some further fighting, if their whisky had not made them go crazy and shoot themselves. I do not know just how many of them we killed, but I believe the number was not more than twenty or thirty, all together. Some of these were during the slow distant shooting time and some were after we had gone among them and found badly wounded men to kill at once. There was no capturing alive. I did not hear any Indian talk of wanting to make such capture.

All of our dead Cheyennes were found, were taken away and were buried. I am not sure about all of the Sioux dead, but it seems they all must have been found, as there was the remainder of that afternoon and much of the next day to make search. The three dead Corn Indians I saw were left where they had been killed.

None of the Custer soldiers came any closer to the river than they were at the time they died. When the first Indians went out and met them, and exchanged shots with them, these soldiers were riding along the ridge far out northeastward.* They kept moving westward along its crest until they spread out on the ridge lower down, the ridge where the most of the battle took place. After about an hour and a half of the slow fighting at long distances, the group of forty soldiers who rode down from the ridge along a broad coulee and toward the river were charged upon by Lame White Man, followed at once by many Cheyennes and Sioux. This place of the first Indian charge and the first sudden great victory is inside of the present fence around the battlefield and at its lower side.

The most important warrior among the Cheyennes was Lame White Man. I believe all of our old men consider him so. Next in importance and usefulness were Old Man Coyote, leading chief of the Crazy Dog warriors, Last Bull, leading chief of the Fox warriors, and Crazy Head, one of our tribal chiefs who had been a warrior society chief when he was a

---

* Many Custer rifle shells have been found scattered along this high far-out ridge, by J. A. Blummer and other residents.—T. B. M.

younger man. The first Indians to go across the river and fire upon the Custer soldiers far out on the ridge were two Sioux and three Cheyennes. These three Cheyennes were Roan Bear, Buffalo Calf and Bobtail Horse. This last named man is still living, his home being on the Rosebud side of our reservation.

Two Moons used to tell white people of his own great importance in the battle. I believe he was brave, like many others there, but he was not thought of as being very important. He was one of the nine little chiefs of the Fox warriors. The only special way I heard him talked about was concerning his having a repeating rifle, the only one of such guns among the Cheyennes in this battle. When the smaller part of our Cheyenne tribe surrendered to General Miles, at Fort Keogh, Two Moons was chosen by him as their one big chief. For several years those Indians were governed by General Miles. From time to time, in the years following, others of our people were added to these. The coming of Little Wolf made a difference, but he lost his place when he killed the Cheyenne. When all of the tribe finally were assembled on the present reservation, the Fort Keogh officers and the government agents still kept Two Moons as the one big chief over all of us. I do not know of there being among us any great dissatisfaction because of this, but I do know that it was General Miles, not the Cheyennes, who selected him as our leader.

There are yet living (1930) among the Cheyennes more than twenty men and about the same number of women who were full-grown people with us in the camp beside the Little Bighorn. I suppose that each tribe of the Sioux have, in proportion, the same numbers. We have many more who were children in the camp and who remember much of what was done at that time. Last Bull, leading chief of the Fox warriors, took his family and joined the Crows after the days of peace came. His two daughters married Crow men. The scared and screaming girl I took upon my horse when the soldiers burned our forty lodges on Powder river has become an old woman, a Cheyenne-Crow woman. She is known to the white people as Mrs. Passes.

Every time I have been where white people have been asking questions about the Custer battle, somebody has wanted to know:

"Where was Sitting Bull during the fight?"

For a long time I did not understand why this question was pressed so strongly. Then I learned that white people had been saying: "Sitting Bull was a coward. He was not with the warriors in the fighting."

I do not know where he was. I had not thought about trying to find out. I suppose he was helping the women and children and old people, where he belonged. He had a son in the fight. Any man having a son serving as a warrior was expected to stay out of battles and give the son his chance to get warrior honors. Lame White Man, the Southern Cheyenne tribal chief who was killed, went into the fight because of his having no son there. I suppose it was the same with Chief Crazy Horse, of the Ogallalas, and Chief Hump Nose, of the Arrows All Gone. I do not know of any other tribal chiefs or old men having mixed into the battle. My father stayed in the camps, but his staying there was not on account of personal fear.

I am not ashamed to tell that I was a follower of Sitting Bull. I have no ears for hearing anybody say he was not a brave man. He had a big brain and a good one, a strong heart and a generous one. In the old times I never heard of any Indian having spoken otherwise of him. If any of them changed their talk in later days, the change must have been brought about by lies of agents and soldier chiefs who schemed to make themselves appear as good men by making him appear as a bad man.

It is comfortable to live in peace on the reservation. It is pleasant to be situated where I can sleep soundly every night, without fear that my horses may be stolen or that myself or my friends may be crept upon and killed. But I like to think about the old times, when every man had to be brave. I wish I could live again through some of the past days when it was the first thought of every prospering Indian to send out the call:

"Hoh-oh-oh-oh, friends: Come. Come. Come. I have plenty of buffalo meat. I have coffee. I have sugar. I have tobacco. Come, friends, feast and smoke with me."

THE END

Legend for opposite map: A.—Near the present-day Crow Agency, Montana.

1. Uncpapa camp circle.

2. Blackfeet Sioux camp circle.

3. Minneconjoux camp circle.

4. Arrows All Gone camp circle.

5. Ogallala camp circle.

6. Cheyenne camp circle.
   Arrows ➝ ➝ show Reno troops' advance and retreat.

7. Reno battle line, for a few minutes.

8. Present Garryowen railroad station.

9. Reno entrenchment hill, after retreat across the river.

10. Present Custer monument, in field enclosed by fence.

11. Broad coulee of Medicine Tail creek just across east from Cheyenne camp circle.
    The long links, ⬭ ⬭ show approach of Custer troops, moving northwestward, along a high ridge. Scattered crossmarks, x x x, show where irregular second camps of Indians were placed.
    Little Bighorn river flowing northwestward.
    Indians forded river at Medicine Tail coulee and also went along hills from Reno hill, 9, to intercept Custer soldiers.

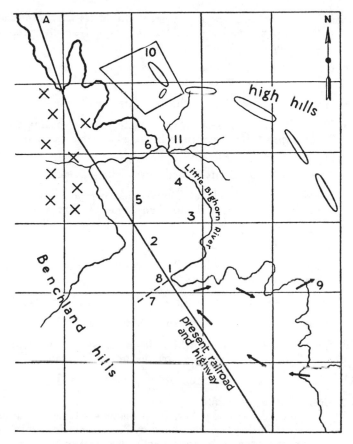

CAMP SITES AND OTHER SALIENT POINTS IN VICINITY OF
CUSTER BATTLEFIELD, MONTANA.

Legend for opposite map: A.—Present-day Miles City, Montana. B.—Present-day Hardin, Montana. C.—Near the present-day Sheridan, Wyoming.

1. Cheyenne camp whipped out and burned, on Powder river, just above mouth of Little Powder river, March 17, 1876.

2. Where Cheyennes joined the Ogallala band.

3. Where Ogallalas and Cheyennes together joined Sitting Bull's Uncpapas. Minneconjoux Sioux also came here, making four separate camp circles.

4. Arrows All Gone Sioux joined here, making five camp circles.

5. Powder river. Blackfeet Sioux made here the sixth camp circle. Other small bands had come, but not enough for tribal camp circles.

6. Camp at Tongue river.

7. Upper Wood creek, where they stayed five or six days, for a great buffalo hunt.

8. The six camp circles on the Rosebud river, about May 19th.

9. Where the Uncpapas had their sun dance, in early June.

10. Reno creek camp, from which the Indians went out at night to fight Crook's soldiers, on the upper Rosebud.

11. Site of the Crook fight, on the upper Rosebud, June 17th.

12. Custer battle, June 25th.
    All moved away together, in the same six tribal camp circles, until they arrived back at 3, east of Powder river. Here the great combined camp was broken up, and the tribes separated, about July 15th.

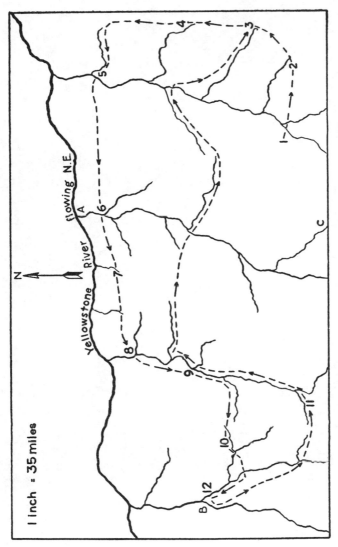

Sketch Map of Hostile Indians' Course of Travel in Montana, 1876.